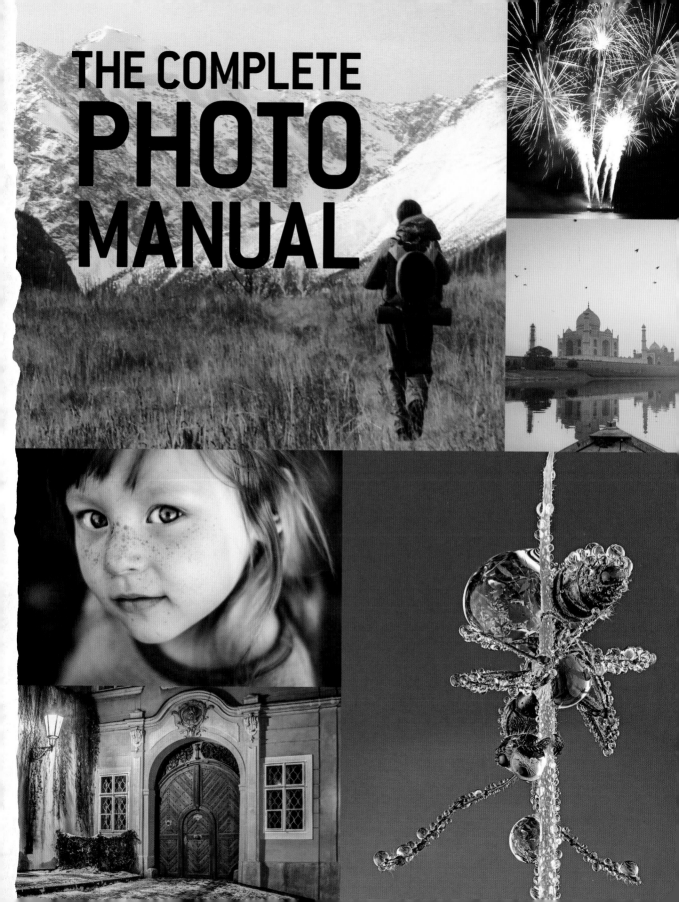

THE COMPLETE
PHOTO
MANUAL

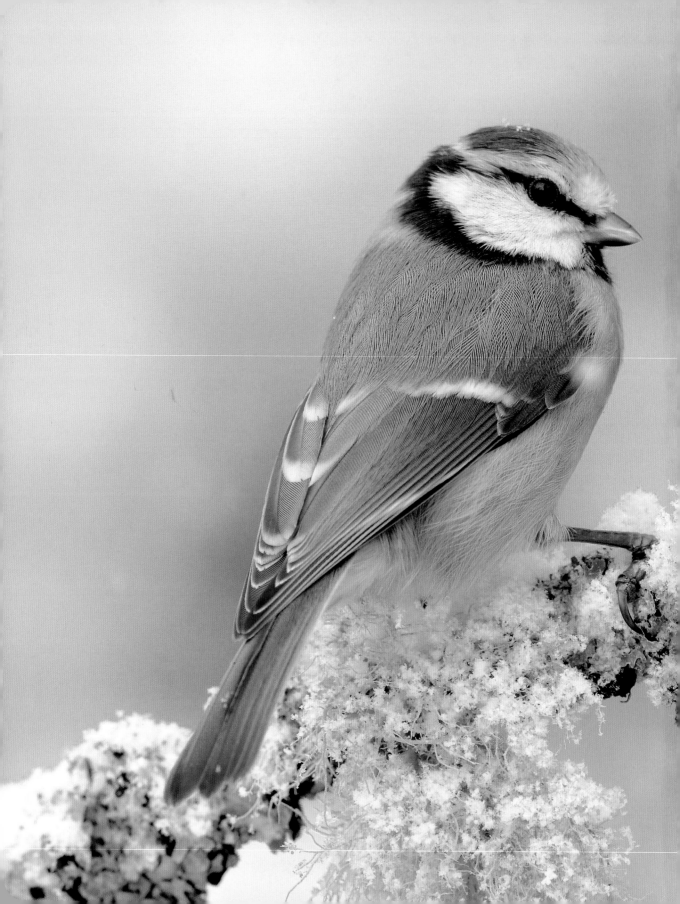

POPULAR PHOTOGRAPHY
THE COMPLETE
PHOTO
MANUAL

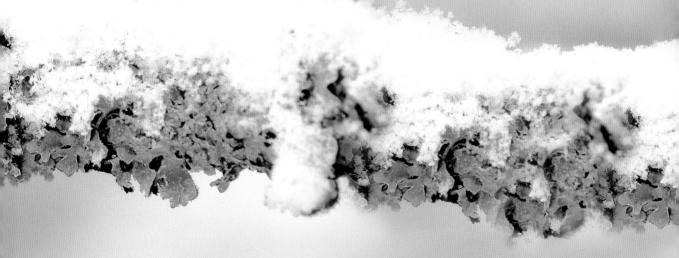

weldon**owen**

CONTENTS

INTRODUCTION

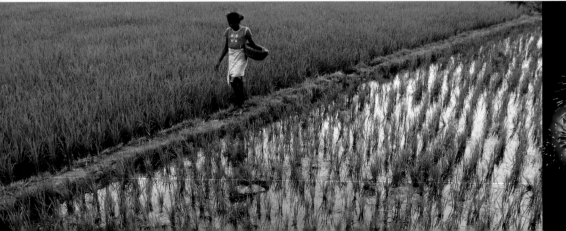
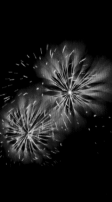

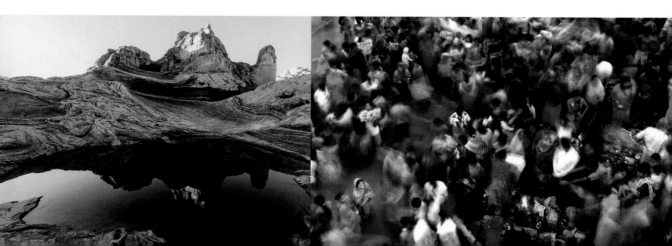

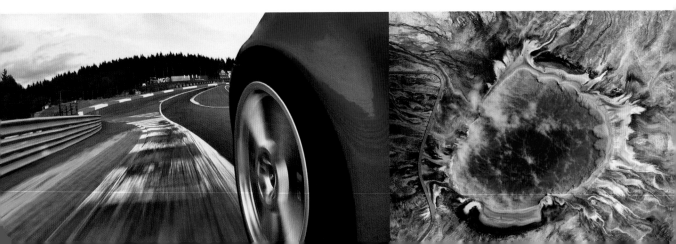

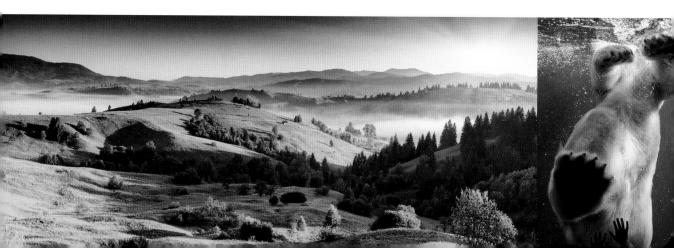

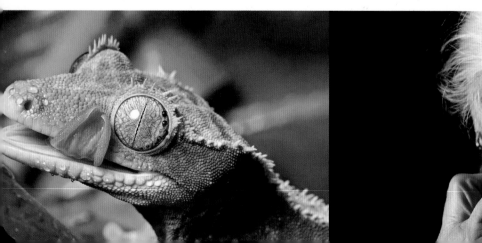

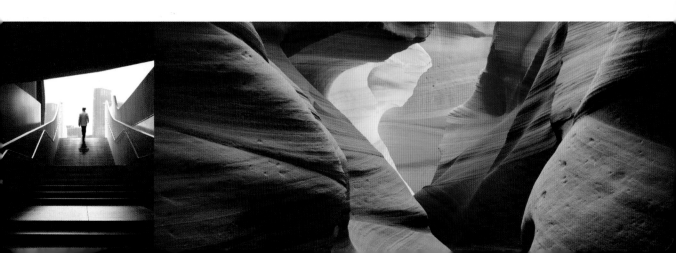

INTRODUCTION

A small, dark-brown box, about the size of a thin brick, sits discreetly on a table in my living room. Pick it up by its leather handle, press a button on top, and a door on the front drops open to reveal a lens in a metal apparatus that's attached to a retractable bellows. This little marvel is my grandmother's first camera, a No. 2A Folding Pocket Brownie Automatic made by the Eastman Kodak Co. of Rochester, New York. My grandfather gave it to her for her 17th birthday in 1912, and it still works perfectly—when I manage to track down film that fits.

A century ago, my grandmother's Brownie—simple to use, small and light enough to carry anywhere—represented the apex of consumer technology. But even the most casual of snapshooters must understand the essentials of photography to take a picture with it. A dial governs the size of an opening (aperture) in the eight-bladed metal diaphragm behind the lens to let light in and expose the film. A lever offers three ways to control how long this diaphragm shutter remains open. And, to focus, the bellows extend to a length determined by a scale marking the distance to the photo's subject.

Today, taking pictures is a whole lot easier and more automatic than it was when Grandmom was a teenager. Yet, to get the photos you really want—whether you're enjoying the incredible convenience of a cellphone camera or exploring the endless capabilities of a digital single-lens reflex (DSLR)—you have to master the same basics: the amount of light coming into the camera at any one moment, how long the light streams in, and the optical properties of the lens that focuses that light. The better you control light and the way your camera captures it, the more satisfying your photos will be—and the more fun you can have with photography.

This book will help you get there. You'll find hundreds of tips for every aspect of photography, from choosing the right gear to setting up your shots to capturing and enhancing your images. You'll discover quick fixes for typical situations and longer projects that will challenge your skills and creativity. You'll learn not just how to best capture the light, but how to shape it for precise pictorial effects. And you'll learn how to translate the scene you see in your mind's eye into a finished photograph that you can share with the world.

Every camera, from my grandmother's Brownie to the latest device you just ordered online, is really nothing more than a dark box with a hole on one side and light-sensitive material (film or a sensor) on the other. The pictures that you make with it are entirely up to you—and this book will get you started on that adventure.

Miriam Leuchter

Miriam Leuchter
Editor-in-Chief
Popular Photography

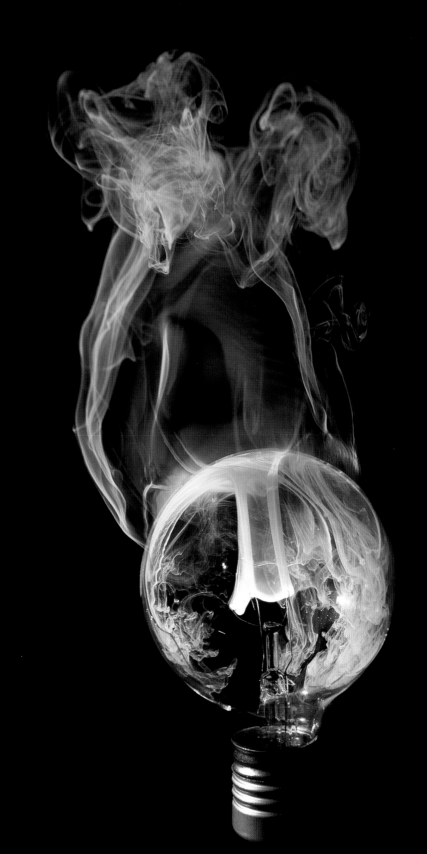

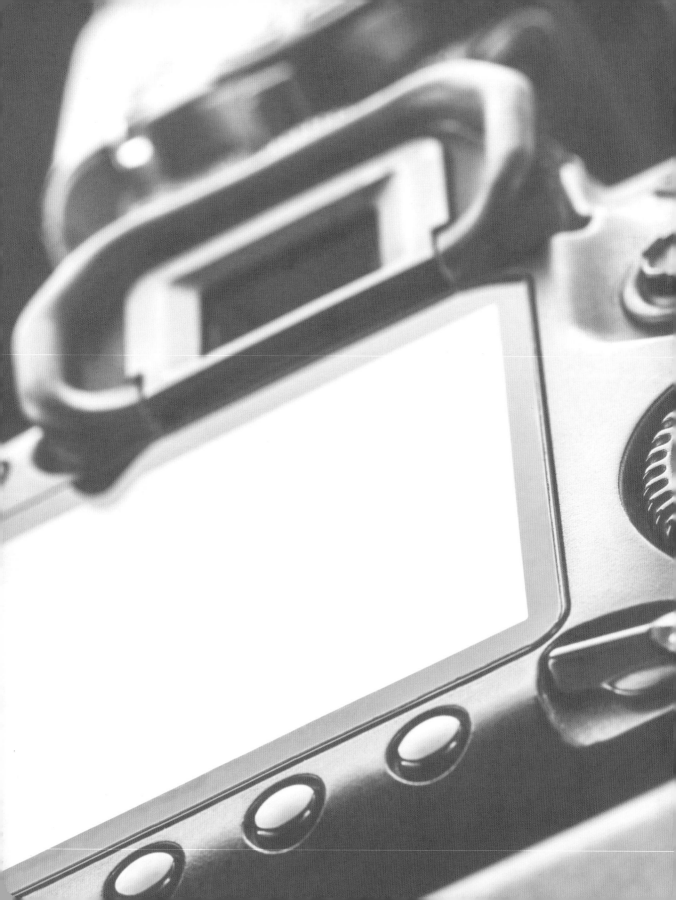

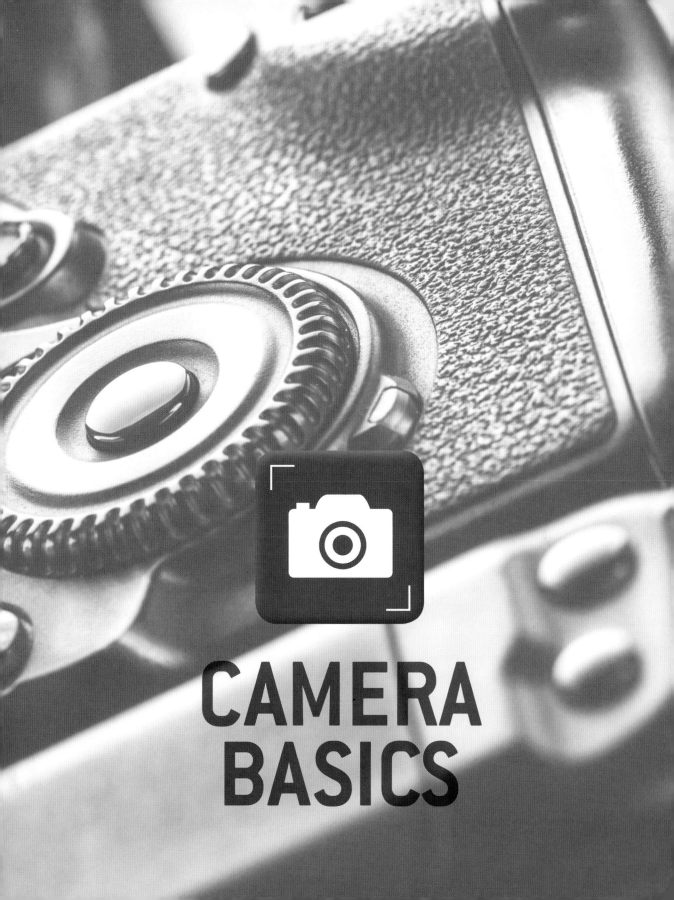

CAMERA BASICS

001 GET TO KNOW YOUR CAMERA

There are two main interchangeable-lens cameras on the market today. The most popular—shown below—is the digital single-lens reflex (DSLR), which views through the lens via a complicated optical system: The scene is reflected by a mirror up to a prism, which flips the image right side up and unreversed to display in the viewfinder or on the LCD screen. The mirror then hinges up out of the way at the moment of exposure. However, an interchangeable-lens compact (ILC) dispenses with the prism and mirror, delivering a direct electronic feed from the imaging sensor to the viewfinder—hence they are called "mirrorless."

Regardless of style, today's cameras come covered in more buttons, dials, and control pads than the cockpit of the space shuttle. Sorting out what they all do, however, does not need to be rocket science.

MANUAL FOCUS (MF) RING
Switch your lens out of autofocus (the switch is on, or near, the lens), and you can decide for yourself where to focus by turning this ring. Some lenses let you fine-tune autofocus with it as well. Note that some lenses do not have an MF ring.

ZOOM RING
Turn this to adjust for wide or long focal length to make your subject appear nearer or farther away. Some cameras may have power zooms, operated by a switch on the lens barrel.

ISO BUTTON
Use this button to set the sensitivity of your camera's image sensor according to how much light you're working with.

IMAGE STABILIZATION SWITCH
This control may be on the lens or on the camera. It lets you shoot static subjects with the camera handheld at shutter speeds that would ordinarily blur the image.

COMMAND WHEEL
On most cameras, you can control shutter and aperture via a command wheel. Some cameras have two—a plus.

HOT SHOE
Used primarily to attach an accessory flash (see #211–215) and other accessories. It is much more than a simple trigger—it can convey lots of information between the camera and shoe-mounted accessories.

LIVE VIEW BUTTON
Push this button to switch from viewing via the optical eye-level viewfinder to the LCD monitor, called Live View.

MODE DIAL
This dial lets you pick a totally automatic way of shooting, an auto mode that lets you have some say in making the settings, or a manual mode that lets you be the boss all the way.

AUTOFOCUS BUTTON
Press this button to select the elements in a scene that you want to appear in sharpest focus.

002 PREP YOUR CAMERA FOR QUICK SHOOTING

So you've unpacked your new camera. You probably want to start shooting immediately—not spend hours reading the instruction manual. Here's what you need to do to get your camera up and running so you can begin taking photographs as soon as possible.

STEP ONE Charge the battery fully—it may take several hours. To insert the battery, find the hinged or sliding hatch on the camera's bottom and slide it in so its metal contacts go in first. Turn the camera on.

STEP TWO Attach the lens to the camera. The lens and camera body often come as separate pieces. To mate them up, twist the protective caps off the camera body and the rear of the lens. Match the mark on the rear of the lens with the one on the lensmount, insert the lens into the camera body, and twist to lock together.

STEP THREE Find the covered slot for the memory card on the camera's side or bottom and slide it in, terminal end first, until it clicks into place. Almost all current digital cameras use Secure Digital (SD) cards, although some take the larger Compact Flash (CF) cards.

STEP FOUR Format the memory card. This procedure readies a card's file structure to properly record images; you'll also need to reformat it every time you want to erase images (after you've downloaded them, of course). Check that manual for the directions.

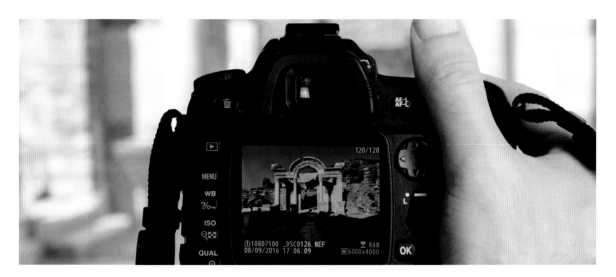

003 WAKE YOUR CAMERA WITH THE HALF-PRESS

The shutter button is the instant On switch for a whole raft of functions. Press it halfway, to the point where you feel some resistance, and your camera goes live: Autofocus focuses the lens on your subject; autoexposure meters the light and sets exposure; the viewfinder and/or LCD monitor displays these settings; image stabilization starts up; and, if the built-in flash is on, it gets a jolt of volts to prep it for firing.

All this is good stuff. But here's the most important part: If you maintain that crucial half-press, it locks in the exposure and focus until you press the button fully to snap the picture, letting you compose without tweaking settings. It's well worth practicing the half-press so it becomes routine. Compose a picture, lock in the settings with the half-press, and then try new angles—all the while holding the half-press.

004 | GET FAMILIAR WITH CAMERA TYPES

Digital cameras vary widely in how much control they offer photographers when it comes to settings. Point-and-shoots, which do everything but click the shutter for you, produce good standard shots. Digital single-lens reflex (DSLR) cameras are your best bets once you've moved past the novice stage, however. Although they require a longer learning curve, they create distinctive, high-quality photos.

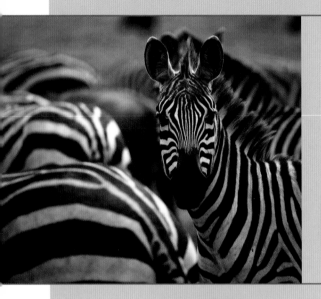

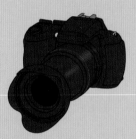

POINT-AND-SHOOT
The most basic model available, this camera automatically adjusts all settings and permits no manual control.

ELECTRIC-VIEWFINDER ULTRAZOOM
This choice is similar to the advanced compact (below), but it has a built-in, large-range zoom lens.

Ultrazooms help get your viewers much closer to far-away subjects, such as the zebras here.

INSTANT PRINT
The beloved Polaroid concept gets an update—some even have macro modes and a built-in selfie mirror.

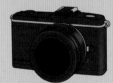

INTERCHANGEABLE-LENS COMPACT (ILC)
The ILC generally has a bigger sensor than other compacts and lets you use various lenses.

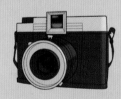

DIANA LOMO
This plastic film camera produces dreamy, streaky low-res images.

A '60s cult classic, the Diana is back, updated with pinhole, panorama, and shutter-lock options.

VIRTUAL REALITY
Often spherical with several lenses embedded in the camera body, VR cameras allow you to capture 360-degrees of a scene for a truly immersive experience.

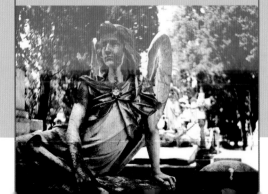

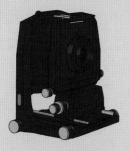

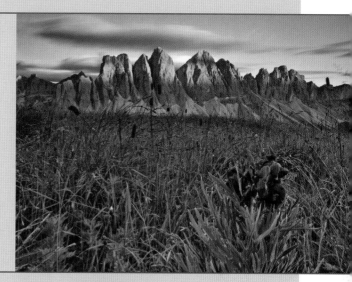

LARGE-FORMAT VIEW CAMERA
This top-of-the-line option has a sensor larger than a medium-format DSLR's to capture astonishing detail.

From still lifes to landscapes, large-format view cameras capture the greatest detail and offer the most precise focus.

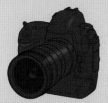

DIGITAL SINGLE-LENS REFLEX (FULL-FRAME DSLR)
A DSLR uses a mirror system to allow you to see exactly what the camera will capture through the lens.

ACTION
Capture your extreme-sport, outdoor, and underwater adventures with these small, rugged video cameras that you can mount to pretty much anything.

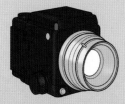

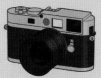

MEDIUM-FORMAT WITH DIGITAL BACK
This double-duty camera can be used with different backs for film or a digital sensor larger than a full-frame DSLR's.

DIGITAL RANGE FINDER
This camera has a bright, oversize viewfinder, which you'll need for manual focusing.

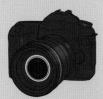

DSLR (SMALL SENSOR)
This alternative has the same functions as a full-frame but a smaller sensor size that is brand specific.

MOBILE PHONE
For shots on the go, this option is increasingly sophisticated, with 2MP or higher sensors, autofocus lenses, and decent color accuracy.

005 GET A GRIP

The way you hold your camera has a big effect on your photos. To grasp it properly, grip the camera body tightly with your right hand with your index finger on the shutter button. (You should be able to depress the shutter without moving the rest of your hand.) Then cradle the camera in your left hand with your palm facing up—you'll use this hand to adjust the lens to zoom or focus. For stability, bring the camera up to your face so the viewfinder rests against your brow bone. It also helps to keep your elbows tight against your body, which braces the camera and prevents image shake.

006 READ THE MANUAL

Sure, we're trying to get you to do a lot of reading, but you'll thank us later. You don't necessarily have to plow through your camera's manual all in one go, though it should be your first resource when questions arise. Wondering how to set in-camera noise reduction to your liking? Wish the thing would stop beeping every time you get something in focus? The manual will straighten you out. And you might find fantastic new tips and tricks in its pages. (Some people suggest you keep it in the bathroom so you'll actually read it.)

007 CAPTURE RAW IMAGES

Your new DSLR likely has lots more imaging firepower than your old camera, especially if you're stepping up from a compact. But to get as much as you can out of your camera, you need to shoot Raw. Not only does Raw give you uncompressed files, but because it captures maximum image data, it gives you more flexibility when you're processing photographs.

Processing Raw files (see #311) is a bit more complicated than working with JPEGs, so if you're new to the mode, set your camera to capture in both Raw and JPEG. That way, you'll have JPEGs to quickly share online and Raw files to adjust in postproduction. Yes, this strategy demands lots of space on your memory card and hard drive, but the payoff is well worth it.

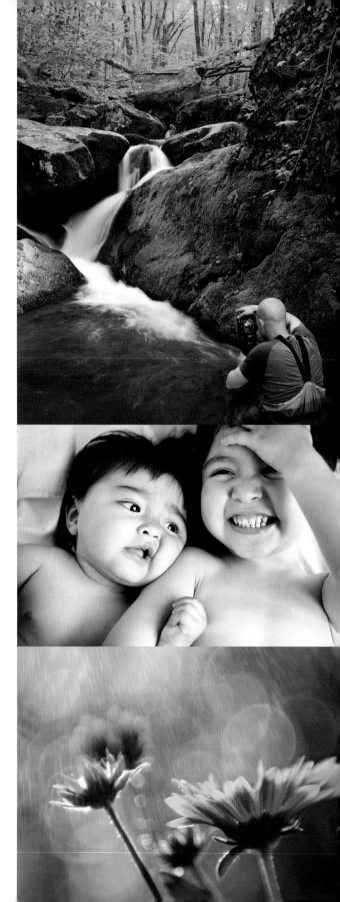

008 START OUT IN PROGRAM MODE

DSLRs are so smart that you can let them do almost everything for you—which is dangerous if you want to learn photography. Instead of starting in auto mode, switch to program (P)—it's still an automatic setting, but it lets you override the camera's robotic decision-making and explore functions such as shutter speed, aperture, and flash. If your previous camera was a compact (or a smartphone), you're in for a wealth of creative opportunities.

After you get a handle on basic functionality, move on up to manual (see #029), which allows you to control every little setting. Wherever you start, keep autofocus (AF) on: DSLRs' AF systems are so sophisticated that they'll adjust perfectly as you shoot.

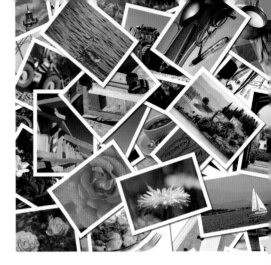

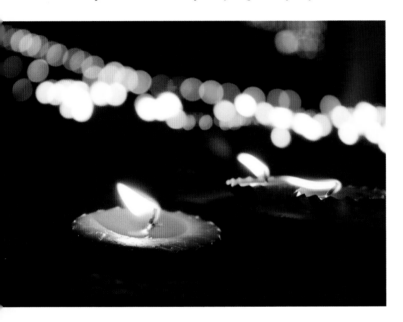

009 GET ORGANIZED

Filing definitely isn't glamorous, but if you don't have your ducks in a row, things can get messy fast. Before you start shooting, choose a central location to store photos and a standardized naming convention for folders and images. The software that you use to import images from camera to computer can help with file arrangement and naming, too. Tag images with useful details so they will be easy to find.

Back up your favorite images in more than one place. Online cloud storage services (see #353) are a good option, as are portable drives that you store at, say, your office or mom's house.

010 LEARN YOUR CAMERA'S LIMITS

When you acquire a new camera, your expectations are naturally high. Yes, it'll behave much better in low light and focus much faster than your old camera, but it can't do everything. Test it by taking a shot at each of its ISO settings—a high ISO setting makes it more sensitive to light, and a low ISO renders it less sensitive. Then find a setting with different light, and do the same thing.

When you look at these images later, you'll learn how the camera performs and which ISO settings work best. Check, too, how the autofocus handles low-light situations, and find out just how fast the high-speed burst mode really is. Exploring these functions prepares you for serious shooting.

QUICK TIP

011 PROTECT YOUR NEW PURCHASE

As soon as you get it home from the store, write down your camera's serial number and put it somewhere safe. Register the camera, too, in case it's stolen or needs service.

012 EXPERIMENT WITH CAMERA FUNCTIONS

If you're new to DSLRs and ILCs, their functions can bewilder you—but learning what they are and experimenting with what they do grants you great control over shots. Below are the key functions of most DSLRs and ILCs—including color, exposure, and image-quality controls and custom settings that handle many other aspects of a shot, though advanced ones sport even more features. Models vary, of course, and some functions are found in on-screen menus and others in external controls. Study your manual before you shoot.

IMAGE-QUALITY AND RESOLUTION CONTROLS
When you're grabbing casual snaps, choose lower-quality, higher-compression settings so your memory card won't overflow. Save high-quality, high-resolution settings for artful images.

IMAGE-SHAPE CONTROLS
Many DSLRs let you select photos' dimensions—3:2 is the most common proportion, but you can choose other shapes to best suit your style.

AUTOFOCUS MODES
These settings allow you to focus in several fashions: Single works optimally on still subjects, while modes such as Continuous allow you to track a moving subject through the frame. Your viewfinder and LCD screen (in Live View) can show you where the camera's autofocus points are, allowing you to center your focus area, place it in the frame, or activate multiple points simultaneously. In some situations, such as when shooting close up in very low light, it may be better to focus manually.

AUTO-EXPOSURE MODES
A DSLR's one-size-fits-all, fully automated setting is called Program. It picks aperture and exposure duration for you. Experienced shooters might select Intelligent auto or auto ISO modes to control their image sensor's light sensitivity (a low ISO—50 to 200—works well in bright conditions; high ISOs are best in dim ones). Tip: The higher the ISO, the noisier your image will be. Choose aperture-priority mode (see #028) when you require a specific aperture for certain light conditions. Freezing speedy action? Pick shutter-priority mode. And full manual mode allows complete control over exposure.

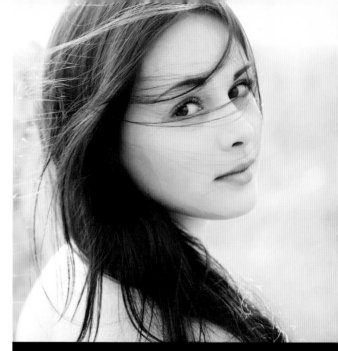

SCENE MODE
This mode contains a menu of settings for specific subjects. Portrait mode instructs the camera to use a short exposure but switch off flash, for example; Foliage mode amps color saturation and sets a small aperture.

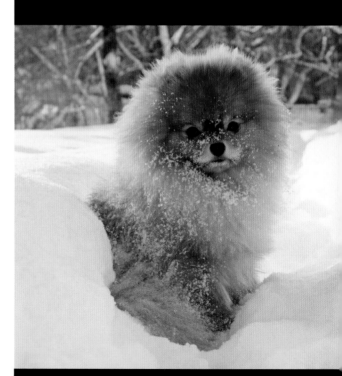

WHITE BALANCE
Choosing auto white balance lets the DSLR define how white areas look in specific lighting conditions, and it corrects all other colors accordingly. Set WB manually when shooting in mixed lighting conditions.

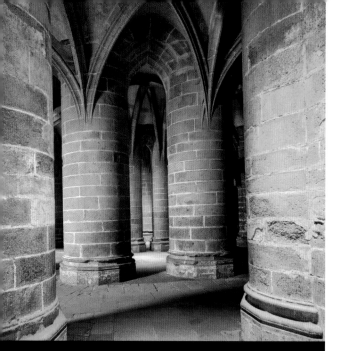

FLASH MODES

In auto mode, the camera's own flash fires when light is low. Turn it off if you don't like flash's hard look or prefer to use a tripod and a long exposure.

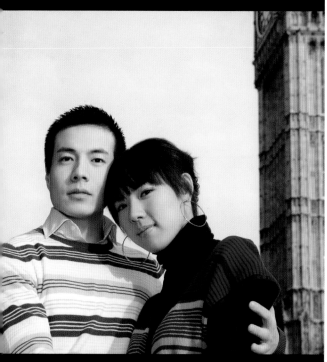

SELF-TIMER

Want to avoid jostling a tripod-mounted camera? Set its self-timer mode, and it will trigger its own shutter after a predetermined period of time.

COLOR-QUALITY SETTINGS

Many in-camera menus offer settings from B&W to pale pastels. Experiment by shooting a subject in several settings to learn their effects.

HOT SHOE

Here you can slot in a flash unit or other accessories; a small cover protects it when it's not in use. Accessory flashes can also sit in L-brackets to the camera's side. Or set them near your subject and fire them via remote trigger.

AUTOBRACKETING

When you're unsure which exposure will work best, employ the autobracketing function to fire off several shots at varying exposures with a single shutter press.

FOCAL LENGTH CONTROLS

When you use a zoom lens, its zoom ring will allow you to set the focal length to control the angle of view and how much of the frame your subject fills.

POP-UP FLASH

Many DSLRs and ILCs include an onboard flash that pops upward—a convenient option if you lack an accessory flash unit.

LIVE VIEW MODE

This mode lets you use the camera's LCD screen as a viewfinder so you can preview framing and composition before you shoot.

BURST MODE

Also known as Continuous shooting mode, this function lets you choose the number of shots your camera fires over a duration with one press of the shutter button. It's perfect for fast-moving action.

IMAGE-STABILIZATION CONTROL

Sitting on the lens or camera body, this control helps you capture sharp images even when you shoot in low light or without a tripod.

CONNECTIONS TO PERIPHERAL GEAR

You'll need to hook your DSLR to a computer or printer at some point. Follow the camera's menu instructions (and consult its manual) to ensure connections work smoothly.

013 UNDERSTAND EXPOSURE

Exposure is the most crucial aspect of photography. To understand this concept, it helps to consider a somewhat odd metaphor: filling a bucket with light.

Think about filling a bucket with water. If you turn on the tap a little, it takes a long time to fill the bucket—say, 4 minutes. But if the faucet is open twice as wide, your bucket fills up much faster, maybe in 2 minutes. And if you open it up to its widest, the bucket may overflow in only 1 minute. The fill level—exposure—is measured by a factor called *stops*. If you double the exposure, it's called adding one stop. If you halve the exposure, you're subtracting one stop.

It's the same with your camera, only your camera's digital sensor is the bucket; the width of the faucet opening is the lens's aperture; and the length of time that the water runs is the shutter speed. To ensure that the sensor receives just the right amount of light to make an exposure, you adjust the size of the faucet opening (aperture) and the amount of time you're letting the light through it (shutter speed). Too little or too much of either shutter time or aperture width and you'll get photos that are too dark (when the bucket didn't fill up all the way) or too light (when the bucket overflowed).

014 LOOK AT A GRAPH OF YOUR EXPOSURE

An excellent tool for evaluating your photo's exposure is your camera's *histogram*, a graph of the range of tones in the scene from darkest (left) to brightest (right). You can look at a photo's histogram post-capture on the LCD screen, or keep it live as you shoot. In general, you want to see an even distribution from right to left, with a gentle peak near the middle. If you see the graph bunched up against the left or right side, you're getting *clipping*: shadow or highlight tones that are too extreme to be recorded by the sensor. Take, for instance, the lost detail in the shadowy, rocky banks in the underexposed image at center, and the blown-out white rapids in the overexposed example at right. Of course, sometimes clipping is unavoidable or even desirable—the trick is knowing when it works for your scene.

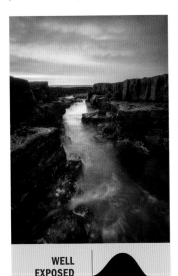

WELL EXPOSED

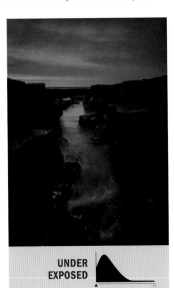

UNDER EXPOSED

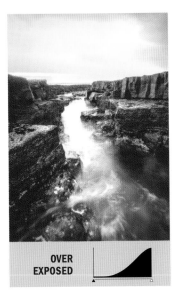

OVER EXPOSED

015 DISCOVER LIGHT METERING

How does your camera arrive at a quality exposure? It uses its built-in *light meter* to measure the light coming through the lens, then creates an exposure setting for a middle tone based on an 18-percent-reflectance neutral-gray card. (In fact, it's common procedure to place one of these handy cards in your scene and take a meter reading off it.)

Your light meter's fondness for midtones creates even exposures, but it can cause problems. If you meter off a light-skinned person's face, for example, that exposure will render the person's face a middle tone. Meter off a dark-complected person's face, and the reading will also render the face a middle tone. Your camera's light meter is pretty smart—it can analyze scenes with complex lighting and make good guesses at the exposure. But it can still make a bad guess—or a good guess that you plain don't like. That's what exposure compensation (see #018) and manual exposure (#029) are for.

016 CHOOSE A METERING MODE

Your camera has up to four metering modes that allow it to set an exposure. Each uses a different tactic to measure the light in your scene.

SPOTMETER The preferred mode for making precise exposures, a *spotmeter* measures the light in only a small circle in the viewfinder or LCD. Typical targets for a middle tone include gray rocks, green grass, and clear north sky midmorning or midafternoon.

LIMITED AREA This mode isn't found on all cameras; also called fat spot, it behaves much like the spotmeter but takes in a wider area.

CENTERWEIGHTED This popular mode surveys the entire area of the frame, averaging its reading for a middle-tone setting.

EVALUATIVE Also known as multipattern, *evaluative mode* reads the light across multiple points and analyzes it in software to arrive at a best guess. It also works with autofocus to bias the exposure to closer objects.

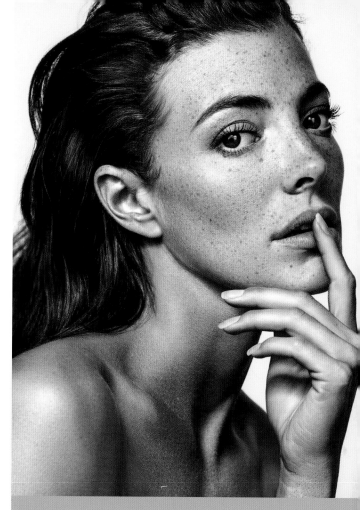

QUICK TIP

017 METER MANUALLY WITH AEL

When you half-press the shutter button, autoexposure locks on an area in the scene. But what if you want to meter a different area without fussing with manual exposure? *Autoexposure lock* (AEL) to the rescue.

On most cameras, AEL is found on a back button convenient to your thumb. To use it, aim the camera where you want to meter in your scene and press AEL. The exposure locks there, freeing you to recompose the shot but keep the exposure. This function is great for spotmetering—landscape shooters, for example, know that many rocks are neutral gray, so they will lock a spotmeter reading off a rock and recompose for the actual shot.

018 FIX PHOTO PROBLEMS WITH EXPOSURE COMPENSATION

Despite all the attention exposure gets, there is no such thing as an objectively correct one. Sure, grievous mistakes—gross underexposure or overexposure resulting in total loss of detail—are bad. But if, in your mind's eye, you see your scene as lighter or darker than reality, go for it. And, if you're working in program, aperture-priority, or shutter-priority modes, here's how: It's called *exposure compensation* (EC).

Your camera might have an actual EC dial, but with most cameras, you access EC via a button with the universal +/- symbol, and then twirl a dial or wheel to make the setting. It's about as intuitive as it can get. If you dial EC in the positive direction, you'll make the picture lighter. Dial it to negative, and the picture will be darker. The EC scale is laid out like a ruler, and the standard big gradation is one *exposure value* (EV), usually called a stop. EVs are very precise steps: Increase by one EV and you double the exposure;

decrease by one EV and you halve the exposure. You can dial in lightening or darkening by 1/3 increments as well. Below are some situations in which EC can really come to the rescue.

STRONG BACKLIGHTING When working in intense backlight, a portrait subject might be a near-silhouette, even with the best efforts of metering. Crank up the exposure by at least +1.0 EV.

AREAS OF BRIGHT WHITE Pale sandy beaches in bright light don't always keep their crisp whiteness. Some smart meters may catch them, but often these scenes will end up gray. Dial up EC by at least +1.0 EV; you may need up to +2.0 EV.

SPOTLIT SUBJECTS Let's say you're trying to photograph performers onstage. The meter may see all that black background and overexpose badly. To fix, take EC down by at least −1.0 EV.

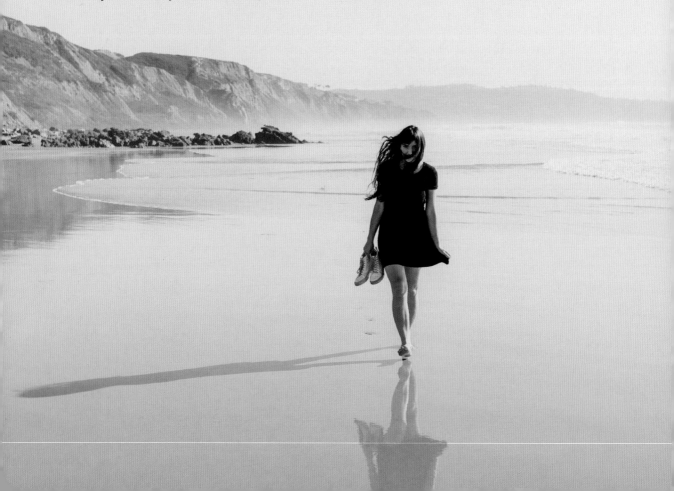

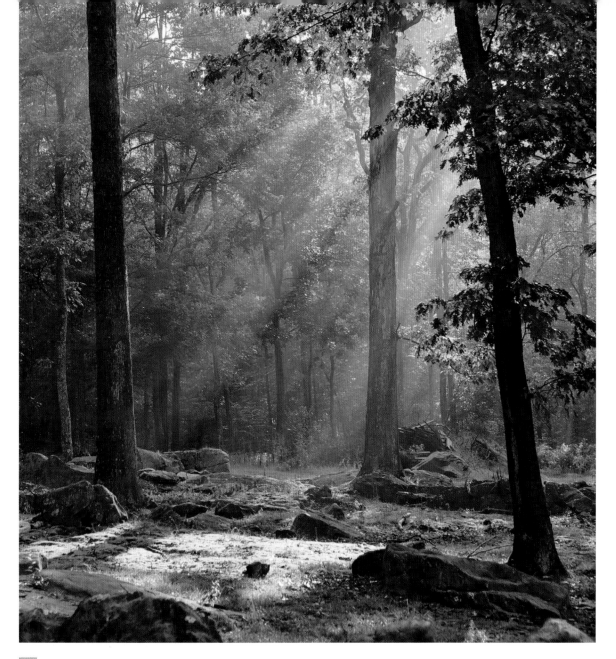

019 BRACKET TO ENSURE GOOD EXPOSURE

Bracketing dates way back to the film era, when photographers learned to nail exposure by shooting one image at the meter reading, then one a bit above and one a bit below. Today, this process is automated so you can set the intervals of your brackets (a third stop, a half stop, etc.) and how many you want to take. Then, when you trigger the shutter, the camera takes all the exposures in a quick burst. Bracketing is useful in scenes with rapidly changing light—for example, concerts with wild strobes—or scenes with a wide range of dark and light, like the forest above. Recent cameras can merge these shots into one perfectly exposed image via *in-camera HDR* (high-dynamic range imaging); check your manual for more details.

020 UNDERSTAND SHUTTER SPEED

The shutter in your camera is a complicated mechanism, but it does a very simple thing: controls the length of your exposure. It's basically a set of curtains in front of the imaging sensor. Press the shutter button, and one curtain opens to expose the sensor to light, and a second curtain then shuts to end the exposure. If the shutter stays open a long time, it lets in a lot of light; if it's open a short time, it lets in little light. The standard shutter timings are 1, 1/2, 1/4, 1/8, 1/15, 1/30, 1/60, 1/125, 1/250, 1/500, 1/1000, 1/2000, 1/4000, and (on some cameras) 1/8000 sec. There are intermediate settings, too, and your camera most likely has slower speeds, down to 30 sec or longer. (This setting, called Bulb, allows for extralong exposures common in nighttime photography or lightpainting; see #130, #268, and #266.)

Beyond helping you land on an ideal exposure, your choice of shutter speed also changes the look of your pictures—sometimes dramatically so. With fast shutter speeds, the camera captures a short slice of time, freezing subjects in action, while at slow shutter speeds, the camera documents a long slice of time, letting motion blur across the frame. Regardless of your subject, learning how to harness shutter speed is crucial to achieving your aesthetic vision.

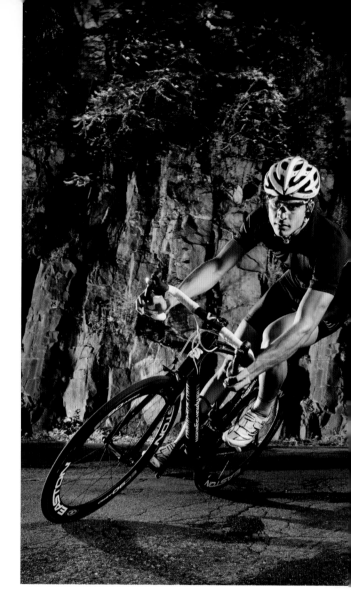

021 FREEZE MEGAFAST ACTION

You don't need specialized equipment or complex image editing to create "frozen" drama—just a camera, a lens that's long enough to get you out of the way of the action, a fast shutter speed, and a subject capable of lightning-fast moves. Use the harsh light of midday sun (or a strobe, as above) to sharply define your subject's details, and set your camera to one of the fastest shutter speeds—1/1000 to 1/8000—with the ISO set high enough to give you sufficient exposure. Then position yourself as close to the action as possible and shoot away. Below is a handy cheat sheet for shutter speeds and their effects.

1/1000	1/500	1/250	1/125	1/60	1/30	1/15	1/8	1/4	1/2

FREEZE ACTION   **BLUR ACTION**

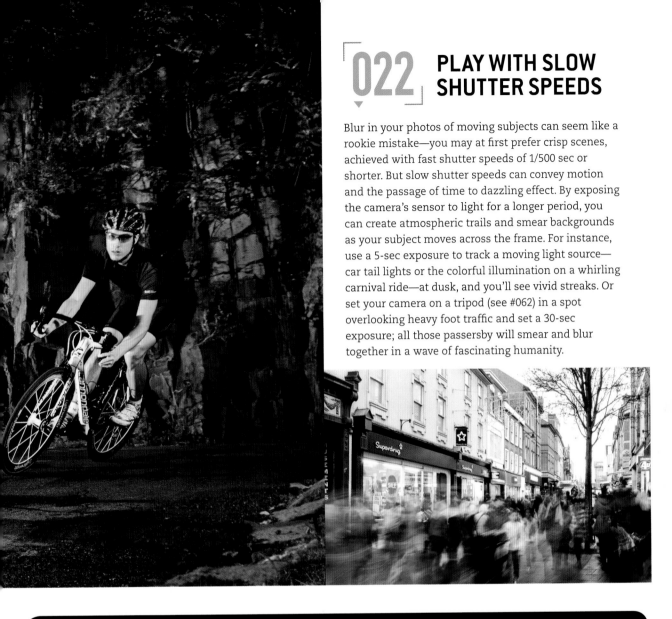

022 PLAY WITH SLOW SHUTTER SPEEDS

Blur in your photos of moving subjects can seem like a rookie mistake—you may at first prefer crisp scenes, achieved with fast shutter speeds of 1/500 sec or shorter. But slow shutter speeds can convey motion and the passage of time to dazzling effect. By exposing the camera's sensor to light for a longer period, you can create atmospheric trails and smear backgrounds as your subject moves across the frame. For instance, use a 5-sec exposure to track a moving light source—car tail lights or the colorful illumination on a whirling carnival ride—at dusk, and you'll see vivid streaks. Or set your camera on a tripod (see #062) in a spot overlooking heavy foot traffic and set a 30-sec exposure; all those passersby will smear and blur together in a wave of fascinating humanity.

023 TAKE FULL CONTROL OF SHUTTER WITH S MODE

To command your camera to use a specific shutter speed without going full-on manual, use the exposure mode called *shutter-priority*. On most camera makes, this mode is denoted simply by S; on a few others, by Tv (for time value). You'll find the setting in the same place where you set program, aperture-priority, and manual (see #008, #028, and #032, respectively). Once in S mode, set the shutter speed that you want using the dial or touchscreen menu, and presto—the camera locks it there. Then, to maintain proper exposure, the camera will automatically adjust the other control—aperture. This way, there's one less thing to think about when shooting.

Don't worry if you get blinky warnings in the viewfinder in some lighting conditions (mainly dim light). It just means that you've exceeded the range of apertures available for your chosen shutter speed. Fix this with flash or by bumping up your ISO (see #033).

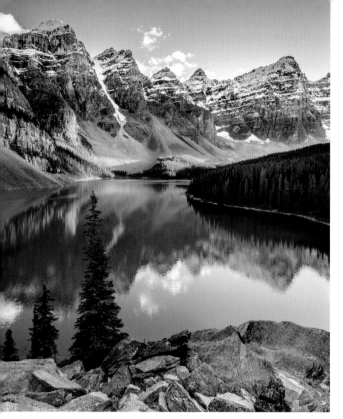

024 UNDERSTAND APERTURE

Like shutter speed, aperture—one of our fundamental camera controls—is also remarkably simple. It's a valve (or a faucet, if you will) inside your lens, with a circular, or nearly circular, opening. Open up the aperture wide, and light will come gushing through the lens; close down the faucet to a narrow opening, and light will just trickle through. Beyond rote mechanics, aperture determines how much of the scene will stay in acceptable focus (called depth of field). The wider apertures (like f/1.4, f/2, and f/2.8) will keep the foreground object you focused on sharp but will blur out the background. Meanwhile, small apertures—such as f/16 and f/22—can render the foreground and background and everything in between sharp, as in this glacial landscape. So you can think of an aperture setting as a slice of space: Shooting with small f-stops will give you a shallow slice of space, while shooting with big f-stops will give you a deep slice of space.

025 GET A HANDLE ON F-STOPS

Aperture sizes are designated by an odd sequence of numbers called *f-stops*: f/1 (which is rare), f/1.4, f/2, f/2.8, f/4, f/5.6, f/8, f/11, f/16, and sometimes f/22 and f/32. (Like shutter speed, there are intermediate settings between the standard f-stops, too.) The small f-numbers—such as f/1.4 and f/2—stand for big apertures that admit gobs of light and result in a shallow depth of field, as in the evocative cityscape at right. The larger f-stops, like f/5.6 and f/8, admit less light. And the biggest f-stops of all (such as f/16 and f/22) let in a trickle of light, creating a deep depth of field that's sharp from front to back.

One caveat: An f-stop is not to be confused with a stop, the unit of measure for how much light enters the lens, determined by the combination of the aperture and shutter speed settings.

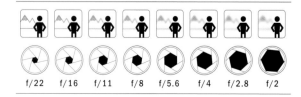

f/22   f/16   f/11   f/8   f/5.6   f/4   f/2.8   f/2

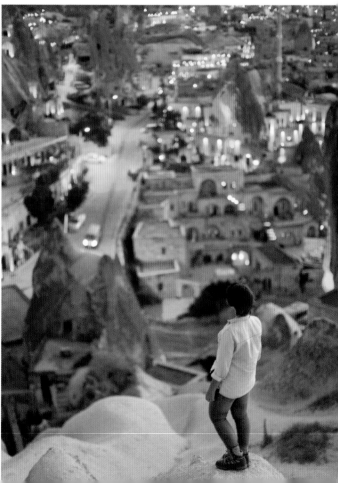

026 GO DEEP—OR SHALLOW

Whether you want a deep or shallow depth of field depends on your subject. For portraits, a shallow depth of field (small f-stop) works best—it blurs distracting background detail. In landscapes, a deep depth (a big f-stop) conveys a sense of dimension. But there are nuances galore. A portrait of, say, a mechanic in his garage would be better with enough depth of field to show his environment, while a study of blossoms will benefit from a gauzy out-of-focus background. So use your judgment.

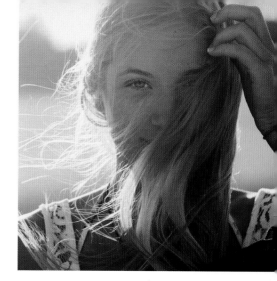

027 EXPLORE THE RECIPROCITY LAW

By now you might be getting comfortable with the two fundamental controls of exposure: shutter and aperture. Long exposures and wide-open apertures admit lots of light to the sensor. Short shutter speeds and small apertures admit less light to the sensor. And you can mix up shutter speeds and apertures in various combinations to get good exposures.

Now for a crucial principle: The amount of light that you gain or lose by going from one standard f-stop to the next (say, from f/2.8 to f/4, or from f/11 to f/8) is equal to the amount of light that you gain or lose by going from one standard shutter speed to the next—from 1/60 sec to 1/125 sec, or from 1/500 sec to 1/250

sec. (These standard chunks of exposure, via shutter or aperture, are called stops, or EV.) So all the settings in the chart at left will give you the exact same exposure.

The more you shoot, the more this principle (called the Reciprocity Law) will become second nature. While these settings result in the same exposure, you'll get different effects. To take two extremes: A setting of 1/2000 sec at f/1.4 will freeze pretty much any action short of a speeding bullet, but it will also give you a very shallow depth of field. In the meantime, an equivalent exposure of 1/15 sec at f/16 will blur tree leaves in a breeze but give you a huge depth of field for the forest.

EQUIVALENT EXPOSURES

Shutter Speed	Aperture
1/2000	f/1.4
1/1000	f/2
1/500	f/2.8
1/250	f/4
1/125	f/5.6
1/60	f/8
1/30	f/11
1/15	f/16

QUICK TIP

028 TRY OUT APERTURE-PRIORITY MODE

Command your camera to use a specific aperture with *aperture-priority mode*, indicated by A or Av and found near the program (P) and shutter (S or Tv) modes. In this mode, the camera automatically varies the shutter speed to create a correct exposure while maintaining your chosen aperture. Note: If you set a small aperture in dim light, the shutter will stay open a long time and cause blur. Get a faster shutter speed by upping ISO.

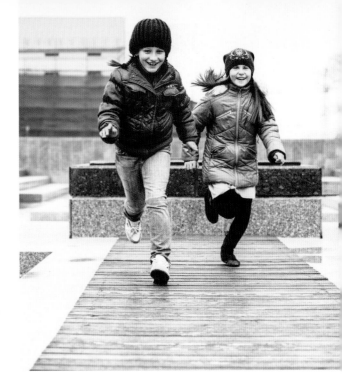

029 MEET MANUAL MODE

Long before autoexposure, photographers set shutter speed and aperture themselves, either in consultation with a stand-alone light meter or an exposure calculator. Today, manual exposure is still ideal in situations that call for precise exposure settings. The key to manual mode is that once you set an exposure, it stays there until you intervene again. There's no interference from an automatic mode—if you move a dish in your still life or have your model change into an outfit of another color, the in-camera meter won't boss you into a different exposure setting. But, of course, this means you're on the hook for making sure your exposure works if you, say, wander into a patch of different light. While it may seem counterintuitive, manual exposure is often a better choice for fast-moving subjects—it will hold on to your set exposure for the subject and not be thrown off by any sudden change in background.

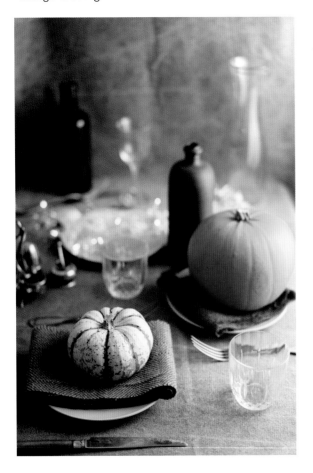

030 PICK THE RIGHT TIME FOR MANUAL

Here are typical situations for use of manual exposure.

STATIC SETUPS Manual is excellent for carefully set-up, unchanging scenarios, such as still lifes, product shots, artworks, and so on.

STUDIO PORTRAITS Opt for manual when the exposure for one particular area is all-important—like a person. You'll want to make an exposure for the model's face and hair, and keep it constant regardless of the lightness or darkness of the outfit or background.

MIXED LIGHTING For setups combining flash and ambient lighting, you may want to set the exposure for the background manually and then leave it there for all subsequent flash adjustments, even when using TTL autoflash (see #215).

QUICK SUBJECTS Paradoxically, manual exposure works better for some stadium sports. Consider a football running back: During a long run, he may pass in front of a bench full of light-colored uniforms, then be surrounded by defenders in dark uniforms—but the light on the runner is the same in both instances. Autoexposures will land all over the place, whereas a manual exposure specifically for the running back will keep the exposure setting constant.

031 COUNT THE CLICKS

You've likely noticed weird intermediate numbers for aperture (such as f/3.2 and f/3.5) and shutter speed (1/40 and 1/50 sec). Each represents exactly 1/3 stop, or 0.3 EV. If you go three clicks, it's exactly a stop, and if you go three clicks with one control, you can shift the other control three clicks to get an equivalent exposure.

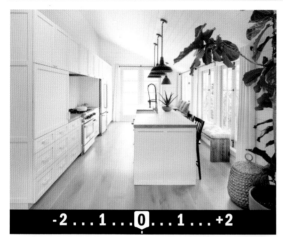

-2...1...0...1...+2

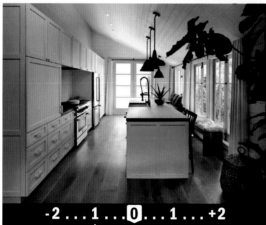

-2...1...0...1...+2

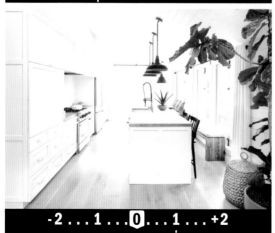

-2...1...0...1...+2

032 SET MANUAL EXPOSURE

How do you know if your exposure is set correctly? With help from the manual-metering indicator, which appears as a graduated scale in the viewfinder or on the LCD screen, either horizontal at the bottom or vertical at the side. It looks like a ruler, and the central zero point is what the camera's meter deems correct exposure. The minus (–) end of the scale indicates underexposure; the plus (+) end of the scale indicates overexposure. The scale is usually gradated two or more stops on either side of the center zero point, in 1/3 stop increments.

To reach a desired exposure, adjust shutter speed or aperture to move the indicator along the scale until it hits zero. If your settings are off the scale, you'll get a warning light in the viewfinder and LCD monitor.

STEP ONE For a quick starting point for an exposure setting, set the exposure-mode dial to P (program).

STEP TWO Pick a light-metering mode: evaluative, center-weighted, or spot (see #016). Aim the spotmeter at a desired tone, then half-press the shutter button.

STEP THREE Make a note of the reading that displays in the viewfinder and LCD screen, then set the exposure mode dial to M (manual) and transfer the reading to your camera.

STEP FOUR Evaluate the exposure and adjust if needed. If you're photographing a landscape, for example, a small aperture (such as f/11 or f/16) may be a priority, so you may have to readjust the shutter speed to recenter the indicator on the exposure scale. If you're photographing a portrait subject, a reasonably fast shutter (1/250 sec) may be essential, so you may have to fiddle with the aperture setting to get back to a centered exposure.

STEP FIVE Can't nail your desired exposure? Raise or lower the ISO to get more or less sensitivity. (Go with higher ISOs for a faster shutter and/or smaller apertures; try lower ISOs for a slower shutter and/or wider apertures.)

STEP SIX Shoot away, adjusting the exposure above or below the center point as you see fit.

033 UNDERSTAND ISO

Sooner or later, you're going to run low on light. Whether you're shooting beach volleyball at sunset or late-night candids in a bar, low light causes the same problem: Despite a wide-open aperture, you can't boost shutter speed enough to prevent blur. Even if your subject is fairly still, it may be tricky to capture his features in such a dark scene. You can't increase light in these situations, but you can turn up your camera sensor's sensitivity to it with the control called *ISO*. ISO numbers run in the sequence 100, 200, 400, 800, 1600, 3200, 6400, and often higher. Every time you double the ISO—say, from 200 to 400—you gain enough sensitivity to go a full shutter speed faster, or to close down the aperture by a full stop.

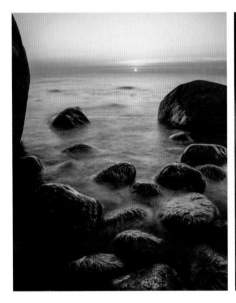
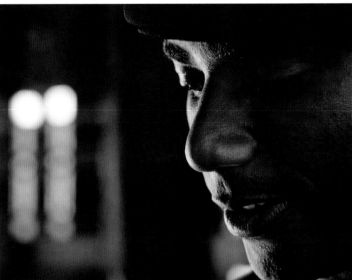

034 MINIMIZE NOISE AT HIGH ISOs

If a high ISO solves so many problems, why not crank it up all the time? There's no free lunch here: At high ISOs, image quality deteriorates, creating *noise*: ugly grain and mottling. Turning up the ISO amplifies rogue electrons in the camera's circuitry. It's a lot like jacking up the volume on a weak radio station—you get more sound, yes, but also more static.

Enter *noise reduction* (NR), a process by which the camera applies a "smoothing" filter to mask noise, but at a cost: Images will be less sharp. At very high ISOs, the drop in resolution can be quite steep, and the images will still be pretty noisy.

All cameras are set to a default NR, which can be turned up or down via your camera's setup menu. In

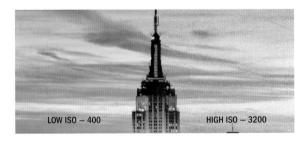

LOW ISO — 400   HIGH ISO — 3200

practical terms, most recent DSLRs and ILCs can produce sharp images with low noise up from ISO 800 to 1600. But by ISO 3200, things get dicey on some cameras, and by ISO 6400, almost all cameras produce images with noticeable noise and/or loss of sharpness.

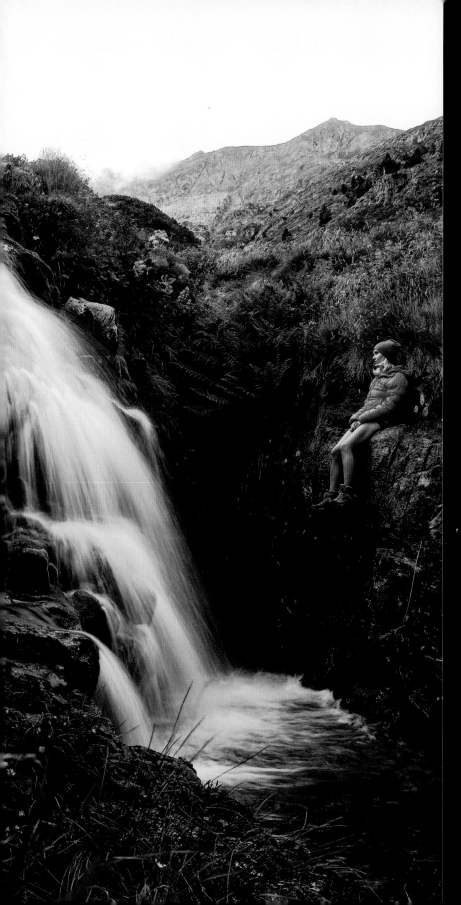

035 GO LOW WITH ISO

What advantage do you get with low ISO settings? First of all, quality, quality, quality.

Pictures taken at low ISOs are sharp, with fine grain and clear rich colors. It's no wonder that landscape enthusiasts will keep ISOs as low as possible, and if they have to lug around a tripod to maintain a low ISO but prevent shake, so be it. And it's why portraitists would rather pour on artificial light than up their ISO.

Keeping ISO low lets you shoot with wide-open apertures to isolate single elements in the frame. And there are times when you really need low ISO settings. For instance, if you want to use a slow shutter speed in a panning action shot (see #208), high ISOs will be only be an impediment, particularly in bright daylight. In a situation like this, even with a very small aperture, you may end up with a shutter speed so fast that an image of a bicycle racer will have little or no streakiness in the background. And if you want to blur moving water and transform it into in a silky, ethereal flow (like at left), low ISOs are a must. And some landscape shooters go for a lot of blur in order to, say, transform a field of wildflowers into an impressionistic field of color. Similarly, if you're doing outdoor portraits and want to blur out the background with a very wide aperture (like f/1.4 or f/2), a low ISO is the only way to go.

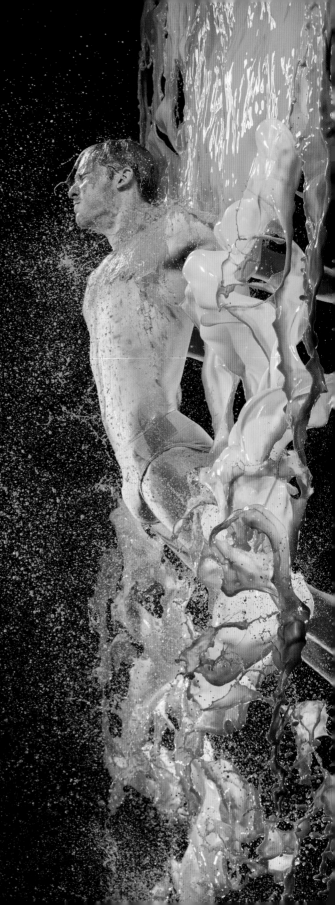

036 CONTROL THE HOW OF AUTOFOCUS

When you half-press the shutter button of your camera, technological wizardry springs instantly to life in a feat called *autofocus*: The camera focuses the lens by itself, moving the lens barrel or elements within the lens to make your subject sharp, all the while displaying your focus points with one or several red dots (depending on your autofocus mode). Autofocus modes determine whether to lock the focus on the original position of your subject, or let the focus roam with your subject. Here are the various flavors to choose from.

SINGLE-SHOT This mode is often designated with an S. Once the AF achieves focus, single-shot mode will lock it there as long as you maintain the half-press on the shutter, and it won't let go until you take the picture. Your subject can move, or you can recompose the shot, but the original focusing point will stay put.

CONTINUOUS To focus on moving subjects such as the dancer at right, Continuous mode (C) is a good tactic. It will focus with a half-press of the shutter, but it doesn't lock on. If your subject moves, or if you re-aim the camera, the AF will attempt to refocus on the subject. You can fire the shutter at any time, regardless of whether the subject is in focus or not. Continuous is often used with burst-exposure mode for rapid-fire shot sequences (see #186).

AUTOSWITCH This mode starts out as single-shot, but if subject motion is detected, it will switch to Continuous.

037 CONTROL THE WHERE OF AUTOFOCUS

In addition to modes that regulate how autofocus works, your camera has different modes that govern where AF looks for focus in the picture frame. Depending on your model, you can select the focus point with a joystick controller, control pad on the back of the camera, or menu on your touchscreen.

CENTERPOINT This is the classic, favored by many for simplicity and reliability. It employs the central autofocus point only, which is almost always the most sensitive one available.

WIDE AREA This works much like center point, except it employs several sensors on the left and right to catch subjects that aren't quite centered—good for less-predictable situations.

MULTIPLE POINT, USER-SELECT This type of autofocus lets you choose the AF point, which is useful for off-center subjects if you don't want to continually refocus and recompose your image.

MULTIPLE POINT, AUTO-SELECT Here, the camera selects an AF point on its own, usually choosing one toward the center or over the closest subject in the frame. Good for tracking action.

MULTIPLE POINT, USER OR AUTO-SELECT Why go with one when you can choose a cluster of AF points? It's great for tracking erratic motion or for scenes with complex patterns. Not present on all cameras.

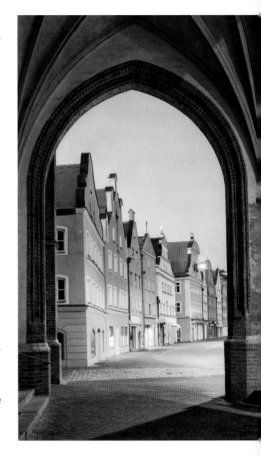

QUICK TIP

038 UNDERSTAND WHY AUTOFOCUS GOOFS (OR QUITS OUTRIGHT)

Here are some classic AF-fail scenarios—if these fixes don't work, try manual focus.

LOW LIGHT AF fails in very dim scenes. Turn up the lights, or deploy the AF-assist beam to light up the scene. If those fail, engage the single and strongest central AF point.

DIM LENS Autofocus can slow at small (i.e., dim) apertures—especially in low light. Manual is your best bet.

EMPTY SPACES Autofocus can't lock onto blank walls or a cloudless sky, which means your shutter button won't depress. To fix, aim at an area of contrasty detail that's the same distance as your subject, then recompose.

COMPETING SUBJECTS When shooting, say, a cityscape in front of a chain-link fence, the AF may focus on the fence. Try moving close enough that you can shoot through it.

039 EXPERIMENT WITH WHITE BALANCE

All light has color, even light that appears "white." Our eye-brain computers adjust automatically to see many colorcasts as neutral or near-neutral tones. But in reality, bright daylight is quite blue, dark overcast bluer still, and tungsten illumination (from household bulbs) is yellow-amber. And your camera's digital sensor will record these colorcasts, unless otherwise instructed by a camera setting called *white balance* (WB), an electronic color filter that compensates for the colorcast of the scene.

White balance is measured in Kelvins. Low Kelvin temps (around 2500 degrees) are very warm, while high Kelvin temps (8000 degrees) are very cool. WB doesn't get any easier than *automatic white balance* (AWB)—it performs great in many situations, particularly in rapidly changing light and when you go from sunlight to shadow or outdoors to indoors. It also knows when

you're using flash. But there are times when AWB just can't render a scene to your liking—if, say, you've got a bright splotch of red in an otherwise neutral scene, it may throw off AWB. Or if you're shooting in nasty artificial light, colorcasts can turn out mighty strange.

When it comes to white balance, neutral is often king: You want to replicate the scene's color as it appeared before your eyes, and you use your camera's white balance tool to correct "misreadings." But sometimes it's more of a creative impulse. Take this foggy mountain view, adjusted a few different ways so you can witness white balance at work. You can try your own white balance experiment; just remember that the white balance setting compensates for the scene's light, so a Kelvin setting in the low end (2500–4000) is a blue filter, and one at the high end (5000 and above) is an amber filter.

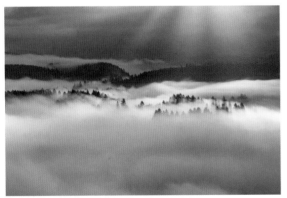

COOL IT DOWN Set to the left of neutral at 3700 Kelvin, this cold touch results in a moody image with bluer tones. This Kelvin setting is a blue filter that compensates for amber light (think light bulbs).

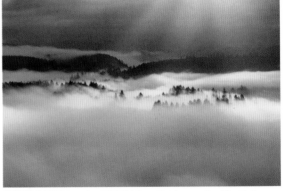

WARM IT UP Here, the 5500 Kelvin setting is an amber filter that compensates for the blue color of bright daylight. You can imagine you're seeing the warm rays of early morning spreading through the fog bank.

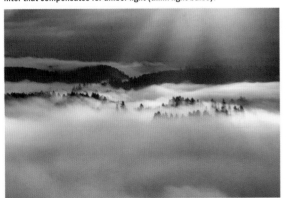

KEEP IT NEUTRAL Processed at 4400 Kelvin, this version of the image is closest to "real." There's a nice range of tones, with warm sun, cool mountains, and silver fog.

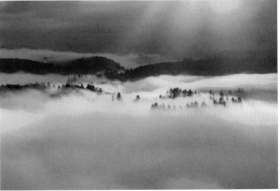

WARM IT WAY UP Here is warmth in the extreme at 6500 Kelvin, without almost any trace of the natural blue. Some would say this is fun with white balance gone too far, but it depends on what you're after.

040 SET A CUSTOM WHITE BALANCE

A simple piece of gray cardboard is your US$3 ticket to neutral color and dead-on exposure—carry one with you to set your WB before you shoot.

STEP ONE Hold (or ask your subject to hold) a photo gray card in the light that you'll use in your shot.

STEP TWO Stand back a few steps, and compose so the gray card fills your frame. Set your exposure accordingly and take a photo.

STEP THREE Navigate your camera's menu options to locate its list of white balance settings. Select the custom white balance option and then choose the test photo you took with the gray card as the reference image.

STEP FOUR Remove the gray card and start shooting for real. If the light changes, take another shot with the card and use it to set a new custom white balance.

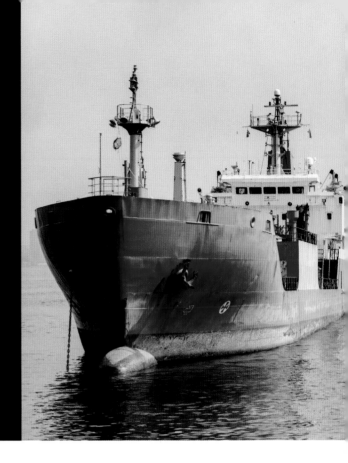

041 CONTROL COLOR MORE WITH PRESETS

Automatic white balance is very smart, but it's not foolproof. Large areas of predominating color in a scene, or a brightly lit object in a darker surround, can throw off AWB. A classic example: sunsets. Our eyes perceive the brilliant golds and reds, but with AWB, they can turn out . . . blah.

This is the right time to opt for a WB preset, a setting that locks in a specific color balance for you. You access presets via a menu; on some cameras, an external button will allow a quick jump to the settings. Presets are denoted by standardized icons, as shown at right. In the case of that gorgeous sunset, use a daylight preset and the colors will come through—the camera won't compensate for them. To use a preset, choose one that most closely matches your lighting situation. One pitfall: If you forget about the setting and the illumination changes, your pictures will show an off cast.

On many cameras, individual WB presets also let you push the balance warmer or cooler via menu adjustments. (These may also allow you to nudge the hue along the magenta-green axis to counteract any green casts caused by fluorescent lighting.) Another fine-tuner found on some cameras lets you move the WB point around on a graph.

Icon	Lighting
☀	Sunny, blue skies with or without clouds; hazy bright
🏠	Open shade on sunny days
☁	Overall cloudy; mists and fog
☀	Tungsten lighting
▤	Fluorescent lighting
▤ 2	Warm-white fluorescent (not on all cameras)
▤ 3	Cool-white fluorescent (not on all cameras)

042 EXPLORE THE BUILT-IN FLASH

A built-in flash, found on consumer-level DSLRs and ILCs, doesn't get a lot of respect from some photo enthusiasts who disdain it as an amateur feature. "Too weak!" "Can't get it off the camera!" "Too automatic!" We beg to disagree. Yes, it has its limitations, but it is bottled light always at the ready, and it is often just the ticket for quick and easy snapshots—especially when working in low-light situations, when your subject is backlit, or when bright sun overhead casts inky shadows that you'd like to open back up. If you're shooting outdoors, popping your flash in broad daylight can also help you achieve richer colors and a certain "pop," as it did for these lovely spring tulips. But the real advantage of speedlight, as it is often called, is that its burst is extremely short in duration—anywhere from 1/1000 sec to 1/20,000 sec. This instantaneous flare enables you to freeze action in low light. It may even help you achieve some surprisingly creative effects along the way.

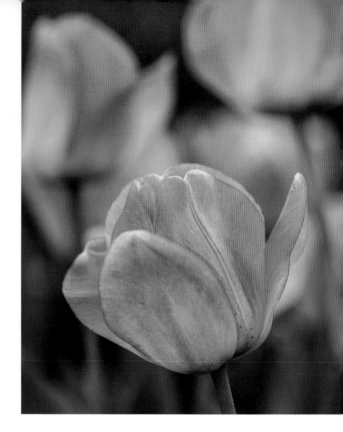

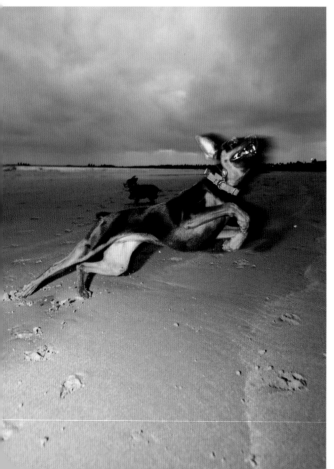

043 CHOOSE YOUR LEVEL OF FLASH CONTROL

Built-in flashes have three levels of automation, which are represented by icons and accessed via a menu or by a dedicated control.

AUTOFLASH This mode decides to fire the flash or not, depending on your scene's light level; it is what you get, without option, in all-auto or scene-exposure modes (see #012). But in P, S (Tv), A (Av), or M modes, you get to choose autoflash or another flash mode. Autoflash limits how low your shutter speed can go, so in low light you may get a dark background.

FLASH ON Here, you're telling the flash to fire every time. Also called fill or forced flash, this tactic helps in bright to medium light when you want to soften harsh shadows in portraits or to pop colors in subjects like flowers. It also limits the shutter speed, so you may get dark backgrounds in dim light.

SLOW SYNC This mode will fire the flash every time, but it won't limit the shutter speed, so you can balance the flash exposure with dim lighting indoors or darkening skies outdoors.

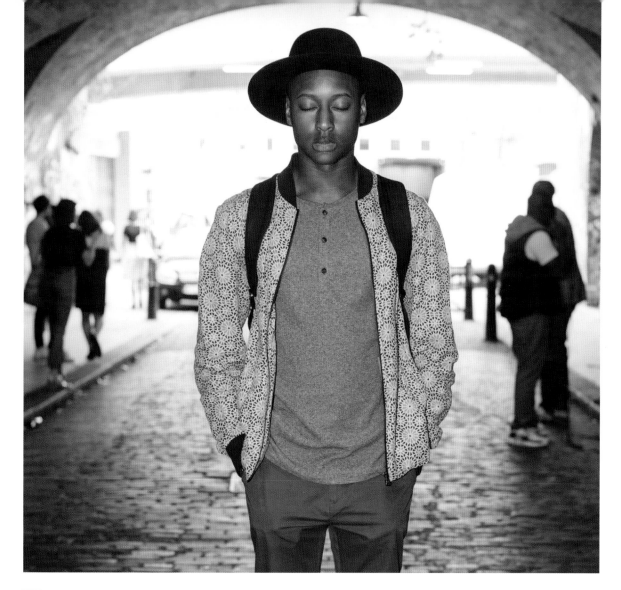

044 COPE WITH THE FLAWS OF BUILT-IN FLASH

You've likely heard that built-in flash has its drawbacks—here are some problems you're likely to run into and simple solutions for them.

LOW POWER A typical DSLR pop-up flash is limited to about 11 feet (3.4 m) with an f/3.5 lens at ISO 100; an ILC flash may have no more range than 5 feet (1.5 m) at the same parameters. Boost the ISO for more flash range. At ISO 400, you can get 22 feet (6.7 m) and 10 feet (3 m), respectively.

LENS SHADOW When shooting very close, or with a big lens hood, or a physically large lens mounted on the camera, you may get the actual shadow of the lens in your shot. To nix it, simply move back from the scene, remove the lens hood, or mount a smaller lens.

THAT FLASH LOOK Direct flash in low light tends to be harsh and unflattering—plus, it creates distracting shadows behind subjects who are standing close to walls and it can cause dreaded red-eye. To fix these problems, try moving your subjects into brighter light, shifting them farther from walls, and using the anti-red-eye setting of the flash (annoying!) or fixing it later in software (better).

045 UNDERSTAND FOCAL LENGTH

Focal length is a key issue in photography—it will surely impact the look of every picture you ever take. Defined as the distance between the lens and the image sensor when the subject is in focus, focal length determines how much, or how little, of a scene you can fit into the frame. Put another way, lenses of different focal lengths can allow you to take in a wide expanse of the world in front of you, give you a view much like your normal vision, or make distant scenes seem closer. These three classes of focal lengths are termed, in order, wide-angle, normal, and telephoto (or simply long).

Focal length is universally measured in millimeters (with 50 millimeters being equal to just about 2 inches). The shorter (smaller) the focal length, the wider the lens's field of view. The longer (greater) the focal length, the more the lens magnifies distant objects, like this lion. Chances are, you have a DSLR or ILC camera that came bundled with a zoom lens—an optic that lets you vary the focal length with the turn of a ring, which is very convenient and adaptable to many shooting situations. But there are also prime lenses, which are fixed at a specific focal length and are beloved for letting in lots of light. See #090 for an overview of lenses to experiment with, and remember: You can always rent before you buy.

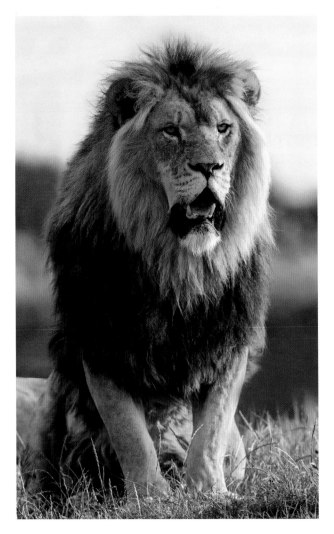

046 TAKE CARE OF YOUR LENSES

It's like medical practice. First, do no harm. Then proceed with great care.

- ☐ PUT IT AWAY PROPERLY Don't leave lenses loose to tumble around in a bag; use lens cases or padded compartments.

- ☐ CAP IT ALL Dust is the enemy of digital sensors. Always cap detached lenses and camera bodies.

- ☐ KEEP 'EM TIDY To clean a lens, start with a no-touch method and use a bulb blower to remove dust. If dust persists, use a soft brush designed for camera lenses.

- ☐ FIGHT MOISTURE Store lenses and cameras with chemical dry packs, especially if you live in a damp environment.

- ☐ FEND OFF WEATHER Protect your lens from rain with a rain sleeve. If a lens does get wet, wipe it off immediately with a microfiber cloth and let it dry at room temperature.

047

UNDERSTAND LENS SPEED

Besides focal length, lenses are defined by their maximum aperture: the widest you can make the hole that lets in light (see #025). Lenses with large maximum apertures, f/2.8 and below, are called "fast" because they let you shoot at faster shutter speeds by letting in a lot of light quickly. A typical kit lens covers a focal length range of 18–55mm with a maximum aperture designation of f/3.5–5.6. This range tells you that the maximum aperture of the lens is f/3.5 at its widest focal length (18) and f/5.6 at its longest (55)—meaning its maximum aperture size changes depending on how close or far its zoom is extended.

048

SEE HOW FOCAL LENGTH MEASURES UP ON DIFFERENT SENSORS

How much of a scene a lens captures depends on the camera's format, which is determined by its sensor size. Cameras fall into one of three formats: full frame (24-by-36mm); APS-C, which is a little less than half the area of a full frame; and Micro Four Thirds (MFT), coming in at one-quarter the area of full frame. The smaller the sensor, the smaller the view that the lens sees. A 50mm lens on a full-frame will give you a true normal field of view. Attach it to an APS-C camera, and you'll see a tighter view. Mounted on a Micro Four Thirds camera, you'll see a still-closer slice. So it's crucial to learn your camera's sensor size before buying lenses.

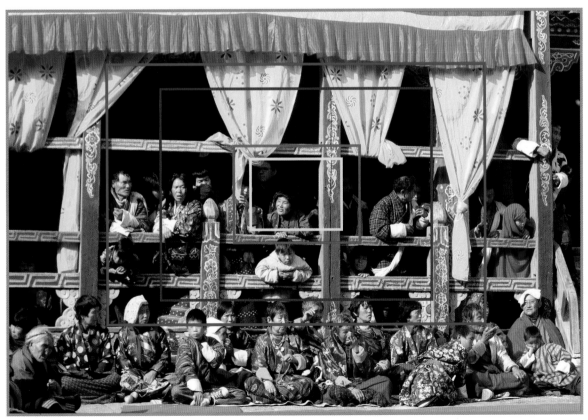

● FULL FRAME   ● APS-C   ● MFT   ● LARGE COMPACT CAMERAS   ● SMALL COMPACT CAMERAS

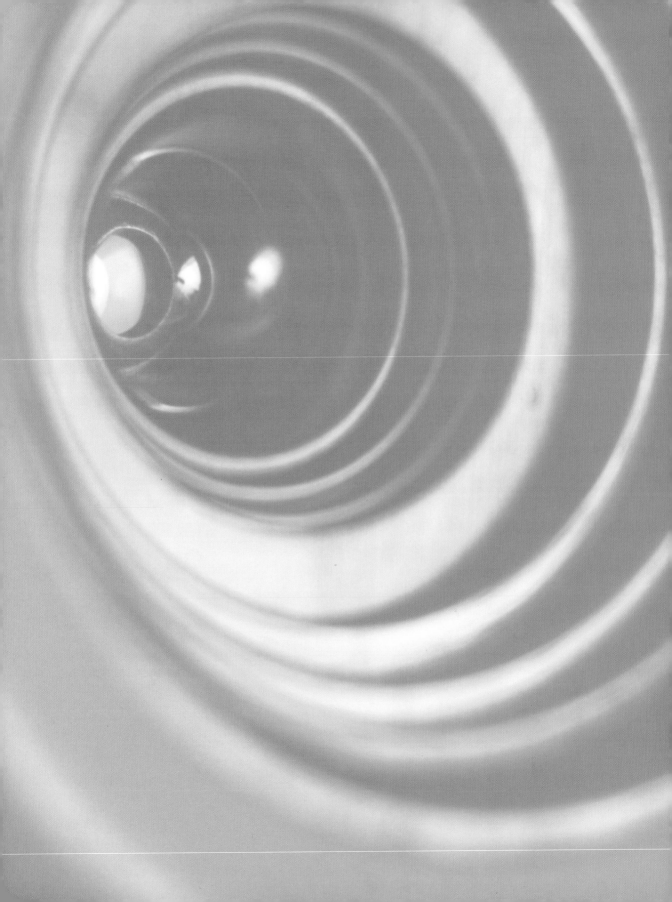

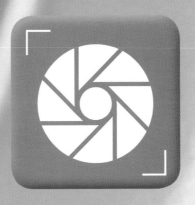

COMPOSING & SHOOTING

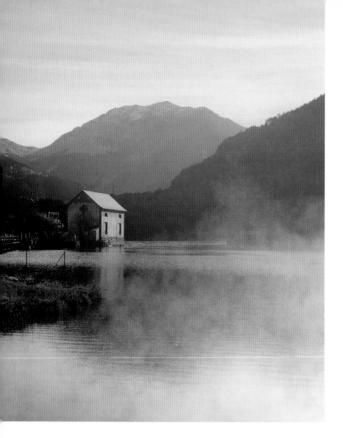

049 | UNDERSTAND LIGHT

Experienced photographers talk differently than snapshooters do. A snapshooter might look at a scene and say, "That would make a great picture!" But an experienced shooter looks around and says, "Wow, look at that light!" If you've ever spent a whole day outside shooting, you probably noticed how the quality of light can change the look of things dramatically. That landmark old house? In angular, direct light, its architectural bones and ornamental detail come sharply to the fore. In mist, a sense of a bygone era—maybe even melancholy—dominates. Your portraits of a male friend? Lit by crisp afternoon sidelight, he may look like a rugged man of action, despite the grin. In overcast lighting, that same grin adorns an open, kind face. That's the power of light: It not only changes the look of your pictures but their emotional impact as well. Learn light and you've learned photography—the rest is technicalities.

050 | GO WITH HARD OR SOFT ILLUMINATION

The softness and hardness of light is determined by the extent of *diffusion*: the scattering of light. Light whose rays go every which way fills harsh shadows, suppresses texture, and lowers contrast. Light whose rays are direct (i.e., parallel or nearly so) deepens shadows, accentuates texture, and boosts contrast. You can harness the effects with simple placement.

GO BROAD OR NARROW The broader the light source, the softer the light. The narrower the source, the harder the light. Makes sense, when you think about it: A wide light source disperses rays across your subject, while the narrow source sends more direct, parallel rays.

GET CLOSE—OR FAR Meanwhile, the closer the light source, the softer the light. The farther the light source, the harder the light. Prime example? The sun, which is so far away that it's just a small ball in the sky, and its direct rays hit us parallel, making for very harsh light.

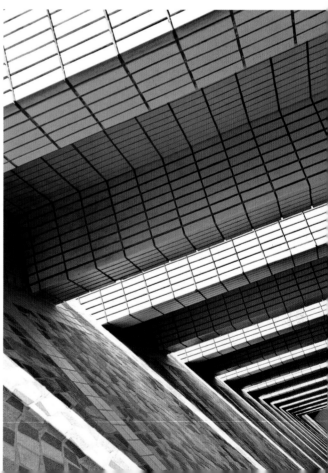

051 OPT FOR DIFFUSED LIGHT

Many shooters like the look of soft, diffused light—generally, it creates a flat, even illumination that saves your subjects from the harsh shadows and distracting glare of undiffused light. Here's how to get it.

GO NATURAL Believe it or not, overcast skies can be your friend. When clouds drift in front of the sun, they act as nature's softbox, making the shadows less distinct. Add fog, and watch those shadows disappear.

SEEK THE SHADE Even on a brilliant, cloudless, blue-sky day, you can escape harsh light by simply going under the shade of a tree or into the shadow of a structure. There will be plenty of soft light for a correct exposure. One caveat: Open shade can be quite blue in color. See #039–041 for ways to control white balance.

BRIM WITH CONFIDENCE A quick and fun fix for a portrait under harsh overhead sunlight is a broad-brimmed hat. Make sure your subject's face is fully in the shadow of the brim, and meter off the face to avoid underexposure. It works well at the beach, where sand can reflect light and open up shadows.

TRY BACKLIGHTING Few subjects are totally backlit—that is, with no light at all falling on them from the front. Someone standing outside with her back to bright sunlight will have light falling on her from the open sky in front of her—and it will be quite soft light at that. The trick will be getting the exposure right.

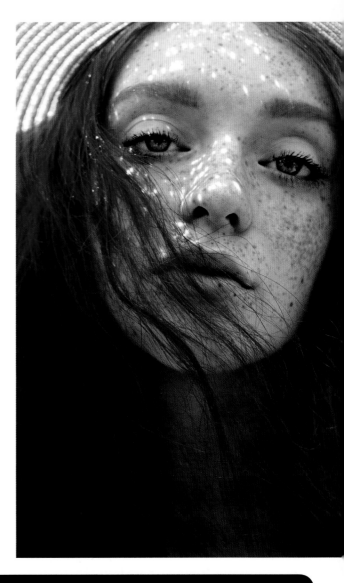

052 EMBRACE HARSH LIGHT

By now you may be thinking that we value soft, diffused light above all others for photography. Not so! Hard light can be very effective for defining shapes and textures, particularly in architectural photographs, shots of craggy landforms and gnarly plant life, and even portraiture—think edgy character studies of weathered faces.

High-contrast light is also very effective in patterns of shadows. Exposure under hard light is trickier than under forgiving soft light; it's very easy for highlights or shadows (or both) to end up getting clipped, making them devoid of detail. To expose scenes like this, try evaluative metering first. Check the histogram and highlight/shadow warnings to see where you may be losing detail. Use exposure compensation (see #018) or shoot in manual mode to tone down highlights or bring up shadow detail. In these scenarios, it's best to follow this rule: Let the shadows fall where they may—that is, adjust the exposure so that it just hangs on to highlight detail while sacrificing deep shadow detail.

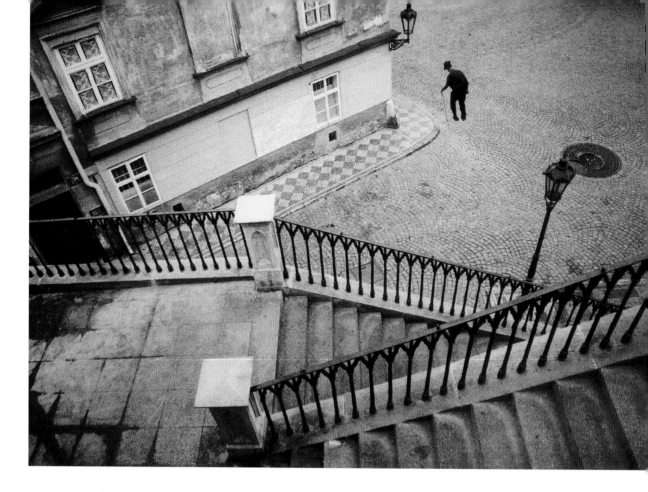

053   LEARN THE ABCs OF COMPOSITION

Whether you're a novice or a master of the lens, the time-tested rules of composition can guide you toward well-balanced, vivid images. Here are some of the best ones to have under your belt.

Keep backgrounds clean and crop out distracting objects. Look for strong diagonals (such as the zigzagging ones above) and leading lines you can exploit by changing your position. Ensure that the frame's borders don't cut through key elements.

You can frame your subject without looking through the finder. Form your thumbs and forefingers into a rectangle to determine the frame's ideal placement before you raise your camera. Examine the scene with the Rule of Thirds (see #060) in mind, and fill the frame with your subject. Step closer and shoot tightly to isolate your subject, or step back if surroundings add to the photo's mood.

Your choice of colors can also aid compositions, especially in scenes without many colors. Remember the color wheel in art class? It taught us that certain hues play well together. Red and green, blue and orange, and yellow and purple are complementary pairs that appear bright and saturated next to each other.

054

EXPLORE AN URBAN CANYON

When you shoot in the city, you usually shoot buildings. Instead, try shooting the spaces between them. That's how Tom Haymes crafted the dramatic abstract at right: by focusing on a narrow, bright slot of sky between skyscrapers.

If you're after a similar shot, pay attention to your light meter. If the reading on the building differs greatly from the reading on the sky, expose for whichever element seems to command the lion's share of the frame.

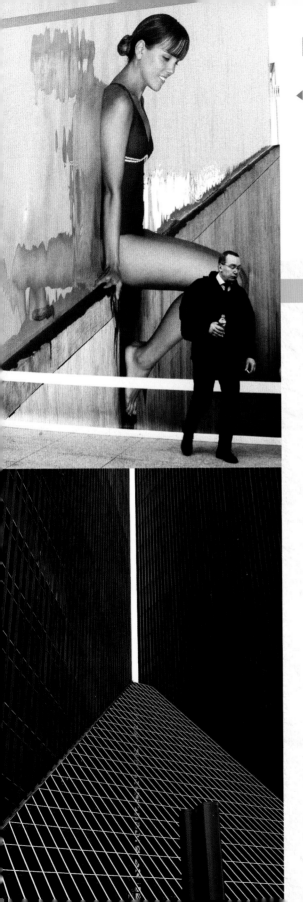

055 MIX UP SCALE

Craft a vertigo-inducing scene by confounding viewers' sense of scale. Take, for example, Guillaume Gilbert's photo at left, in which the model seems to loom above a passing pedestrian and break out of her frame. You can imitate the shot by locating a vivid billboard that contrasts with its streetscape. Visualize your framing, then wait for someone to amble into sight. Twist your camera and shoot quickly to produce an intriguingly scrambled shot.

056 BREAK THE RULES

Some of the greatest photos blatantly defy photography's "laws." So now that you know the rules, go beyond them.

☐ **DON'T FILL THE FRAME** Students learn to move close and zero in tightly. But there are reasons to leave negative space or wide patches of color in the photo frame: They're powerful elements that make your center of interest pop to life.

☐ **SHOOT IN DIRECT SUNLIGHT** You might just love those noonday effects everyone warns you about: desaturated color, flare, comet-shaped lens aberrations, and erosion of sharpness and detail. So go for it.

☐ **LISTEN TO NOISE** Photographers avoid noise by setting the lowest possible ISO for their light, producing crisp images. But shoving ISO sky-high can add a gritty, raw mood.

☐ **TOSS OUT THE RULE OF THIRDS** Set the horizon dead center, not one-third of the way from a landscape's top or bottom. Symmetrical subjects, such as the mountain reflected in a lake in the photo below, are the best candidates for such lawbreaking.

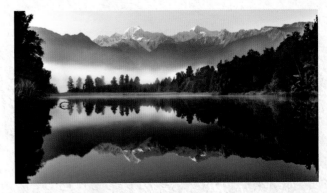

057 PICTURE NATURE'S PATTERNS

Everyone loves a sweeping landscape, but there's more to great nature shots than jaw-dropping scenery. Study natural details to discover an infinite variety of photogenic patterns in subjects tiny and towering, from lichen to thunderheads.

As you shoot, consider a few compositional tips. Think about the emotional impact of the pattern's lines. Towering verticals connote grandeur; spirals, curves, and horizontals tend to impart calm. Avoid highly static, regular patterns. Include some wild cards—a few tumbled trunks in a treeline, for example—to animate a shot. "Interrupting" elements, such as a sharp-edged rock in a soft dunescape, lend visual interest, too.

When a photo's abstract, color is more important than ever. Complementary hues soften a pattern; conflicting colors throw it into high contrast. On your first pattern hunts, tackle just a few subjects, taking lots of shots and playing with settings to capture a beguiling pattern in all its beauty.

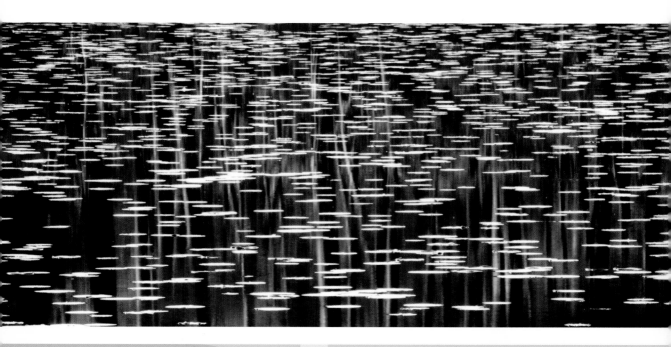

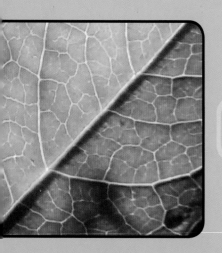

MOBILE TIP

058 ADD FUN LENSES TO YOUR PHONE

These days, the market is brimming with a host of simple, low-cost lenses that you can clip onto your smartphone. From macro tools that let you home in on tiny details to wonderfully weird fisheye attachments that morph and stretch the world, there's something for everyone—even miniature telephotos that make nature photography a breeze when you're on the go. Seek out models that are compatible with your smartphone; for optimum optics, buy lenses made of thick, high-clarity glass.

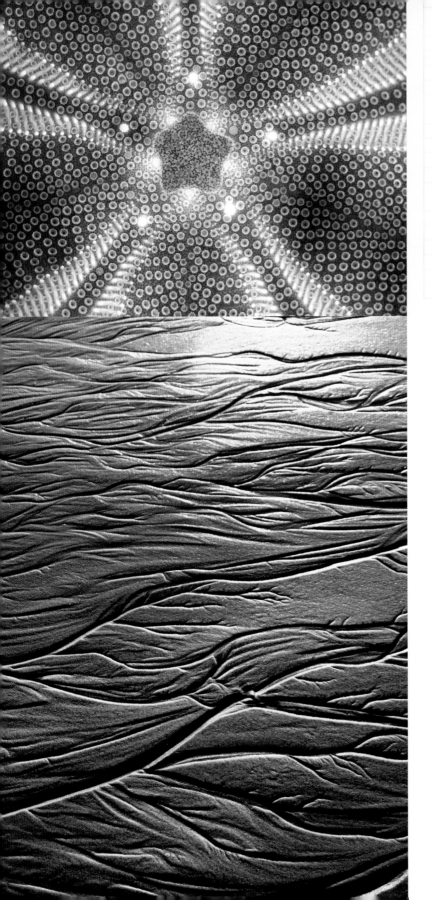

My grandparents were visiting, and I wanted to show them how my new remote flash worked. So I decided to photograph a sea biscuit: shells that have an intricate pattern that's difficult to see in normal light. After propping the shell between two stacks of books, I placed my flash underneath it and, using my cable release, exposed and captured it from above.

—DANIEL WHITTEN

059

PICK A LENS FOR PATTERNS

You can use any lens for pattern studies, but telephoto and macro lenses are the most reliable workhorses. Short to medium telephoto zooms in between 70 and 400mm really close in on subtle, small patterns. (Remember that pricey macro lenses aren't absolutely necessary. Inexpensive extension tubes and front-mounting close-up lenses do good work, too.)

Depth of field can be a problem when you shoot at a sharp angle from your subject's plane of focus, so use small apertures to get clear detail across the composition. Live View mode and DOF preview will help you achieve critical focus and optimal aperture. And remember, a sturdy tripod is always a helpful friend on uneven ground.

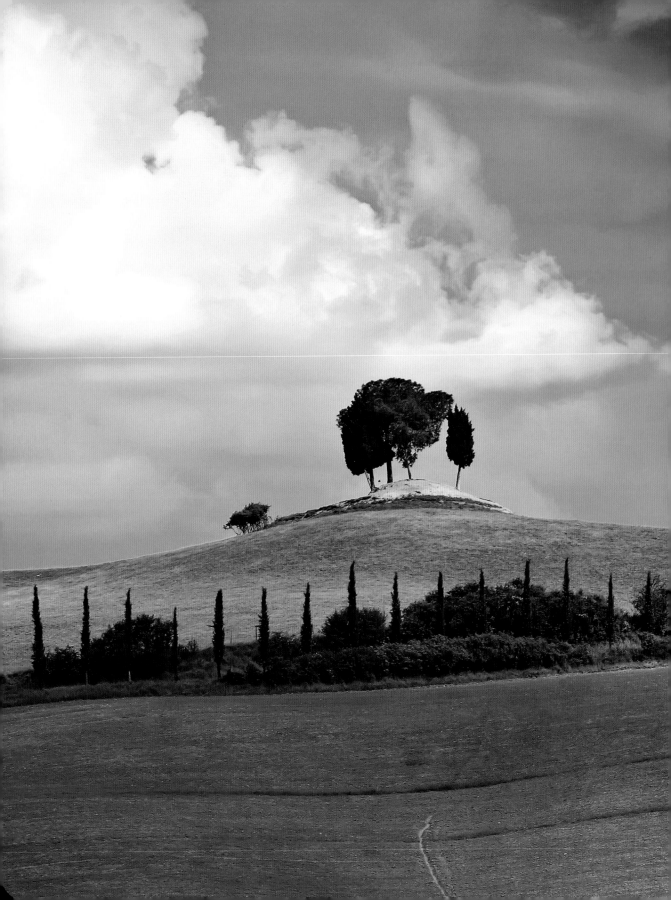

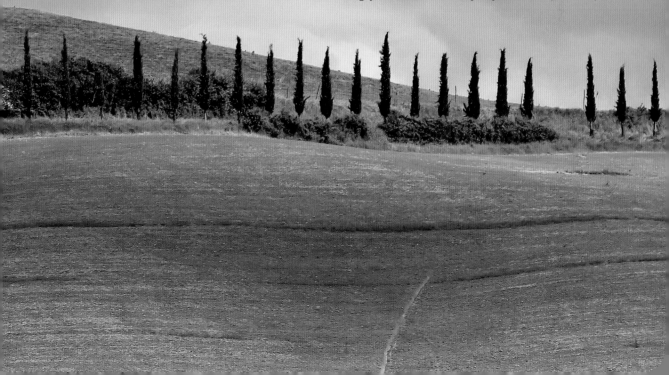

060 FOLLOW THE RULE OF THIRDS

The Rule of Thirds gets more ink than almost any other photography tip, and for good reason: It creates dynamic and interesting shots—and it's easy to apply. When you're framing an image, imagine it's divided into a grid of nine squares, then maneuver until the image's key elements are located along those division lines or at their intersections.

Need an example? Look at this shot. The horizon crosses the page about a third of the way up from the bottom, while a small group of trees anchors the image about one-third of the way in from the left edge.

061 LEVERAGE THE LANDSCAPE

For extra visual impact, make the most of geometry. Pull viewers into the scene by including interesting objects in a picture's foreground, such as the faint vertical lines in the grass found in this image, which draw the viewer's eye up into the landscape.

As any student of the Rule of Thirds knows, horizons generally work best in the top or bottom third of a composition. If you don't keep them straight when you're shooting, you can fix them in postproduction (see #380).

062 GET TO KNOW TRIPODS

Want to keep your shaky hands from blurring images during a long exposure? Dangle your camera over a railing to grab a unique perspective? Capture a moving subject with a mount that swivels at the same speed? There's a supportive rig for your every photographic need and whim.

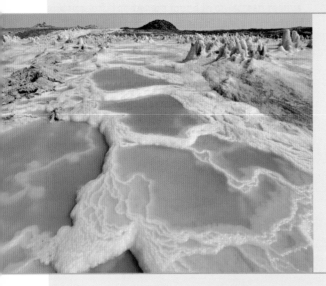

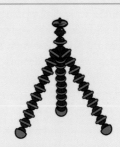

BENDABLE SUPPORT
This prop's flexible legs wrap around objects, so it's more versatile than other tripods.

Difficult-to-capture outdoor shots, such as this hot-springs image, need pliant, reliable field support.

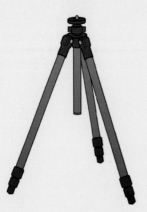

TRIPOD
This invaluable three-legged basic steadies the camera so you can capture a sharp image.

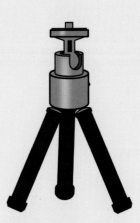

TABLETOP TRIPOD
A mini version of the classic, it sits low to the ground and provides light, portable support.

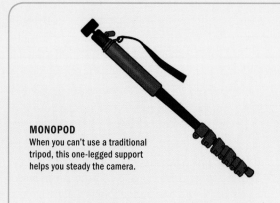

MONOPOD
When you can't use a traditional tripod, this one-legged support helps you steady the camera.

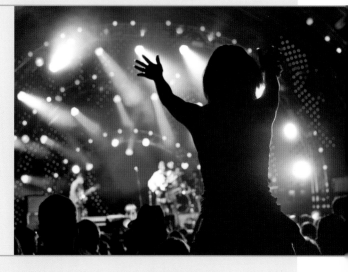

Monopods are ideal for crowd shots: Lift them above surrounding heads to capture the action.

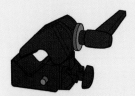

CLAMP
This versatile support latches onto nearly anything—from tabletops to windowsills—to hold your camera or light gear.

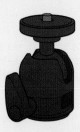

BALL HEAD
Thread a camera onto a mounting plate atop a ball set into this head's base, and you can adjust the head with just one action.

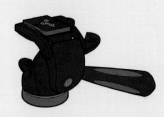

PAN/TILT HEAD
Aim your camera up, down, right, left, or in a circle with this head for perfect position.

Pan/tilt heads are a great aid when you're panning to freeze motion against background blur.

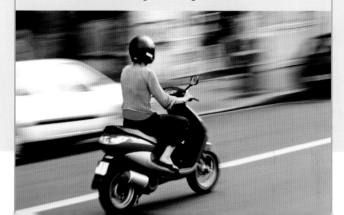

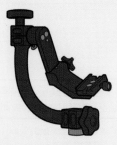

GIMBAL HEAD
This head moves in all directions and supports and balances a camera and heavy lens at their natural center of gravity for worry-free stability.

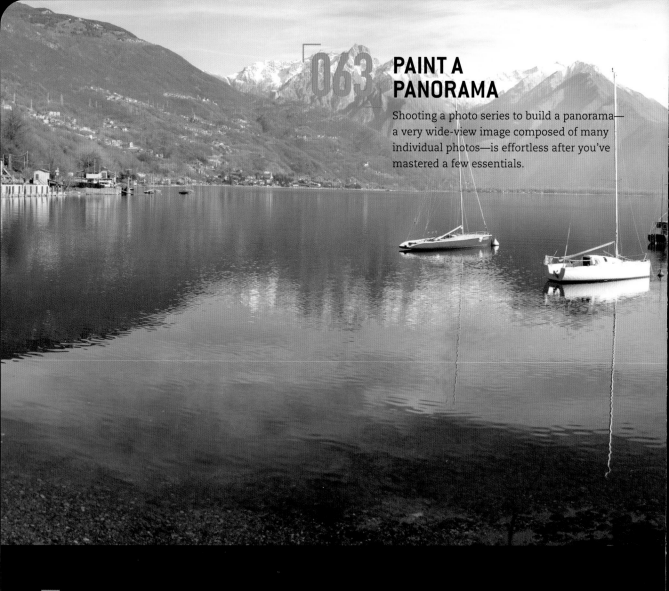

063 PAINT A PANORAMA

Shooting a photo series to build a panorama—a very wide-view image composed of many individual photos—is effortless after you've mastered a few essentials.

064 FIND THE NO-PARALLAX POINT

Finding the no-parallax point (or nodal point) of a lens is key to panorama creation. Parallax occurs when a camera and lens don't rotate properly around the lens's entrance pupil, shifting fore- and background among images—a problem hard to fix in software. Most lenses have one point around which you can rotate a camera without parallax. Some photographers locate it by trial and error, while others use a nodal-point adapter on a tripod. It moves a camera backward till the no-parallax point aligns with the tripod head's axis of rotation.

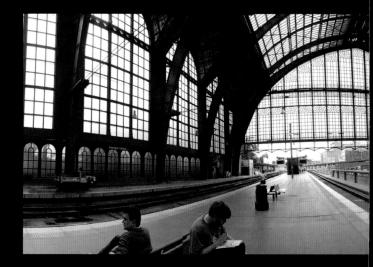

TURN OFF AUTOEXPOSURE Shoot in manual mode, or your camera will automatically readjust exposure for each shot. Subtle changes in light can make corresponding areas of overlapping photos look quite different.

SHUT OFF AUTO WHITE BALANCE Set it manually, or it, too, might readjust with each shot.

CHOOSE A SINGLE EXPOSURE SETTING Determine the shutter speed/aperture combination that works for your full range of shots. Again, your goal is even exposure across your series.

USE ONE FOCAL LENGTH Each shot in your series should have the same point of view. Setting your lens to a long focal length minimizes distortion. Keep nearby foreground objects out of frame, as they're usually the ones that warp most and cause problems when you're combining shots.

AXE THE FLASH It's another cause of inconsistency among photographs.

TRY A TRIPOD Not strictly necessary, tripods do help the camera remain on the same plane throughout the series. In a 360-degree panorama, a tripod ensures that your first and last shots line up with each other.

OVERLAP SHOTS Shoot each photo so that it overlaps from one-quarter to one-half of the area of the prior photo. The wider your lens, the more area you will have to overlap to avoid distortion once the series is combined. For guidance on assembling panoramas with photo software, see #369.

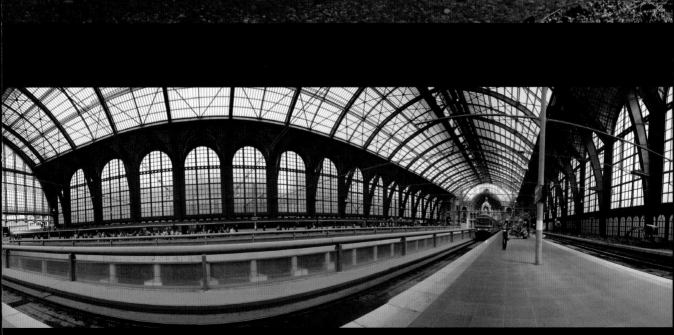

065

STYLE A FOOD SHOOT

Delicious food shots don't require a fake lacquered turkey. With a little forethought, your meal can look as good as it tastes. Start by choosing the right food "models." Whatever your ethics and taste buds say, meat is murder—at least, it can be from a photographic standpoint. It tends to be brown (or an oozy red), oily, and one of the hardest things to shoot. Focus in on colorful fruits and veggies instead—or at least use them as garnish to distract the eye from that slab of unphotogenic roast.

While you're thinking about the composition of the plate you're shooting, remember that a little dishevelment adds homey authenticity (so don't line up your carrot sticks in size order). But unappealing smears and spills should be nowhere in evidence. As for tableware, plain dishes—in colors that contrast with the food or, better yet, old reliable white—will make food pop in images.

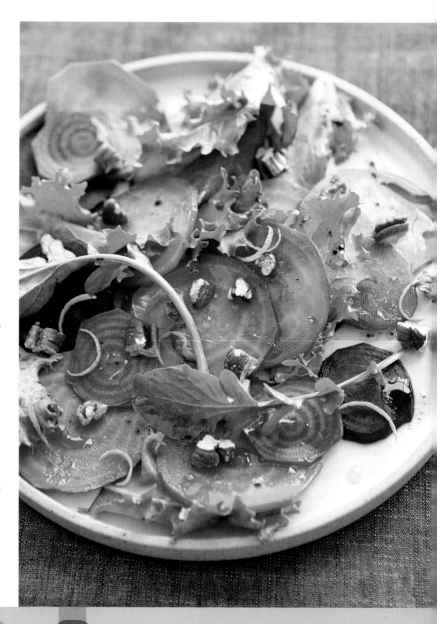

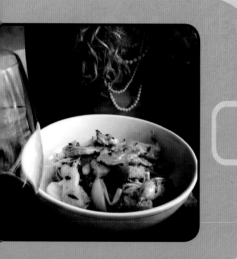

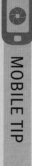

MOBILE TIP

066

RESPECT THE RESTAURANT

Got your smartphone out to snap pics for your food blog? Don't wreck other patrons' meals—not to mention your shot—by using flash. A more subtle solution is to ask a dining companion to use her phone's flashlight app to illuminate the plate you're shooting while you fire away with the camera on your phone. It's a win-win: a better picture and less intrusion.

067 SHOOT DINNER FROM ABOVE

Shoot from an overhead angle—you may want to use a low table, or even climb a ladder—to capture a feast and give the viewer a sense of what the Italians like to call *abbondanza*. To convey a mouthwatering sense of this-is-your-plate urgency, keep the front edge of the table in the forefront of the picture. That composition also bounces the eye back up to the meal, which, after all, is what food shots are all about.

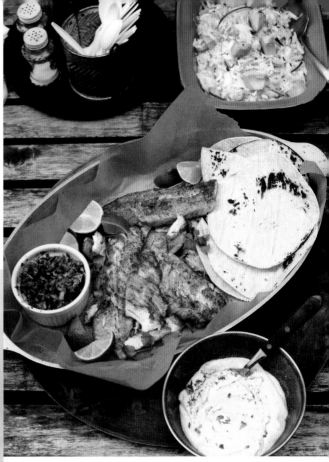

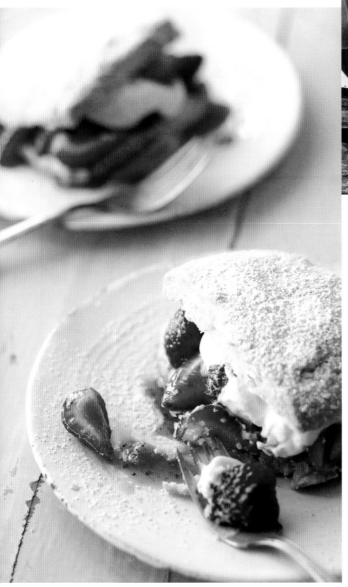

068 FLATTER YOUR FOOD

Diffuse natural light brings out the best in food. If you're picnicking on a cloudy day, you've got it made in the shade—literally. If you're indoors, set up near a window or switch on some lights. Use sidelighting when you want to shoot from above and emphasize texture. If you want to make the overall effect more even, try using a reflector on the opposite side to fill in some of the shadows. And when you're aiming for all-out foodie drama, go for backlighting.

One method for ensuring an attractive plate portrait is to light it the way you would a face. Whether you're using sunlight, accessory flash, or strobe, your primary goal is to illuminate your subject without creating glare. To scatter sunlight, put diffusion paper over a window or just use a sheer curtain. If you're going with artificial light, accessories such as umbrellas, softboxes, or beauty dishes will help soften the effect.

069 PROTECT YOUR GEAR IN EXTREME CLIMATES

Don't just outfit yourself for wilderness adventure—take care of
your camera equipment as well. These items will help you get
through a wildlands excursion with your gear intact.

FOR HOT SPOTS

☐ **SILICA GEL PACKETS** are great for
absorbing humidity. Use the
desiccant envelopes that come with
cameras and other electronic
equipment.

☐ **A SOFT INSULATED COOLER** is a
better choice than your camera bag
to protect your gear from the heat.

☐ **A BLOWER BULB** is a must to keep
sand off your lens.

FOR WET PLACES

☐ **WATERPROOF CASES** protect both
cameras and gear when you're
transporting them.

☐ **SPORTS AND RAIN SHIELDS** protect
your gear while you're shooting.

☐ **RAINSLEEVES** are good for boating
and other watery activities, too.

☐ **A BUBBLE UMBRELLA** offers
protection without limiting visibility.
Buy a large, clear one.

☐ **FOG-CLEARING CLOTHS** in
individually wrapped pouches
are easy to transport.

FOR CHILLY CLIMES

☐ **TRIPOD SNOWSHOES** prevent your
tripods from sinking into the snow
just as ordinary snowshoes keep
your feet topside.

☐ **CHEMICAL HANDWARMERS** are
great for gear as well as fingers. Put
one in your pocket along with a
spare battery, and if it's really cold,
attach one to the base of your
camera with a rubber band.

☐ **NON-RECHARGEABLE LITHIUM
BATTERIES** are your best bet when
you're out in truly frigid weather.

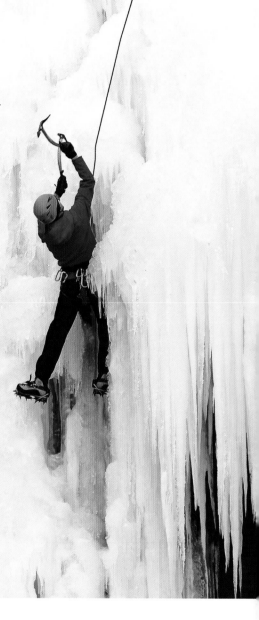

070 TRACK LIGHT WITH A COMPASS

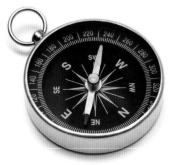

Not only is a compass nifty for figuring out where the heck you are, it's
also useful for photography, since you can use one to anticipate where the
light will be at different times of day. Eastern-facing features will be lit
early in the day; western-facing ones will glow as the evening closes in.
An old-fashioned compass is perfect, or use the one on your smartphone
or other newfangled device.

071 EXPLORE A CAVE

One of the most exciting realms a photographer can explore is the one below. From a photographic standpoint, there are two main types of caverns: well-lit "show caves" and undeveloped ones where you have to bring your own lighting. Show caves are easy to get into and often have dramatic lighting that gives you built-in special effects. But that access often comes with limitations on tools such as flash and tripods, so check in advance. (Caves.org and cavern.com are good places to start your research.) With luck, you may find a cave operator willing to make special arrangements for photographers.

Undeveloped caves require a more adventurous spirit (you can walk into many, but you'll have to rappel into others) and a lot more lights, because they are usually totally dark. If you can, pack in multiple slaved flash units to illuminate deep into the cave. Chances are you won't be able to move too far from your subject, so a wide-angle lens may be all you'll need.

072 SEEK OUT A SHERPA

When the going gets tough, the tough (or at least the smart) photographer gets a guide. If you're venturing out of your comfort zone to photograph glaciers, newly formed lava flows, or other unpredictable terrain, do yourself a favor and hire an expert to take you out on your own or with a group. A good guide will not only keep you safe—she'll help you find the right place and get there at the right time so you can snag the most amazing pictures.

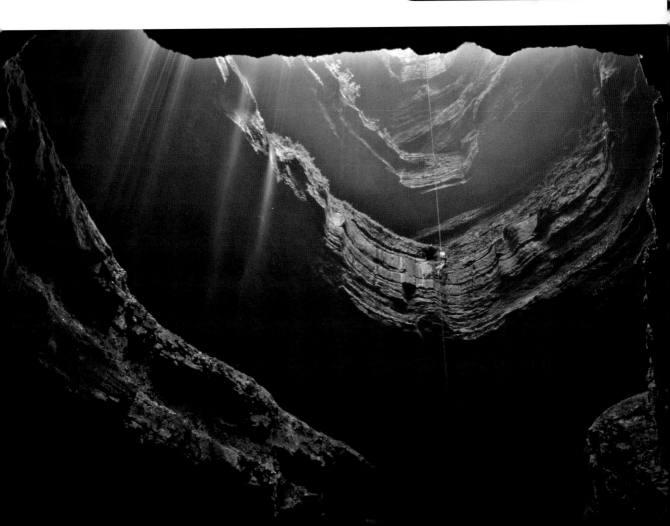

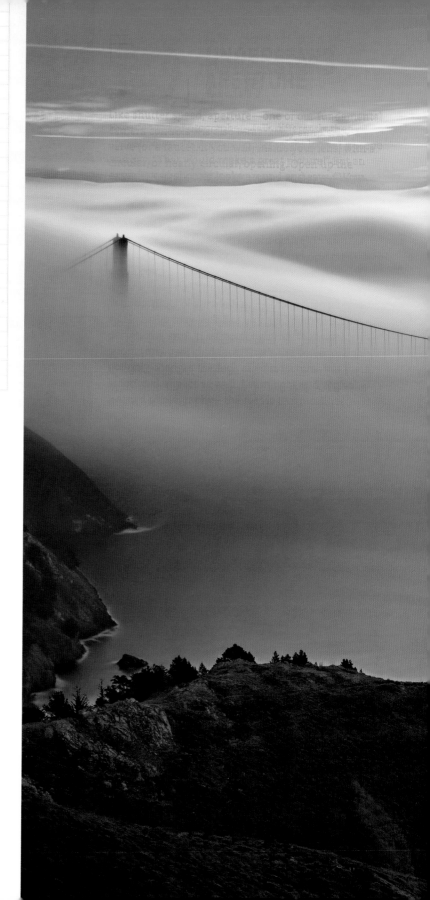

Two years ago I saw an image of fog rolling over the Golden Gate Bridge and became determined to capture it in that state. I monitored the weather and drove up there more than 20 times. There were always obstacles—the fog was too thick or thin; too many boats—so I used the time to scout. One morning I returned to a favorite location. I wanted a long exposure to smooth the fog, and the hills would prevent empty space. As the sun was about to appear, I released the shutter.

—JAVIER ACOSTA

073

SCOUT SITES

You've got to be at the right place at the right time to capture a compelling nature shot. And that requires both luck and research.

Before visiting a new locale, tour it on Google Earth and look at others' shots on Instagram. If possible, head out in person to get a sense of the light and traffic patterns. Consult forecasts, pack food and warm clothes, and go early to avoid crowds at popular sites. Meter off the sky, then shoot in Raw to fine-tune colors afterward. Bracket shutter speeds (see #019) and play with angles, compositions, and croppings until you ID the ideal shot.

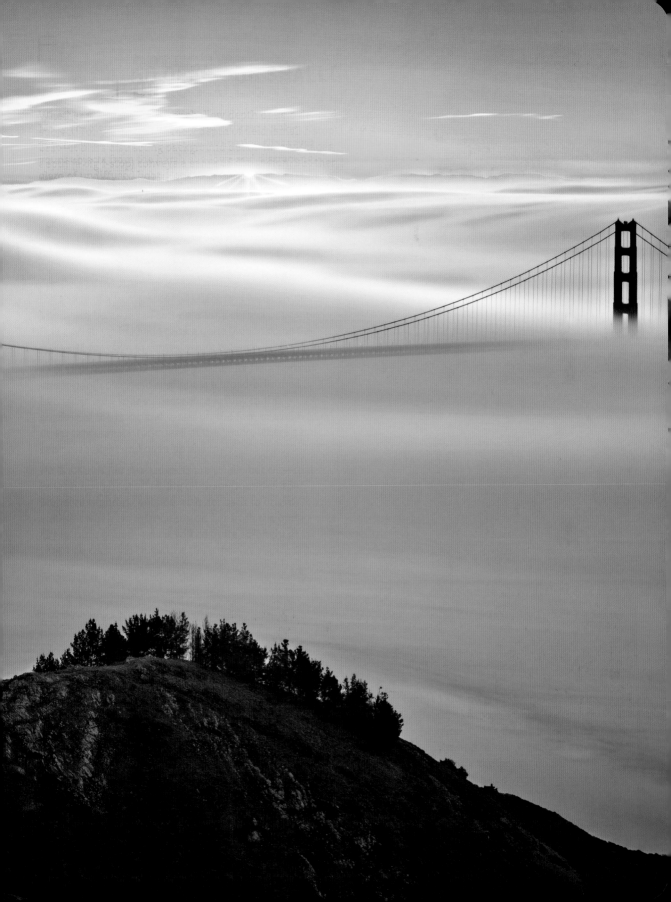

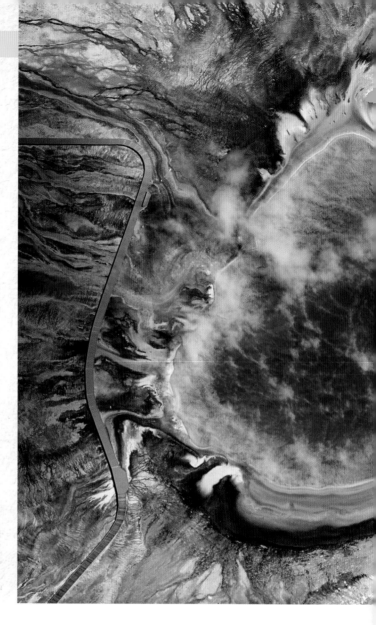

074 SHOOT SKY-HIGH PHOTOS

If you're lucky enough to soar above a lovely landscape in a light plane or helicopter, bring along a DSLR to capture the beauty below. Seek out pilots accustomed to photographers: They'll probably be willing to fly a bit low or slow for a good shot. (For tips on drones, see #271–273.)

☐ **OPEN A WINDOW (OR COPTER DOOR)** Your shots will thus be crisp and you needn't fight flare, scratches, or reflections. But before you lean out, securely wrap your camera strap around your arm so your expensive DSLR won't bean some poor earthbound soul (or smack an engine or tail rotor).

☐ **GO WIDE** Depth of field is a nonissue here, so use the widest possible aperture.

☐ **TACKLE TURBULENCE** Tripods are useless at altitude, so wrap both hands around your camera and lens and prop the back of one hand on the seat cushion in front of you.

☐ **SHOOT PLENTY OF FRAMES** Air pockets will scotch some shots no matter how well you prop your camera, so keep firing.

☐ **CARRY BACKUP MEMORY CARDS** You'll quickly fill them shooting Raw.

☐ **LOOK ON THE SUNNY SIDE** Last, don't despair if your tour day is cloudy. Sunshine enables the most precise earthside images, but clouds soften light and are themselves fascinating subjects.

075 SHOOT THROUGH A WINDOW

On commercial flights, you can't open windows to shoot. But just look at that beautiful countryside and cloudscape unscrolling below you—who can resist a photo? Preflight, book a front-of-cabin window seat for views unimpeded by the wing. Avoid sitting behind the wing, as engine exhaust warps images. And consider your clothes: Black is best, since bright clothing reflects off windows. As for your camera, preset it so you're ready to shoot when you cross dramatic vistas. (But don't shoot during takeoff and landing. Cameras count as the kind of electronic gear you must shut off.) Superwide-angle lenses capture great swaths of ground and clouds, and a lens hood deals with inevitable window reflections. Don't press the hood against the window—vibration will blur your shot. No hood? Cup your hand or drape an airline blanket over the lens. Polarizing filters (see #148) produce color banding from the windows, so leave them in the bag unless you like their effect. Autofocus can zoom in on window scratches, so use manual.

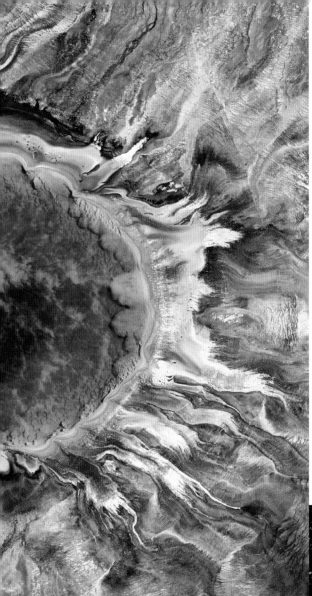

076 GO FLY A KITE

Keep your feet firmly planted on terra firma while a kite captures dizzying aerial photos, looping, zipping, and diving to carry your camera through a funhouse of views. Rigs range from the staggeringly complex to the soothingly simple; we suggest you start your kite-photography capers with the latter.

Buy a stable, single-lined kite. Parafoils are nice: They pull strongly on the line yet are modestly sized.

Now you need a camera rig to stabilize and protect your camera. Buy one if you're not a DIY geek. But if you are, head to your workbench. Basic rigs consist of sheet-metal strips bolted into open squares. Bolt your camera (choose a light one that you don't mind crashing) via L-brackets to the square's bottom. Atop the square, bolt on a horizontal X made of two sheet-metal strips. Attach an eyehook at each of their four ends. Thread extra line through these hooks and attach the whole thing 4 feet (1.2 m) below the kite via a carabiner clipped to the kite line.

Wait for a gusty day, and program your camera to take photos at set intervals or remotely trigger it from the ground. Now hold on tight, send it aloft, and grab yourself an aerodynamic artwork.

077 BAG A BIRD'S-EYE VIEW

For an unusual (and heart-stopping) view of the earth, charter a plane with clamshell doors. Set in the floor and intended for cargo loading, they open for a straight-to-ground view. Muster your courage and lean over for vertical shots of frame-filling wonders, from natural features such as coral atolls and volcanic caldera to manmade creations such as highway cloverleaves and skyscraper tops.

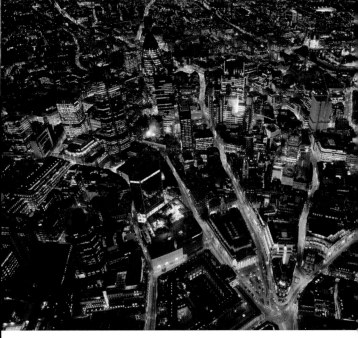

078 LOCATE LOST SITES

Ghost towns, archaeological sites, shuttered factories, forsaken roads and railways—all are magnets for photographers eager to record places on the verge of vanishing forever. The best way to uncover them? Befriend other photographers, especially members of urban explorers' clubs. (Be patient and learn as much local history as you can before you ask anyone to discuss his favorite shooting sites, though.) Open houses, walking tours, and preservation-league websites are other good ways to scout out ruins. Once you've chosen a site, investigate it via GPS and satellite mapping technology, including such free online research tools as Bing's Bird's Eye View and Google Earth, to plan out precisely how you'll access the place.

079 EXPLORE SAFELY

If you're shooting ruins, take some basic precautions. Check the weather forecast, dress accordingly, and wear sturdy clothes. Boots and work gloves will protect you from broken glass and rusty metal. A face mask will help shield your lungs from dust and hazardous particles. Always carry a first-aid kit and flashlight, and be alert to signs warning you of hazards such as rotten stairs and unstable floors. Some ruins are havens for illegal activity, from graffiti tagging to drug dumps, so bring a companion and a cellphone that's been programmed to speed dial for help.

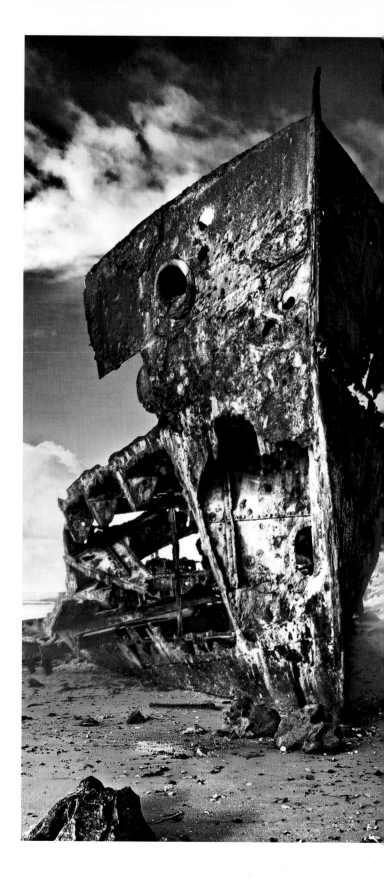

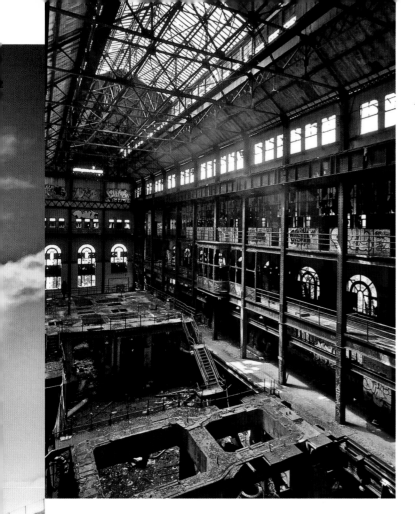

080 GET THE OK TO SHOOT RUINS

Exploring privately owned abandoned sites is considered trespassing, and shooting in civic ruins such as old subway stations and other decrepit infrastructure is usually against the law. But you needn't trespass to take shots of ruins, such as the abandoned turbine hall at left shot by Justin Gurbisz. Just ask permission first. Property owners, park rangers, and caretakers might welcome you if you're candid and able to chat about site history and photography.

"Once security guards understand you're going in there to photograph, not to steal or vandalize or drink—the first things that they'll think—they generally let you go," says ghost-town veteran Troy Paiva. If you must sneak, do your best to get in and out of there inconspicuously. And if you're caught, don't run. Be polite and maybe you'll get only a slap on the wrist. "Grovel, if necessary," Paiva advises.

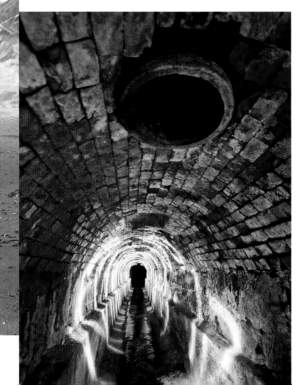

081 LIGHT UP HIDDEN SPACES

Many ruins are, by their nature, very dark. Combat the lack of ambient light with long exposures—from a few seconds to a few minutes—and a DSLR with image stabilization and good performance at high ISOs. Most cameras' auto settings can't cope with such difficult conditions, so manually control aperture and speed. You also need a light field tripod or beanbag supports for lengthy exposures.

Sometimes these lighting strategies aren't enough, especially in underground or windowless spaces. Use a flashlight or a smartphone flashlight to illuminate parts of the ruin and give viewers the sense that they're exploring it alongside you. Flash or off-camera strobe can blast away details. Use them with caution.

082 REIMAGINE A MONUMENT

As a rule, tourist destinations tend to be overcrowded. So it's no surprise that these spots overcrowd the world with pretty much the same photograph—of the exact same place, shot from the exact same angle.

Anyone can get a great picture of a classic building, monument, or landscape; they're icons because they're so visually striking. But how do you work something so familiar into a composition that communicates your unique experience of a place and doesn't join the stack of tired, same-old snapshots? Beyond arriving early or late in the day to beat the crowds (which can really clog up your shot), try to put a unique twist on your image: Show it from an unusual angle or through an interesting framing mechanism. Or add an element to the scene, such as passing planes or crashing waves. You can also plan ahead to capture a site during a special event or a rare phenomenon to ensure your take is one of a kind. Out of ideas? Pray for rain: Few casual shooters are likely to venture out in inclement weather, and the results can be dramatic.

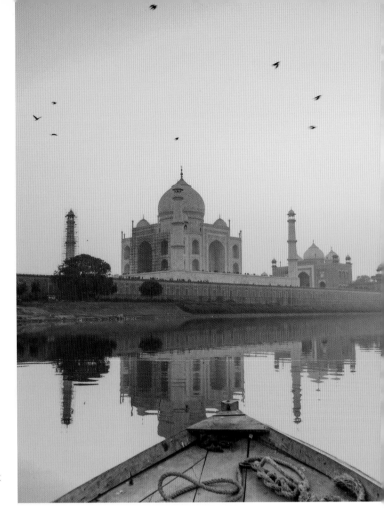

083 THEME YOUR TRAVEL SHOTS

When we travel, we tend to notice more—our eyes are naturally more open to a destination's unique details, and our minds seek to discern patterns among them. Next time you're on the road and observe, say, the intriguing shapes of highway rest stops or arched Gothic doorway after arched Gothic doorway, get out your camera and start snapping photos. Focusing on the challenges posed by these recurring subjects is great for your personal photography practice, and it will link images from your trip into a compelling and surprising study of place.

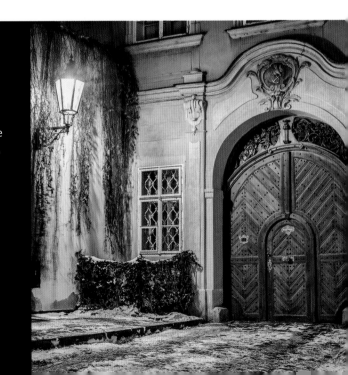

084 TELL THE STORY OF YOUR JOURNEY

One way to make your travel photos intriguing is to craft a narrative (rather than shoot the usual collection of unrelated snapshots). Aim for the following array of photos that, once paced in an album or slideshow, will make your adventures seem cinematic.

LEAD THEM IN Your opening image should spark curiosity—think of it as an advertisement for the photos that follow. It can take any form (landscape or portrait, action or still life), and it can clearly declare your vacation's locale or offer only the faintest of clues, but it must arrest the eye and capture the imagination.

SET THE SCENE Your second image should back up and establish the scene of your story. Here, a wide-angle shot of a telling—but not tired—vista will help ground your viewers in your destination and subject.

INCLUDE PORTRAITS Remember, the people make the place. Whether you shoot candid street photos of locals or pause for a more posed portrait of a travel mate, it's important to occasionally introduce people—they provide a sense of scale against landscapes or monuments and help humanize your story. It also helps viewers imagine themselves in the moment, fostering a sense of wanderlust.

DELVE INTO DETAILS To transcend the trite and capture a place's true essence, isolate specifics that give a deeper look. Seek out high-contrast hues and lots of textures, as well as a balance of pattern and randomness that creates visual tension. Shooting from above can turn the picture into a nearly abstract study in color, shape, and texture. And try going in tight, which strips away extraneous environmental information.

SUMMARIZE THE SCENE As you wind down your narrative, be sure to include a photo that captures the key elements of your story in a telling moment.

FRAME UP A FINALE End on an image that evokes the emotion you want the viewer to leave with: wanderlust, inspiration, or even elation.

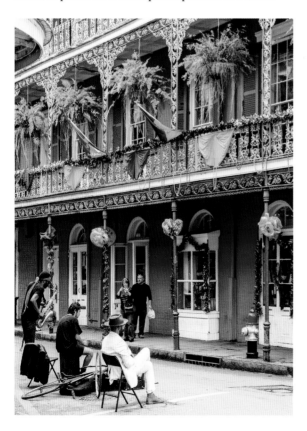

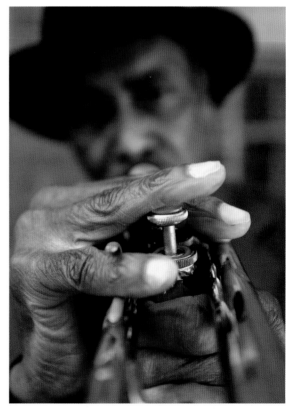

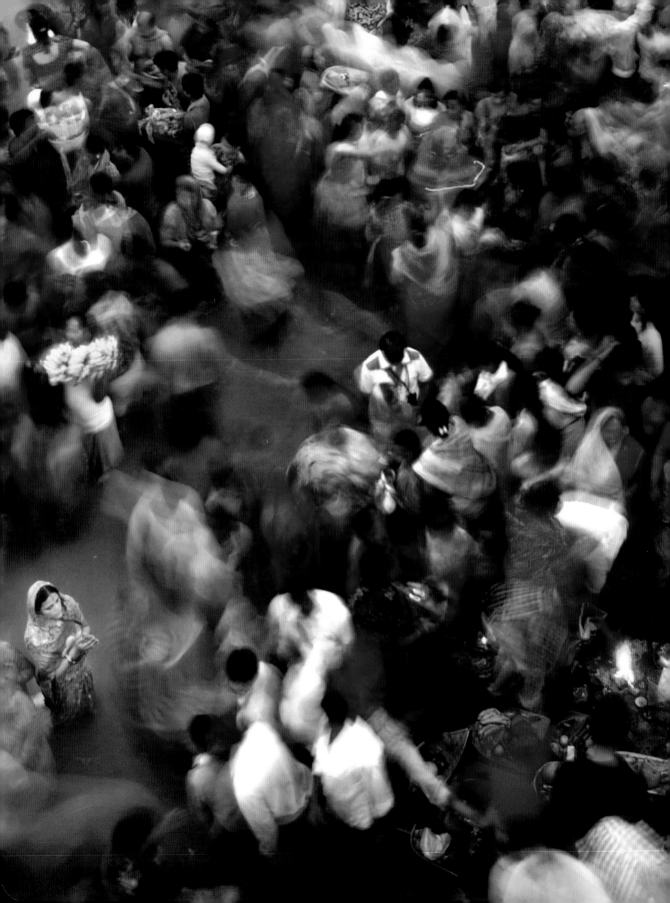

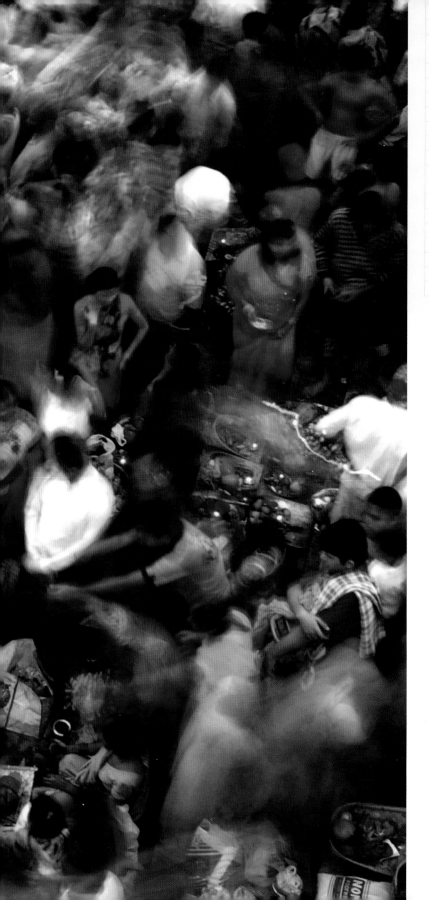

This was taken in Mallick Ghat, West Bengal, India, during an ancient Hindu festival called Chhath Puja. It's to thank and pray to Surya, the Hindu sun god. I was photographing the crowd from a rooftop, watching people move about as they prayed. At last one woman became totally still, capturing the right sense of divinity.

—SUBHAJIT DUTTA

085 SHOOT OVERSEAS

A fantastic travel photo shows more than an exotic locale—the most meaningful subjects are a land's culture and people. In a new country, think as a photojournalist, not as an observer with a camera. First, don't play tourist—avoid tours and well-trafficked sites; hire a local guide to take you to out-of-the-way places and translate for you. Bring minimal gear—you'll be less of a mark for thieves and won't barge in with a big setup. Research local etiquette so you know how to dress, how to greet people, if it's okay to talk to women, and if photos are permitted at all. Once there, keep your camera under wraps until you befriend residents. Later, if you explain which shots you want, most people will let you shoot them. If a small tip is customary, oblige, and let people look at your camera's rear monitor as you work (kids love this). If people ask you to mail them their photos, keep your promise.

086

POSE A NUDE PORTRAIT

Whether you're shooting a friend, partner, or model, nude portraits require you to be both professional and casual. Talk with your (clothed) subject before a shoot to build trust and let him or her know which poses you'd like and the mood you wish to capture (artistic, abstract, suggestive, or downright erotic). Supply a quiet, warm room with a private changing area, plus a few pieces of furniture upon which a tired model can rest.

Once you're set up, run through the classic poses as you shoot: reclining, sitting, kneeling, and standing. All poses depend primarily on leg position, so begin by arranging legs and feet, and then concentrate on arms, hands, and head. Back views—which expose few intimate areas and help keep you on the side of good taste—are great choices for novice models, as are close-ups of features such as hands and the neck. Your subject's glance is also essential. Put psychological distance between model and viewer by directing her to look slightly to the camera's side, or create intimacy by asking her to gaze straight at the lens. (If she's shy, you might crop out her face altogether.) Finally, ask your subject for her own pose ideas. She probably knows which stances make her body look best.

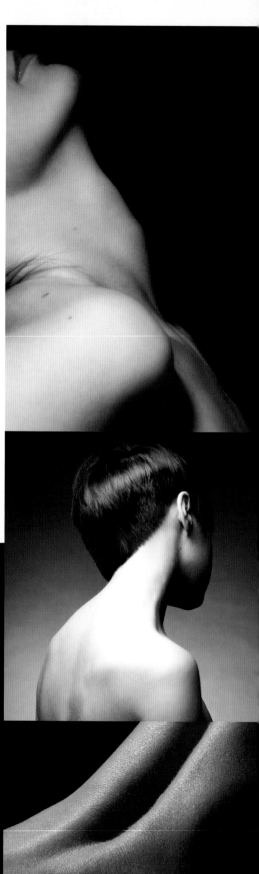

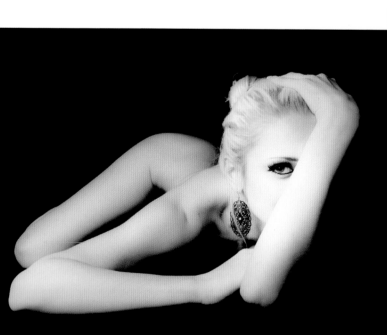

087 LIGHT THE BODY'S CONTOURS

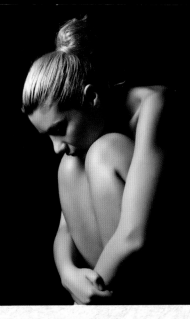

People have painted and photographed the human body for eons because of its sculptural qualities. Make the most of them with canny lighting strategies. Soft, diffuse light, such as that produced by a softbox, window, or (if your model is willing) an open, overcast sky, flatters most bodies. But hard, directional light, such as that from strobe or even snoot- or barn-door-modified light, is arresting, too. Especially when used with a black backdrop, it casts muscles and flesh folds into sharp relief via strong shadows and reveals skin's texture. Backlighting generates striking silhouettes (see #134 and #137), and angled sidelighting accentuates muscles and curves. In any lighting setup, ask your model to slowly and completely turn around so that you can shoot several frames and decide which lighting angle is most compelling.

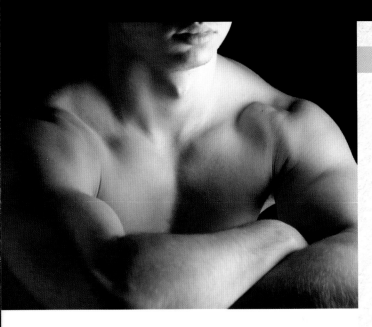

088 WRITE A BASIC MODEL RELEASE

Photo agencies offer free, downloadable release forms, and you'll find them in consumer legal publishers' guides as well. Smartphone model-release apps are easy to carry and let you customize, modify, and store releases on the spot. Whichever you use, ensure the form covers these points:

☐ Explicit permission. For example, "I [model's name] hereby give permission to [your name] to use my photographic likeness and name in all forms and media for all noncommercial, lawful purposes."

☐ Model's printed name and signature.

☐ Model's stated age.

☐ Date signed.

More complex forms delve into topics such as compensation received by the model, how the image itself can be treated (for example, no distortion or overprinting), and other matters. But a basic release will cover you in most situations.

089 ALWAYS GET A MODEL RELEASE

Technically you need a release only when you use a photo for commercial purposes (advertising, posters, cards, endorsement, or trade). Even if you sell a fine-art photo or use it in an editorial context (such as newspapers, magazines, personal websites, social media, or books), you don't need one. But if you sell a photo to stock agencies or commercial websites, you do. Otherwise an agency or publisher might decline it—and your subject could take legal action against you. Especially when shooting a nude, you should play it safe by getting a release and establishing the model's proof of age.

090 GET FAMILIAR WITH LENSES

Understanding the capabilities and applications of lenses—in short, what they can do for your photos—is crucial to taking the best pictures you can. Once you're aware of the full range of possibilities, pick the lens that's suited to the image you're after. Keep your go-to favorites on you and you'll be ready to swap out lenses for the perfect pic—whether telephoto for creature cameos or macro for detail shots.

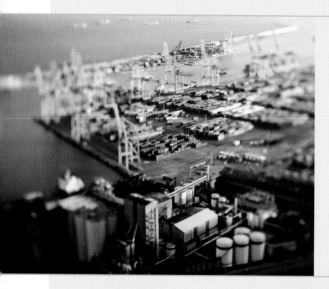

LENSBABY
This selective-focus lens swivels and tilts, and allows manual focus on a small area.

A selective-focus lens allows you to create blurred areas while keeping others crisp.

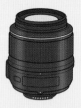

NORMAL PRIME
Choose this model (which refers to a 50mm lens on a full-frame sensor or a 25 to 35mm lens on a smaller sensor) for natural-looking perspectives.

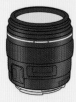

TELEPHOTO PRIME
To magnify distant objects using a single long focal length, go with a telephoto prime.

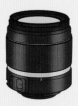

KIT ZOOM
Shoot at many different focal lengths with this lens, which often comes packaged with cameras.

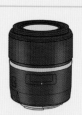

MACRO
Use this lens for magnification of small objects and for close-up focusing.

A macro lens allows you to close in on fine detail or tiny subject matter.

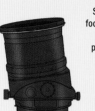

TILT/SHIFT
This lens can be used to correct perspective distortion and to adjust depth of field.

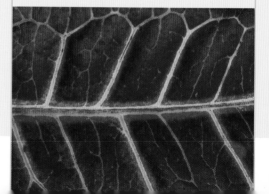

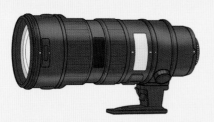

TELEPHOTO ZOOM
This lens magnifies like a telephoto prime, but it also offers variable focal length.

A telephoto zoom lens makes distant subjects seem very close—and it's flattering for portraits, too.

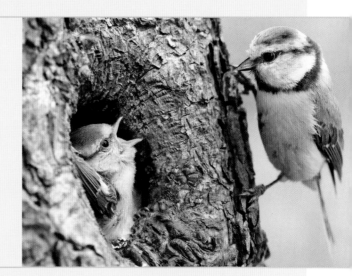

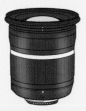

WIDE ANGLE
Its short focal length allows you to capture a fuller area of view.

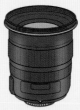

ULTRAWIDE ANGLE
This lens offers you the widest possible angle of view, without distorting straight lines.

FISHEYE
This lens captures an extremely wide angle of view but makes straight lines look curved.

The characteristic distortion of a fisheye lens adds a compelling quality to very wide-angle shots.

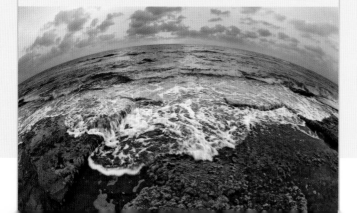

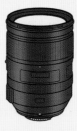

ALL-IN-ONE ZOOM
With wide-angle to telephoto focal lengths, often with a small maximum aperture, this lens is very versatile.

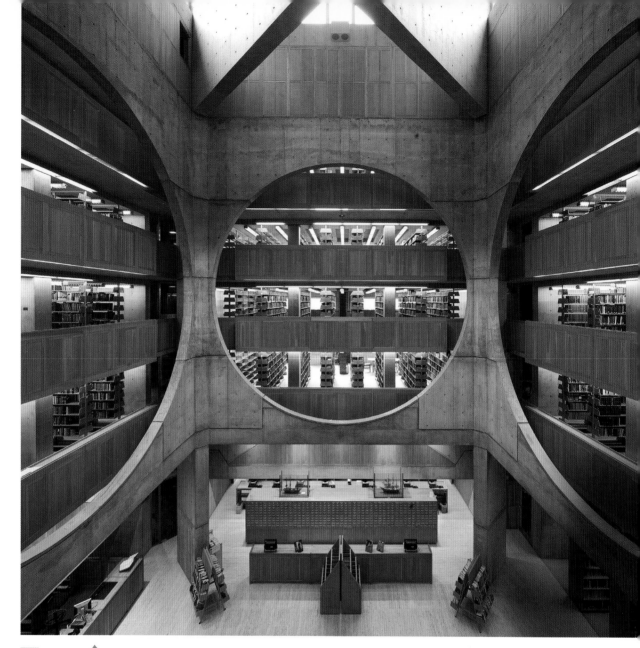

091 STAY STRAIGHT WITH TILT/SHIFT

Tilt/shift (T/S) is a superhero. It can straighten tall buildings, give insanely deep focus without insanely small apertures, and limit focus to the width of an eyelash. And it performs its stunts while you shoot.

Architectural photographers love T/S for its "anti-topple" effect. Usually, when you shoot a tall structure, its parallel lines seem to converge as they rise, but because a T/S lens casts a bigger image circle

than conventional lenses, you have leeway to move the sensor or film plane up, down, or sideways in that circle. Keep your lens parallel to the building, shift the T/S lens upward (a bubble level in the accessory shoe squares the camera with the building), and shazam! You've got more structure and less foreground.

T/S works in the opposite direction, too. Shooting from a tower or ladder top? Shift the lens downward.

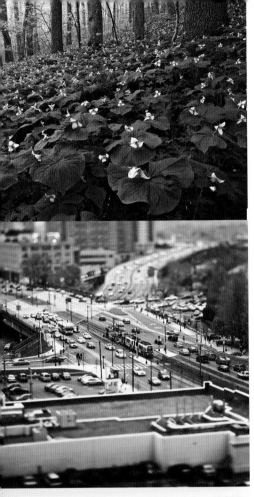

092 PLAY WITH THE SCHEIMPFLUG EFFECT

This delightful term refers to the apparently infinite depth of field a T/S provides—with moderate apertures and fast shutter speeds to boot. By tilting the plane of focus in the same direction as the plane of a subject, much more of that plane is in focus, from fore- to background. Nature photographers love T/S, since it's a great way to freeze a subject such as a breeze-tossed flower against an in-focus field or forest.

To harness this power for yourself, place a camera on a tripod, zero your T/S, and focus about one-third of the way into the zone you wish to keep sharp. Tilt or swing the lens toward the subject plane, then fiddle with focus again. Check depth of field by stopping down the lens to the desired shooting aperture.

093 REVERSE THE SCHEIMPFLUG EFFECT

This amazing trick confines focus to a single area of a composition. By tilting the T/S lens in the direction opposite the one that would produce depth of field, you limit sharp focus to the narrow pivot point of the plane of focus, while the rest of the image blurs. Street photographers use this loopy effect to turn city scenes into toylike miniatures, and portraitists to zero in on a single facial feature.

As with ordinary Scheimpflug, trial and error can help you master the reverse method. Focus with the lens straight and centered on the feature that you want in focus (here, the cars in the midground). Tilt the lens counter to the subject plane (the plane of the streetscape). Play around for a pleasingly uncanny combination of delineation and blur. You can also fake it in postproduction.

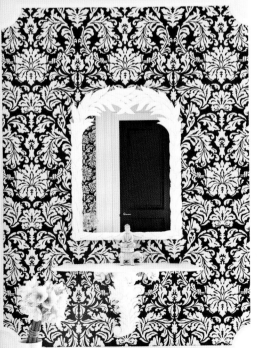

094 DO THE VAMPIRE TILT/SHIFT

Here's a trick to frighten your friends: Shoot into a mirror without your (or your camera's) reflection showing up in the image. More seriously, it's a useful trick when you're photographing indoors, especially when capturing decor details and real-estate shots.

As is often the case when you're being tricky, you'll need a tripod. Set it and the camera parallel to a mirror, then step yourself and your setup out of the reflection. Shift the lens sideways toward the mirror and your image will look as if you snapped it straight on.

Fangs and black cape? Strictly optional.

095 IMPROVISE A MACRO LENS

Without a macro lens but keen to come in close? If you've got a normal lens with an aperture ring, here's an economical choice that can turn that lens into an extremely powerful close-up tool.

All you need is a reversing ring, a simple adapter that you thread onto the front-barrel threads of your lens. Then attach the lens to your camera's lens mount—backward. You won't be able to focus to infinity, but you're ready for bugs and buds. Of course, you'll need to focus manually, and meter manually at stopdown aperture—turn the aperture ring to your desired aperture for this.

No aperture ring? You can still mount the lens with a reversing ring, but, in most cases, you will be stuck with the smallest (dimmest) aperture. To focus, try Live View with LCD brightness and/or exposure compensation turned up.

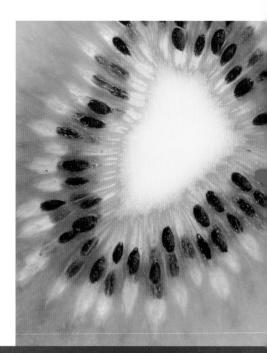

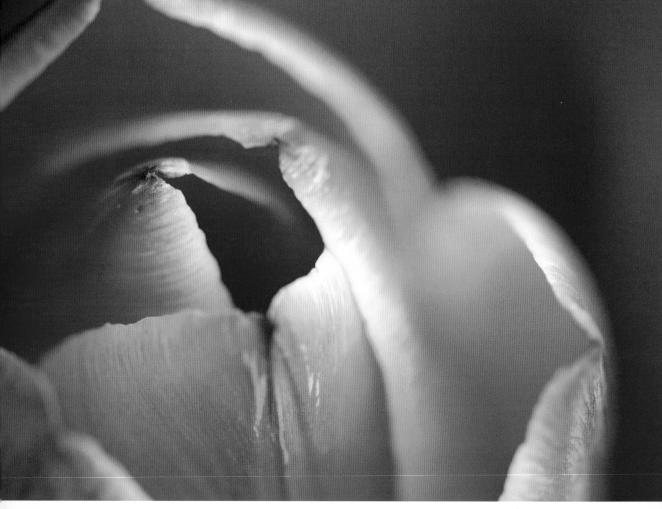

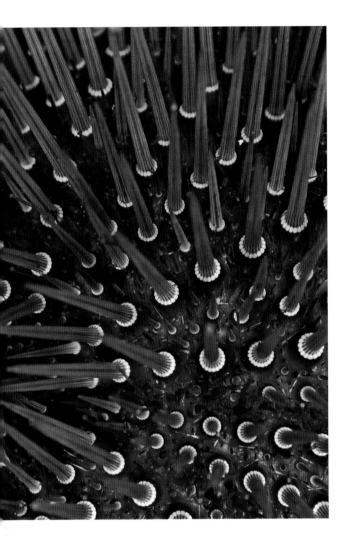

096 DO THE MACRO MATH

Want to know how big you can go? If you have a metric ruler and know the size (in millimeters) of your camera's sensor (or film plane), you can figure out the magnification you're working at for any given focusing distance. Place the ruler where your subject is, focus on the millimeter lines on the ruler, then count the visible lines from left to right. Divide the sensor length by the ruler length visible in the finder, and that's the magnification. So if you see 36mm across, and you're working with a full-frame DSLR (which has a 36mm sensor), the magnification is 1:1. Count 18mm? You're at 2:1, which is twice life size.

097 LEARN FOCUS STACKING

Probably the greatest and most startling advance in macro photography in recent years has been focus stacking. It's a nifty solution to an inherent limitation of macro photography: the greater the magnification, the shallower the depth of field.

Focus stacking involves taking many digital exposures of the subject, moving the focus point slightly from frame to frame. The in-focus points of those frames are then "stacked" in software (Helicon Focus and StackShot are two popular programs). The result: a single image that's as sharp as a tack—from front to back.

098 INVEST IN MACRO TOOLS

If you're really interested in focusing on the small stuff, you'll want to make a few investments. For starters, you might want to score a macro lens that allows you to take life-size shots (designated in the lens specs as a magnification ratio of 1:1) of your subjects. If you're keen to delve even further into the tiny world, invest in a macro lens with greater than life-size magnification. And if you're that committed, you also might lust after a macro focusing rail. Without one, you'll have to contend with the tedium and inaccuracy of conventional manual focus at tight distances.

QUICK TIP

099 USE A BEANBAG SUPPORT

Beanbags are great support for when you're shooting at ground level. Not only do they let you go low, they're not fiddly, since unlike a tripod, there are no knobs or levers.

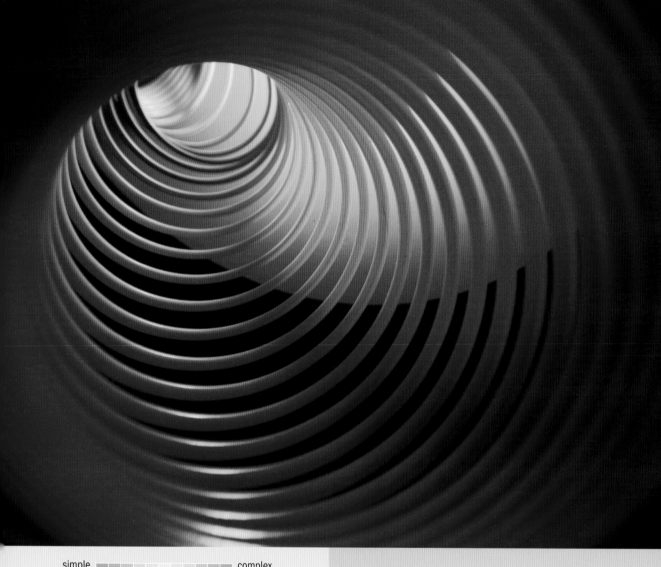

simple ▬▬▬▬▬▬▬▬▬ complex
▲

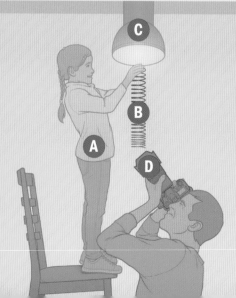

100 MAKE EVERYDAY OBJECTS APPEAR COSMIC

Remember those 1950s sci-fi flicks with pie-pan flying saucers and actors lurching around in rubber alien suits? British doctor Andy Teo does, and he pays homage to them with quirky trompe l'oeil shots of stuff he finds around his house. "My daughters get involved and it becomes a form of family fun," he says. In a series Teo calls "Let's Pretend Space Travel," he

101 TOY WITH ABSTRACTION

You can find delightful ideas for abstract photographs without walking out your front door. Kids' toys, kitchen utensils, the stuff in your toolbox and junk drawer—all are fodder for whimsical photos.

STEP ONE Gather the goods. Assemble intriguingly shaped or colored objects and try shooting them with unusual lighting or close focus.

STEP TWO Enlist an assistant. It's hard to juggle subject, gear, and lights solo. Corral a helper to reposition things while you work the shutter.

STEP THREE Use the right gear. A macro lens can make a little toy seem to tower above the viewer. An ultrawide one can distort or exaggerate an object's shape.

STEP FOUR Play with your subject. You can position it under various lights, fill the frame with it, or add visual weight by including an out-of-focus background.

STEP FIVE Experiment with exposure. Under- or overexposure adds dimension and drama to the most mundane subjects. Make a rubber duck menacing or a kitchen sponge mysterious.

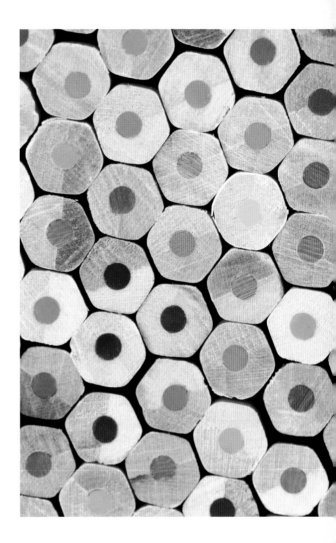

BIG PROJECT

reenvisions the ordinary: Cheese graters become spaceship power generators, cookie cutters morph into metallic snake monsters, and, as seen here, Slinkys transform into time-travel tunnels. As Teo observes, old movies loved to depict time travel "as a journey down a tube with twists, and a Slinky is just that: a long, flexible tube with recurring concentric circles and twists."

To arrange this abstract shot, Teo asked his daughter (A) to hold one end of the multicolored toy (B) up against the dining-room ceiling lamp (C). Teo held his camera and ultrawide lens (D) at the toy's open end and fired away. The ultrawide lens exaggerated the toy's length, rendering close rings enormous and distant ones small. Teo kept the toy somewhat compressed so the dining room's real-world background could not peek through its eerie rings and spoil the mood. Finally, he underexposed the shot for dramatic intensity and darkened its corners to emphasize that beckoning vortex. Despite the photograph's alien colors, Teo used nary a tinted gel or filter. Dr. Who would be very proud of Dr. Teo.

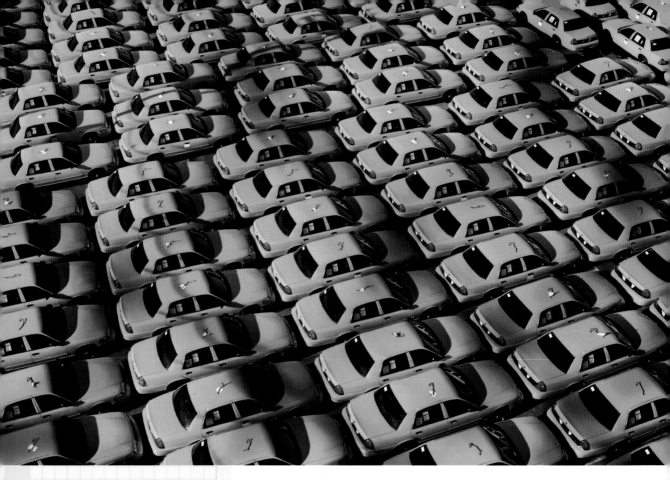

Photographer Dan Bracaglia spotted a taxi lot in Hoboken, New Jersey, filled bumper to bumper with shiny new yellow cabs. He stood atop a bridge to record this field of automotive gold with a 35mm f/1.4 lens, shooting at 1/3200 sec and ISO 500.

102

PROWL FOR URBAN PATTERNS

The city is as rich a source of pleasing patterns as the countryside: Just scout out repeating shapes and dynamic spacing. Repetitious shapes can be found in details, like brickwork, or by focusing on the big picture, such as orderly rows of rooftops. For dynamic spacing, choose repeating elements that don't touch, or shapes that bunch and merge to propel the eye through the scene. Remember, patterns aren't always static; they can also be on the move, like passing clouds. They can be parallel, symmetrical, or include wild cards—such as the taxis parked at different angles in Dan Bracaglia's composition—that supply surprise and a focal point.

Telephoto and macro lenses are patterns' best friends, as is close command of depth of field, so set small apertures (f/16, f/22, or smaller) to ensure sharp focus throughout the image. Taking pattern photos requires patience and a keen eye for the world's subtleties, but once you get it down, the rewards are worth the effort.

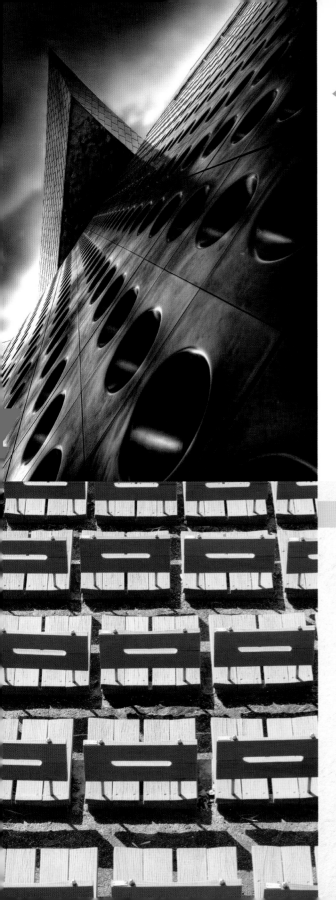

103 CONSIDER ALL THE ANGLES

With its stark, dynamic lines, modern architecture is an ideal subject for photographic abstracts. Capture your perfect shot through careful study and composition.

STEP ONE Pick your perspective and light. Walk around the building. Get as close as you can and examine it from various viewpoints and at different times of day. Look for evocative shapes, curves, and contrasting elements, such as a grid of windows topped by an arching roofline.

STEP TWO Experiment with gear. Choose a wide-angle lens for a vertiginous upward shot of a skyscraper, or a polarizing filter to ensure that interesting reflections don't disappear in ambient glare.

STEP THREE Take lots of practice shots, then delete distractions. For a purely abstract shot, eliminate visual clutter, such as passersby, from your frame or crop them out later.

STEP FOUR Finally, finesse your settings. Bump up contrast to stress shapes, if needed.

CHECKLIST

104 GO ABSTRACT

Bored with the usual subjects? Shoot abstract images—photos that play with pure pattern, line, texture, or color. You'll not only hone your skills as a photographer, you'll stretch your perceptions.

☐ **OPEN YOUR MIND** See a chair, and you'll photograph a chair. But view it as a collection of visual ingredients, and you can craft an innovative shot like the one here.

☐ **PICK OUT DETAILS** Focus on a compelling element of your subject by selecting a long focal length.

☐ **CROP OUT UNWANTED ELEMENTS** If your gear won't let you fill the frame with your composition, shoot broadly and crop in later.

☐ **TRY B&W** Monochrome alters the colored reality we see, so it is the first step on the road to abstraction.

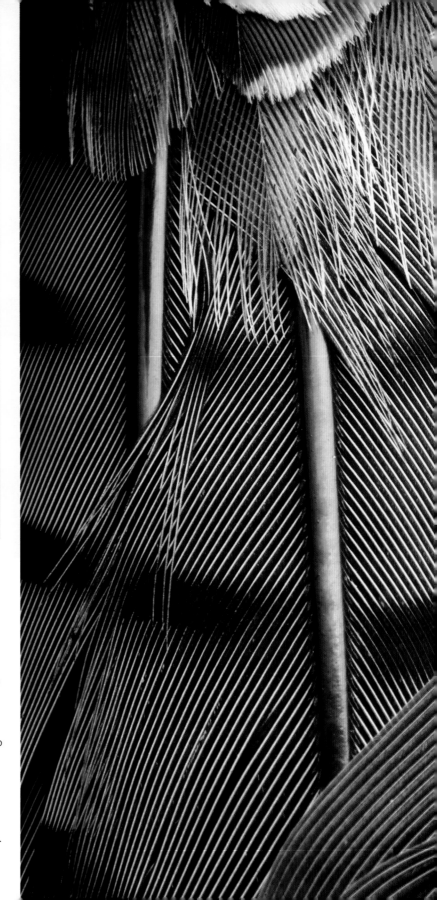

It was a nice warm day, and my wife and I had all of the windows open. A blue jay was chasing dragonflies, and he flew right into the house and landed on a coffee table. We gingerly picked him up and brought him into the little studio I'd set up in the living room. The light from my ring light was very strong, but it just wrapped around him beautifully. My wife held him, and I managed to shoot a few shots with a DSLR and 60mm macro lens. It lets you focus to a 1:1 (life-size) ratio, which is how I got such a tight shot. Then we let him go. Now he's more careful near the door.

—AARON ANSAROV

105

HIGHLIGHT DETAIL WITH A RING LIGHT

To capture minute detail such as the iridescent plumage in the photo at right, zoom in with a macro ring light that fits on your lens to illuminate tiny objects. These lights, often used in food and botanical photography, heighten detail without shadow interference.

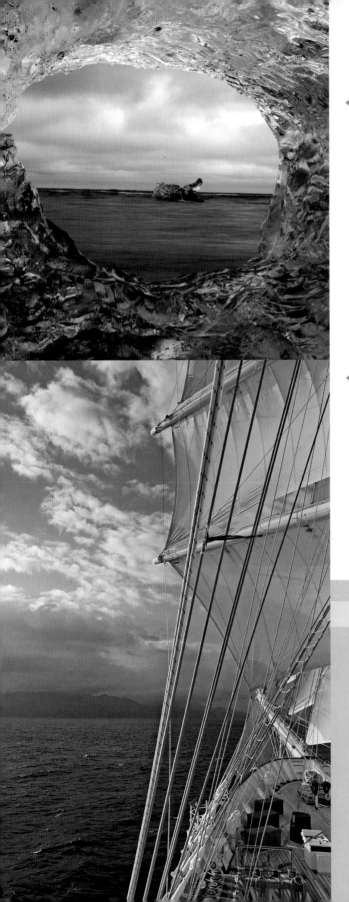

106 FRAME WITH THE FOREGROUND

One of the most striking field techniques is foreground framing, which directs the viewer's eye straight to the photo's star attraction. A foreground frame can also depict a subject in relation to its surroundings. At its most dramatic, as in the shot at left, it produces a 3D effect in which the scene sweeps from front to back. Keep an eye out for anything you can use to frame your subject: tree branches, architectural elements, rock formations, flowers, or even the outstretched arms of a companion.

107 SWITCH THE PERSPECTIVE

When should you shoot a vertical? Whenever you shoot a horizontal—though many photographers overlook the advantages of the vertical shot. This type of shot lets you get a wider angle of view with the same focal length, since it can take in low foreground detail without losing the background. Plus, tall things seem to cry out for the vertical treatment: skyscrapers, redwoods, statues, giraffes—and the intricate rigging of this boat's sails. Try getting up high and shooting down for an unexpected angle on a vertical scene.

108 CLEAN A LENS WITH VODKA

If you're out shooting and discover that your lens of choice is dirty, don't panic. Just stop by the nearest bar and order a vodka. Moisten a clean microfiber cloth with the hooch, then wipe your lens as if you were using cleaning fluid. Avoid flavored vodkas, though—they may leave a residue.

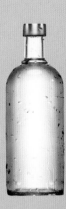

109 LOOK DEEPLY INTO A SUBJECT

Depth of field (DOF) is the amount of space that's in focus in the foreground and the background of a photo—and controlling it helps you craft artful images. A deep DOF captures detail in every part of your composition, from nearby subjects to faraway ones.

If you're striving for the deepest possible DOF, remember that small apertures—those with high f-stop numbers—increase DOF. Experiment with distance from your focal point, moving back to increase DOF. Finally, choose the right focal length for your lens. The shorter its focal length (in other words, the wider its angle of view), the greater your depth of field will be.

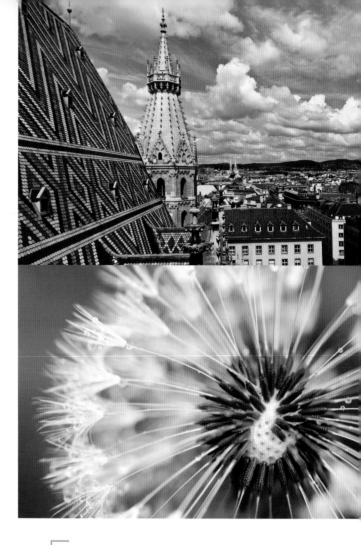

110 BE SHALLOW

Using a shallow DOF in your photos allows you to direct your viewer's attention exactly where you want it: on a face, a flower, or a single detail of your composition. To narrow your DOF, adjust your aperture's size. The f-stop plays a huge role in determining DOF—when the aperture is wide open (at a low f-stop number), your image's main focal point will be crisply defined. The rest of the image will be somewhat blurred, an effect often called *bokeh* (see #258). Your distance from the focal point also determines DOF. For a shallow one, move closer. Lens choice is another factor—a macro or telephoto decreases DOF.

111 STRAIGHTEN OUT A SKYSCRAPER

When shooting a skyscraper from ground level, what your eyes see as a rectangle will be distorted in the image: broad at the bottom, narrow at the top. You can blunt this effect, called keystoning, with tilt/shift lenses or view cameras (see #091), and you may be able to use software to correct it. But the cheapest and easiest method is simply to use a wider focal length.

Move back as far as you can while maintaining an unobstructed view of the whole building, keep your camera perfectly level, and shoot. (Hot-shoe-mounted bubble levels are handy, as are built-in levels for the pitch axis, or up/down tilt.) You'll suck in a big expanse of unwanted foreground at the bottom of your shot; crop it out afterward.

112 FAKE DEPTH

To simulate increased focal depth in your photographs, turn your camera vertically to a portrait rather than a landscape orientation.

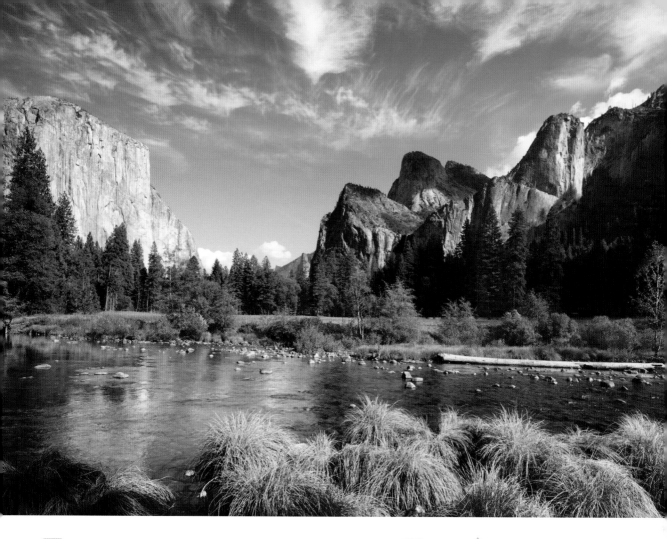

113 GET HYPER ABOUT FOCAL DEPTH

To capture a sweep of precise detail from the foreground to the horizon—especially desirable in landscape photos—focus at your lens's hyperfocal distance. This is the point at which you have the greatest possible DOF that includes infinity. Set your aperture 1 stop below the lens's smallest aperture, switch the lens to manual focus, and then focus to infinity. Now stop down the lens to shooting aperture using the camera's depth-of-field preview button or lever. The viewfinder will be quite dark, so use the camera's Live View, if it has it, and lighten the LCD display so that you can see detail in the frame. Now manually focus back from infinity until a foreground detail just comes into focus. If infinity is now out of focus, go to a smaller aperture (larger f-number) or move back. Conversely, if you have leeway in your DOF, move closer and/or go to a wider aperture. The end result? A sharp shot from foreground wildflowers to distant snowy peaks.

114 HOLD THAT HORIZON

Inside your DSLR is a landscape lover's savior: the in-camera leveling guide. If your horizon tilts in a shot (likely when you're on uneven terrain), you could level it in postproduction, but you'd lose some frame edges. Alternately, you could use a tripod or a hot-shoe level, but these don't let you compose and level at the same time. A built-in electronic level, which you'll see in your viewfinder, permits both. Some cameras also have a level for the pitch axis. Built-in levels are a boon when you seek landscapes off the beaten path, but you don't want to lug a tripod around solely for its leveling head.

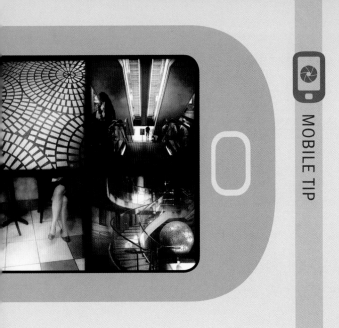

115 SHOOT WITH A MOSAIC IN MIND

Out and about without your high-tech DSLR and favorite filter? You can still capture the magic of the moment—or several moments digitally stitched together into a stunning package. To create a spontaneous but artful array of photos such as the one here, download a mobile-phone app that allows you to create a quick grid or other graphic array of images. Then use the same app to upload your collage or send it to a friend.

116

ZAP SPECKS WITH DUST MAPPING

Your camera sensor shakes to remove dust, and a blower can gently loosen dirt from the glass plate in front of the sensor. Basic camera hygiene also keeps away dust. Change lenses carefully, and never leave a camera body or rear lens element uncapped.

Despite your best efforts, you might still get some dust spots in your photos. To eliminate these bugbears, call on your camera's dust-mapping software. The program photographs a blank white surface, and then an image-editing feature uses that data to fill in dust spots via interpolation.

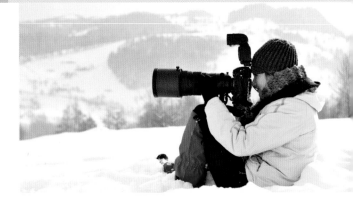

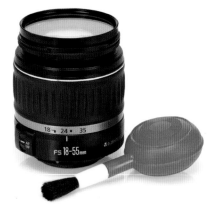

117 FIGHT ZOOM CREEP

Zoom lenses with loose turning actions often suffer from something called zoom creep. It can be vexing when, for example, you hike with a long zoom lens hanging from a neckstrap and it slowly extends from a conveniently compact state into a longer, chest-thumping log. Zoom creep can also reduce sharpness. With a loose-turning lens, when the camera is aimed up or down, the zooming elements can move during exposure, resulting in a softer image. To prevent creep, some lenses have a zoom lock to maintain a compact profile. Lock it down or (as pros who shoot from the rafters of sports arenas do) use gaffer's tape to tame that creep.

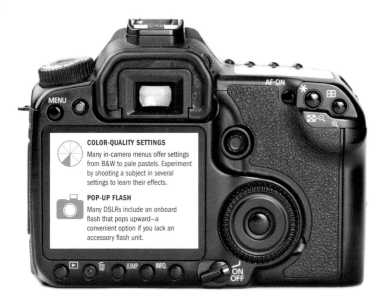

COLOR-QUALITY SETTINGS
Many in-camera menus offer settings from B&W to pale pastels. Experiment by shooting a subject in several settings to learn their effects.

POP-UP FLASH
Many DSLRs include an onboard flash that pops upward—a convenient option if you lack an accessory flash unit.

118

TAKE NOTES WITHOUT A NOTEBOOK

Your camera's voice memo feature lets you record voice clips via the camera's built-in microphone and embed them in image files. Thus you need not schlep notebooks or handheld devices to note down stuff that doesn't get into exchangeable image file (EXIF) format data, such as names of people and places, directions to shoot locations, hair-raising or amusing midshot happenings, and the like. Use it to take field notes when location scouting, to create shot-list reminders, or to tag photos for later identification. The capability used to be the provenance of high-end DSLRs, but it has begun to migrate down the market.

119 CREATE A PORTABLE CAMERA MANUAL

Can't remember what all your camera's fancy functions do? Shoot close-ups of the pages in your manual that explain each one. Load them on a memory card and take it along when shooting. In playback, zoom in with the magnifier function so the text is legible. Use the same shortcut to record instructions for any procedure that chronically slips your mind. Presto—a weightless manual for the field.

120 PERFECT YOUR OPTICS WITH LENS CORRECTION

There's no single perfect lens on the market, search as we might to find one. Even top-shelf optics can produce distortion, light falloff in the corners, and soft images at certain apertures. Many cameras now flaunt built-in fixes that correct barrel and pincushion distortion and corner vignetting. Some can counteract chromatic aberration, too, which robs your images of sharpness and causes color fringing (this function is found in the Raw conversion menu). Bear in mind that such functions sometimes work only with a camera maker's own lenses, not with independent optics. Remember, too, that lens correction is a default setting in some cameras. Switch the function off in the setup menu if you prefer distortion or want to avoid the frame-edge cutoff that such correction sometimes causes.

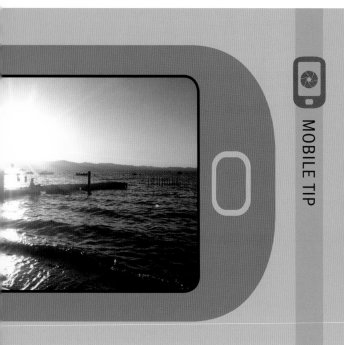

121 ADJUST EXPOSURE ON YOUR PHONE

Here's one trick many smartphones have over your DSLR: You can tap their screens to improve focus and exposure. To choose a focus area, simply double-tap on it. And to adjust exposure, press your screen at a good metering spot, then use the pop-up slider to brighten or dim. Many camera apps have an AEL function similar to your DSLR (see #017): Hold your finger on your chosen focus/exposure point until an "AE/AF Lock" label pops up, then recompose and shoot. You can also try your camera's HDR function, which captures images at slightly different exposures.

122 MAKE THE MOST OF LIVE VIEW

Live View on cameras lets you use the rear LCD monitor to set up shots, not just review them after the fact. You can experiment with exposure and white balance before you shoot, and most cameras can display your histogram using exposure simulation. If you adjust exposure compensation, the LCD immediately shows you the result. All that means you don't need gobs of test shots, which is great when you're working in fast-changing light. Live View's brightened LCD display is terrific in low light, too—when the viewfinder is too dark for accurate manual or autofocus. Menu settings turn the auto-brighten feature on and off, or you can simply increase exposure compensation to brighten the LCD image. That way, you can shoot in shadows and shade without shooting in the dark. Some monitors are articulated—you can pop it out away from the camera body and swivel it, allowing for easier viewing at awkward angles.

123 CONSIDER COLOR

Digital photography enables you to precisely control photos' color. But what, exactly, is color? Simply defined, color is our visual perception of various wavelengths of light. Learning to adjust and deploy it for artistic and emotional effect is a key task for every photographer.

Since color is so important, an advanced camera is chock-full of tools that let you capture and adjust it. These allow you to choose specific saturation levels, mimic black-and-white and sepia-toned photography, and set white balance (WB) to record true color in all kinds of light environments.

But the best way to control color is to shoot with neutral settings and in modes that record and store shots as Raw files. These tactics conserve the maximum amount of image data because images aren't compressed or processed as you shoot. That gives you leeway to use software later if you decide you want to alter, amplify, or soften color.

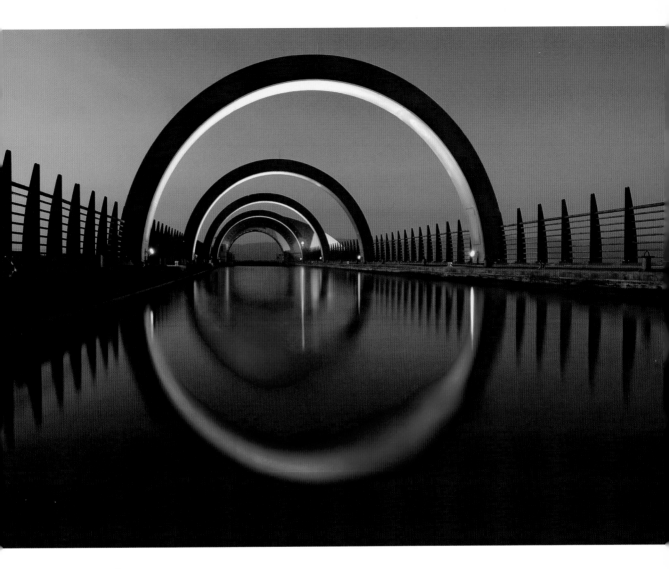

124 COPE WITH COLOR IN MIXED LIGHT

To photograph Scotland's Falkirk Wheel—a rotating canal-boat lift—Kenneth Barker made do with light of four varieties: a low sunset, LEDs in the lift's hoops, incandescent uplighting, and distant city glow. The next time you confront similarly varied (and tricky) lighting, try following these steps.

STEP ONE Select your file format. Shooting in the Raw format is ideal, because it captures the most data and gives you options later. But if your camera can't do it or you need JPEGs (for quick uploads, for example), pick a key object, determine its color temperature, and select a preset white balance or create a custom one.

STEP TWO Bracket color temperature. Dial through your camera's scenic presets and select the one that's closest to the scene that you're shooting.

STEP THREE Bracket exposure to control color richness and saturation. Dialing down exposure compensation saturates color through underexposure. Setting it in plus range desaturates it via overexposure.

STEP FOUR Compose for color. When the light is dramatically mixed, color is your true subject. Compose to fill your frame with contrasting and complementary hues, both natural and manmade.

125 FLOAT ABOVE IT ALL

When Sandy Honig was 17, she learned to levitate for a high-school project. Or at least to look like she was floating in midair. Wondering how she created this seemingly magical self-portrait?

As most magicians will admit, it's all about props. Honig's was a chair, which she set up in her yard so she could capture two images of the scene. One contained nothing but foliage, trees, and the setting sun; the other was of her lying across the seat of the chair. She then layered the images in Adobe Photoshop, and finally erased the chair from its layer, revealing the foliage in the layer below. Presto!

To put on your own photographic magic show, find a suitable background with great light (A). Mount the camera on a tripod (B), as the camera must remain absolutely still between exposures. Compose the scene, then place your chair (C), manually prefocus on it, and take test shots to determine exposure. Focus, then set the exposure and white balance with manual settings to prevent them from changing between shots. For the first exposure, set the self-timer, fire the shutter, and then lie rigidly on the chair (D). To nail identical lighting, take your second shot right after the first: Remove the chair and shoot only the background.

Later, combine the exposures in image-editing software. Check out entry #374 for specifics on making a confounding composite like this one.

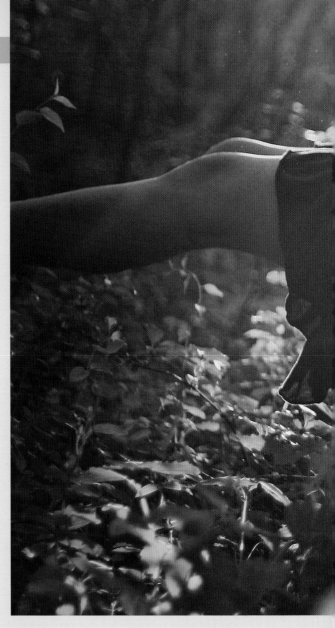

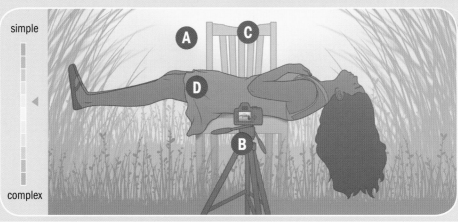

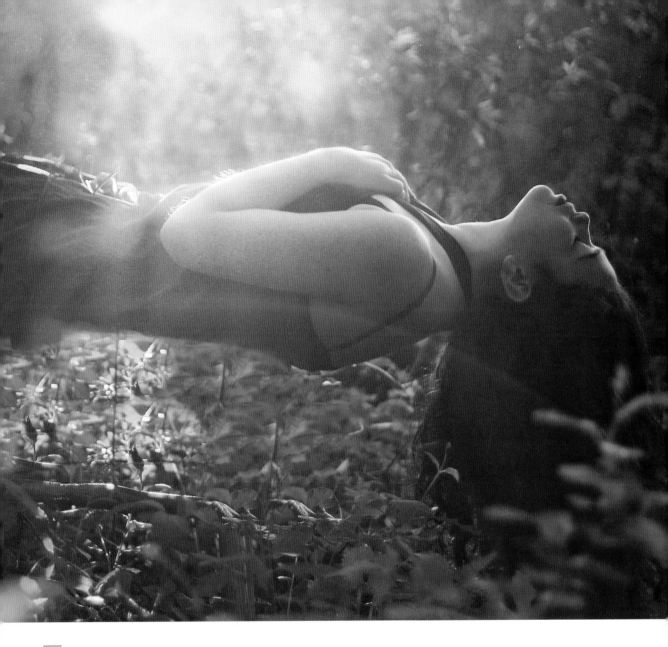

126 EXPERIMENT WITH FLASH EXPOSURE

It sounds odd, but it's actually true: Any photograph that you shoot with a flash is in fact a double exposure. The scene's own ambient light produces the first exposure, while your flash illumination produces the second. Use the exposure dial to tweak ambient exposure for intriguing effects, making it equal, slightly unequal, or wildly unequal to your flash exposure. Or adjust shutter speeds so that one

exposure is motion-blurred and the other appears razor-sharp. You can also give each exposure its own color balance.

Here's an experiment: The next time you shoot a subject against a background of foliage or a sunset, turn off auto settings and separately set ambient and flash exposures to create a range of looks. Such games make flash photography fun—and versatile.

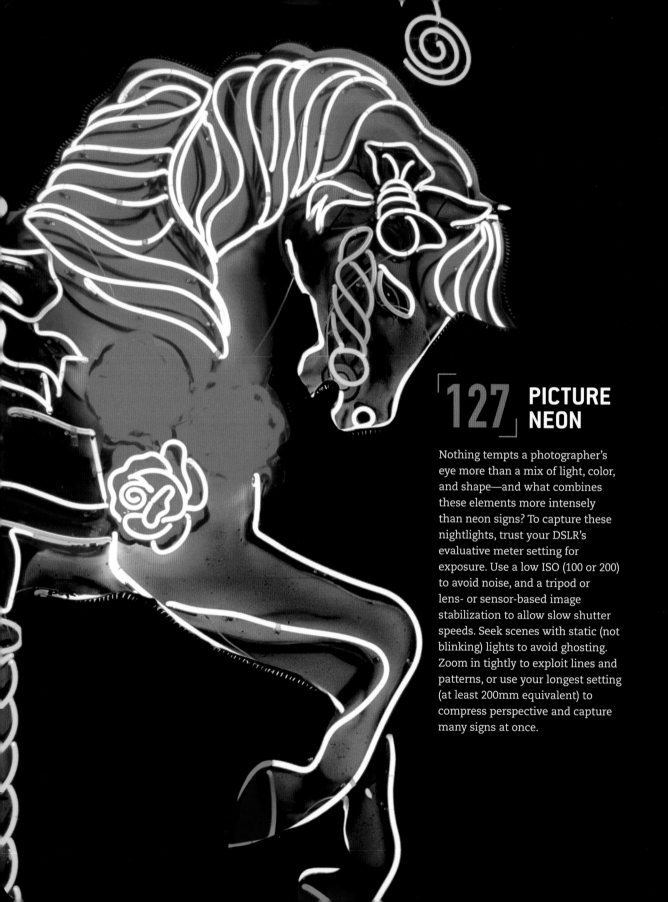

127 PICTURE NEON

Nothing tempts a photographer's eye more than a mix of light, color, and shape—and what combines these elements more intensely than neon signs? To capture these nightlights, trust your DSLR's evaluative meter setting for exposure. Use a low ISO (100 or 200) to avoid noise, and a tripod or lens- or sensor-based image stabilization to allow slow shutter speeds. Seek scenes with static (not blinking) lights to avoid ghosting. Zoom in tightly to exploit lines and patterns, or use your longest setting (at least 200mm equivalent) to compress perspective and capture many signs at once.

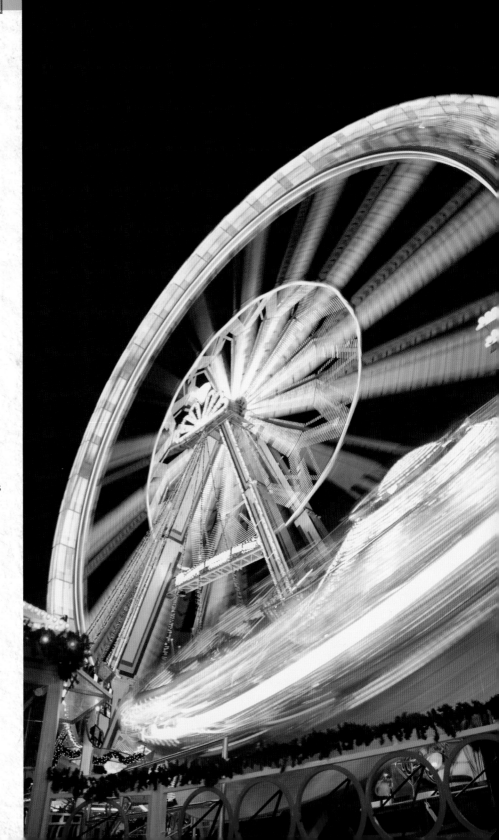

128

SHOOT FAIRS AT NIGHT

The thrill of the carnival at night: bright lights, shriek-inducing rides, and campy merriment. Here's how to capture it.

- ☐ **PREPARE AHEAD OF TIME** Scout rides in daylight. You also might want to take some shots at twilight, when you can catch a sapphire-blue sky behind the rides' lights.

- ☐ **SET UP THE SHOT** Pick a dark, out-of-the-way vantage point to avoid lens flare and jostling crowds.

- ☐ **EXPERIMENT WITH SHUTTER SPEED** Add creative blur to moving rides by using a tripod and long shutter speeds (1/4 sec to 30 sec).

- ☐ **ADD SPEED** Zoom during long exposures to add an extra element of motion.

- ☐ **TIME YOUR SHOT** Let rides get going before shooting. Or, for sharper shots, wait for the pauses when rides are loading or unloading.

- ☐ **BOOST TONE** For HDR, bracket shots widely.

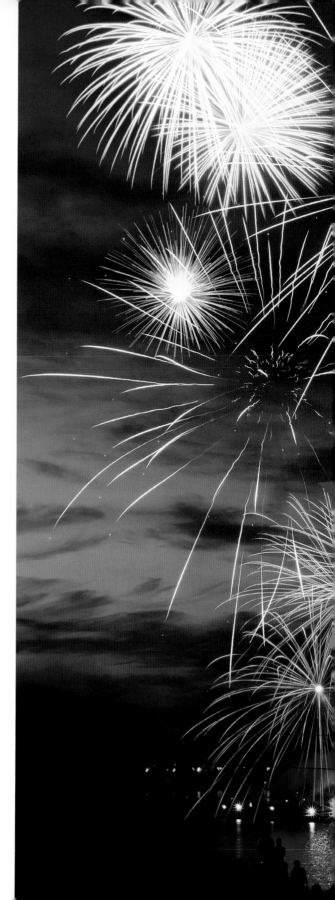

129 GET FIRED UP ABOUT FIREWORKS

Literally dazzling when seen live, fireworks can fizzle out in photos. To avoid that, crank up the color saturation in your camera's setup menu. And make sure you don't go too wide while shooting. Yes, shorter focal lengths capture complete bursts, but they can appear mighty puny in your shot. Instead, compose to include a bit of foreground material (trees, people, and architecture) to provide a sense of scale.

Don't worry if you have to crop out some of the airborne action—you'll still capture plenty of fiery light. Shoot in manual exposure, turn off autofocus, and manually set the focus to infinity. Put your flash to bed; you won't need it.

Keep shooting. Pyrotechnic photos have a low keep-to-delete ratio. For every great shot, you'll get 20 duds, so get that shutter finger clicking!

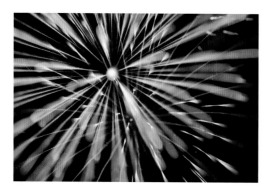

130 SNAG MANY SALVOS IN ONE SHOT

The easiest way to get multiple bursts in the same photo is to shoot the finale—but its smoke might mar your image. Instead, try a long exposure that fills your frame with overlapping bursts. Use a tripod, and focus and set exposure manually. Set the shutter to Bulb, which lets you hold the shutter open (a cable release will keep you from jostling the camera). Hold a black card in front of the lens. Open up the shutter and, as a rocket bursts, remove the card for a few seconds. Cover the lens again when the burst subsides, keeping your shutter open. When the next firework explodes, pull the card away again. Repeat the process several times, for a total exposure time of about 15 to 20 sec.

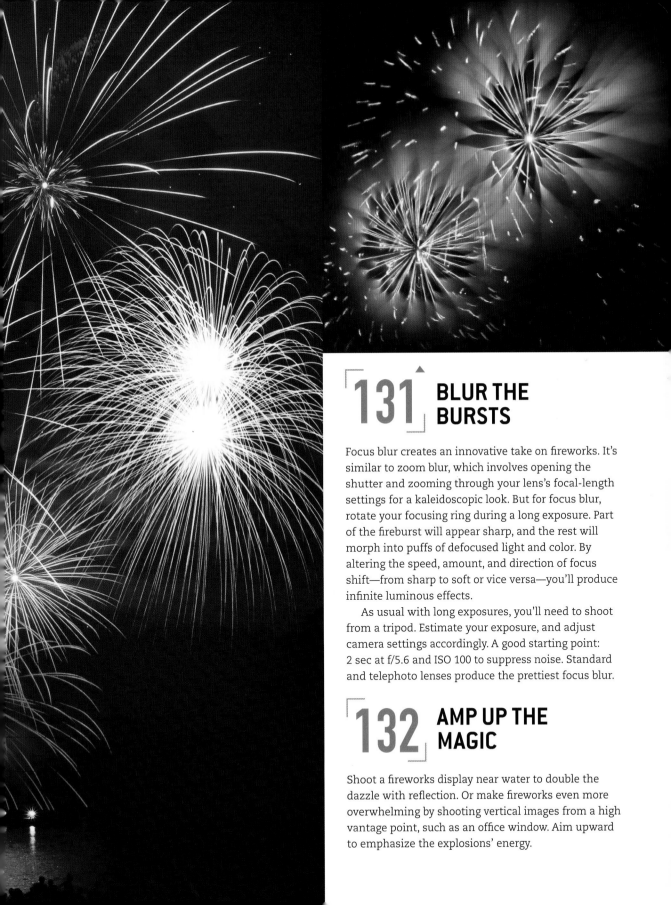

131 BLUR THE BURSTS

Focus blur creates an innovative take on fireworks. It's similar to zoom blur, which involves opening the shutter and zooming through your lens's focal-length settings for a kaleidoscopic look. But for focus blur, rotate your focusing ring during a long exposure. Part of the fireburst will appear sharp, and the rest will morph into puffs of defocused light and color. By altering the speed, amount, and direction of focus shift—from sharp to soft or vice versa—you'll produce infinite luminous effects.

As usual with long exposures, you'll need to shoot from a tripod. Estimate your exposure, and adjust camera settings accordingly. A good starting point: 2 sec at f/5.6 and ISO 100 to suppress noise. Standard and telephoto lenses produce the prettiest focus blur.

132 AMP UP THE MAGIC

Shoot a fireworks display near water to double the dazzle with reflection. Or make fireworks even more overwhelming by shooting vertical images from a high vantage point, such as an office window. Aim upward to emphasize the explosions' energy.

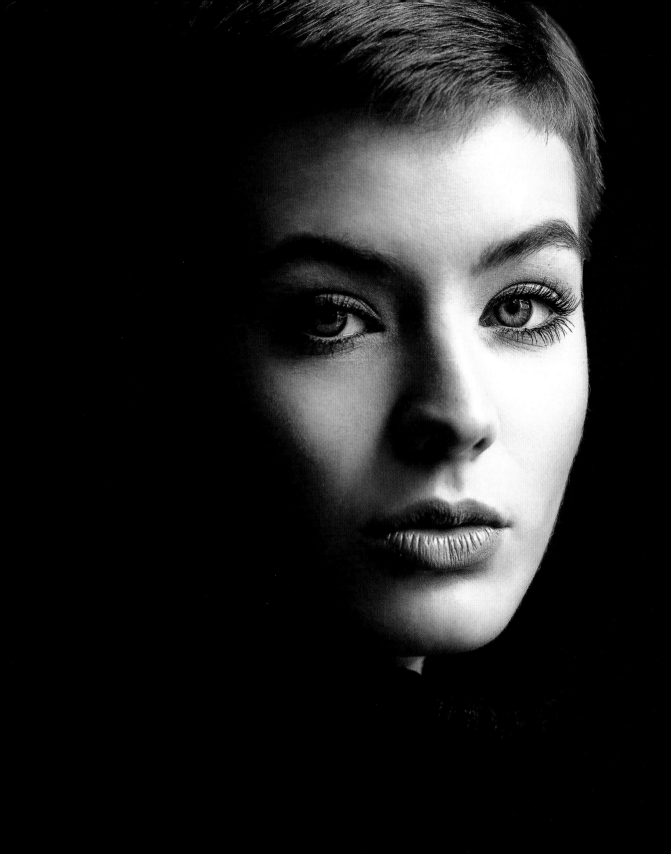

133 LIGHT A PORTRAIT LIKE REMBRANDT

When it comes to portrait lighting, here's a sure bet: Merge the power of two classic formulas, Rembrandt and window lighting, as the German portrait and fine-art photographer Andreas Jorns did here. Rembrandt lighting (named after the Dutch master whose portraits epitomize the style) is prized for its ability to bring out facial modeling—its signature is a triangular highlight under the eye on the shadowed side, which helps the adjacent shadow pop the model's nose forward and sculpt the line of the left cheek. Add to that the flatteringly soft quality of diffuse window light—so forgiving of complexion issues—and you've got a successful portrait.

FOR REMBRANDT LIGHTING Place your main source to the left or right side of the subject and aim it down at her face at about a 45-degree angle. Keep adjusting its position until you see the telltale triangle and the shadow to the side of and slightly below the nose.

FOR WINDOW LIGHTING When working with south- or southwestern-facing exposures, shoot early or late on a cloudy day with diffuse light. If circumstances require working on a sunny day, use light from a north-facing window or hang a white sheet in front of the window to mimic the effect of an overcast sky. Conversely, if the sky is heavily overcast and its light weak, put your subject as close to the window as possible. The window shouldn't be too large, but, if possible, it should reach down to the floor, especially if your model is seated. If your window lets too much light into the room, hang black flocking in front of it.

134 EMBRACE THE DARKNESS

We often associate darkness with obscured subjects and blur. But darkness can be a blessing: If photography is writing with light, darkness is the punctuation. It defines shapes, makes two dimensions look like three, and heightens drama. It can even be a subject in itself. Here's how to achieve dark victory.

FRAME WITH DARKNESS Use a tunnel, a dark window, or a backlit landform in the foreground as a natural framing device. Be sure to expose for the scene that's inside the frame, not for the frame itself.

SNAG A SILHOUETTE Try defining forms by reducing them to dead black, called a *silhouette*. For a perfect silo, meter off the bright background and allow the edges of your subject to be rim-lit by a light source behind it.

DELIBERATE UNDEREXPOSURE For a dramatic portrait in a dark outdoor scene at golden hour, allow just enough exposure to define the subject's face, and let the background go underexposed.

DIY CHIAROSCURO Try negative reflectors—black cards also known as flags—to tone down bright areas, prevent light spillover, and define shapes.

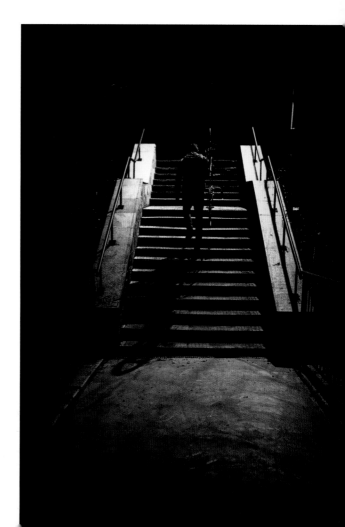

135 LIGHT THE WAY WITH CANDLES

Candlelight produces evocative photos, lending still lifes a golden glow and warming up portraits. Here are five tips for making the most of the flickering glow.

- ☐ **USE A SLOW SHUTTER SPEED** and a tripod or a self-timer to avoid blur. If you can, employ image stabilization.
- ☐ **SET YOUR WHITE BALANCE TO DAYLIGHT,** as candlelight is red. Otherwise your camera will cancel out the very tones that you want. If your shots turn out too red, try the incandescent light setting.
- ☐ **AMP UP THE MOODY FEEL** by underexposing shots. Your digital camera's instant feedback will guide you to the right exposure.
- ☐ **SHIFT THE CANDLE CLOSER TO YOUR SUBJECT** if your shots prove dim, or you can arrange more candles around it.
- ☐ **COMPOSE SHOTS WITH DARK,** distraction-free backgrounds. Whether you're creating a still life or photographing a child's face, foreground is the key to a classic candlelit image.

136

SHARPEN SHADOWS

When you photograph delicate, small, or highly detailed objects, pinpoint light sources can solve the vexing problem of blurred, imprecise shadows. Positioning a penlight to the side of your subject and using a long exposure will help you capture an intricate play of solids and shadows.

Other light sources—from small flashlights to sunlight streaming through holes in an old wall or pierced fabric—can also produce patterned or repeating shadows. Photograph those—or use them to highlight portions of a model's face or body, adding mystery to a straightforward portrait.

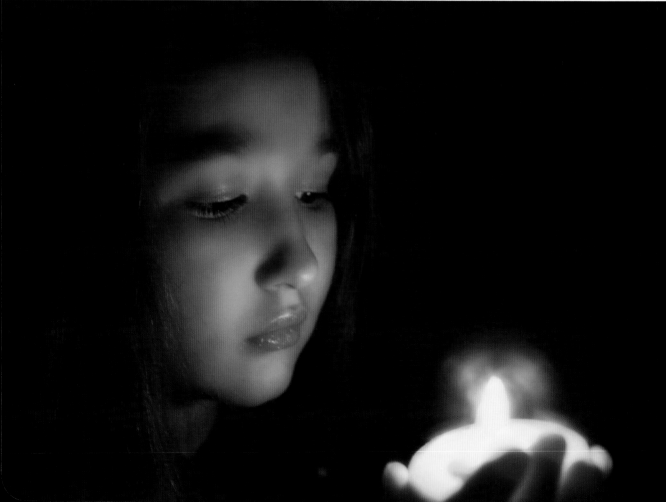

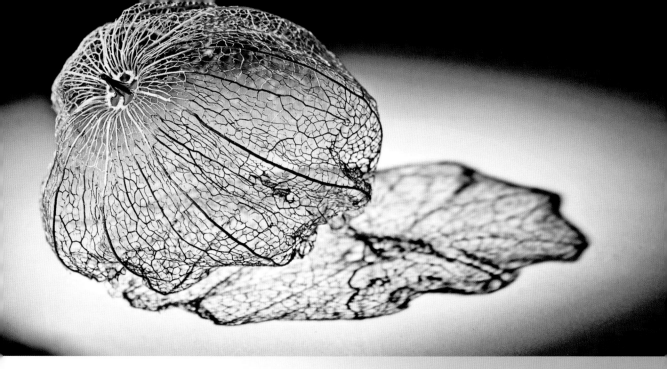

137 EXPLORE THE DARK SIDE

Photographers tend to think of shadows as things to manage and wrangle, forgetting that they can be the subject of potent photos. Wherever you find yourself, chances are you can find—or create—stunning shadow photographs. If you have a willing model and a frosted glass sheet, backlight him and shoot through the glass to produce an eerie, surreal silhouette with areas of both precise detail (fingers pressed to the glass's surface) and evocative blur (the head inclined away from it). Find frosted glass at home stores, or put your shower door to use. Outdoors, choose a compelling object—flowers, rock formations, a length of translucent fabric—place it on a texturally intriguing surface, and shine light on it. Shoot the shadow itself to give darkness center stage.

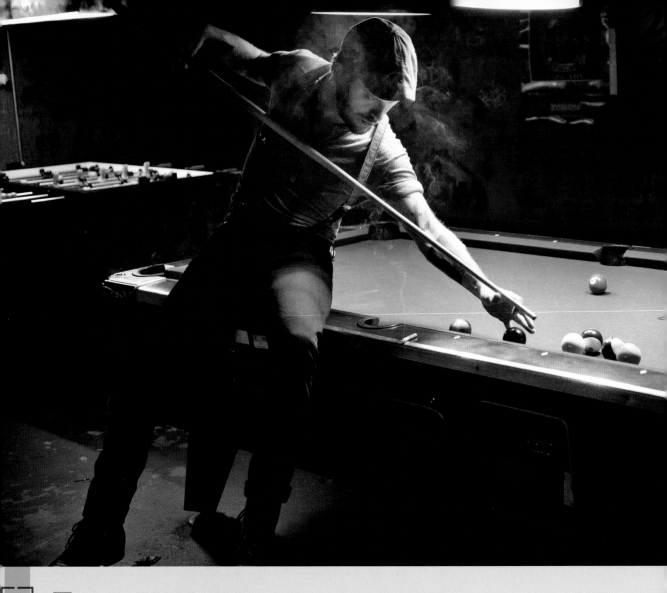

138 WORK WITH AVAILABLE LIGHT

Why drag around strobes, snoots, and umbrellas to create the right light when the stuff may be on the scene already, just waiting for you to notice it? Complex setups have their place, but for Cary Norton's gritty, Southern-flavored shot of rock star Matthew Mayfield, the lights of an Alabama dive bar provided the perfect down-home color and contrast. Working with available light isn't easy—you must have the skill to spot it, as Norton did when Mayfield's cigarette smoke emphasized the three cones of light streaming down from the lamps above the pool table. Norton used both the fluorescent lights (A) over the foosball table and the three shaded incandescents (B) above the pool table. He handheld his camera (C) and used a high ISO to capture sharp detail, choosing an angle that created a dynamic diagonal composition of tables, pool cue, and player. Later, he fixed the fluorescents' and incandescents' conflicting color temperatures in postprocessing. "I enjoy finding good light instead of making it," Norton says. "I tend to shoot from the hip." With practice, you, too, can achieve high drama from low lights.

139 FACTOR IN COLOR TEMPERATURES

To wrangle the light in your photos, you need to know a bit about bulbs. Fluorescent bulbs (3,200 to 5,500 Kelvin, or K) emit whitish light. Electronic flashes imitate midday sunlight (which hovers around 5,600 K). Tungsten (2,700 K) lights, be they halogen or incandescent, are amber in hue. You can compensate for competing light sources by setting your camera's white balance manually while you shoot, or capture Raw files and work it out later using conversion software or other programs.

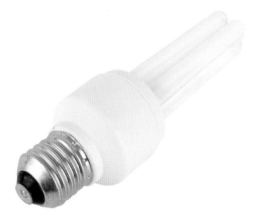

140 SHOOT OUTDOORS WITH AMBIENT LIGHT

Cost-free and hands-free, ambient light comes in all varieties: flat, high contrast, bright, and dim. Outdoor photographers who work without supplementary lights often stalk a site, revisiting it many times to nail the ideal light. Prized as "golden hours" by painters and photographers, sunset and sunrise tend to yield more nuanced shots than the hard light of noon.

Dramatize an outdoor subject with elements that direct ambient light, such as a filtering screen of leaves or the angle of a wall. To avoid blown-out or black areas, search for light that's reasonably even across a composition. Finally, don't sweat a little blur: It makes outdoor scenes look more natural.

simple ▬▬▬▬▬▬▬▬▬ complex
▲

A

B

C

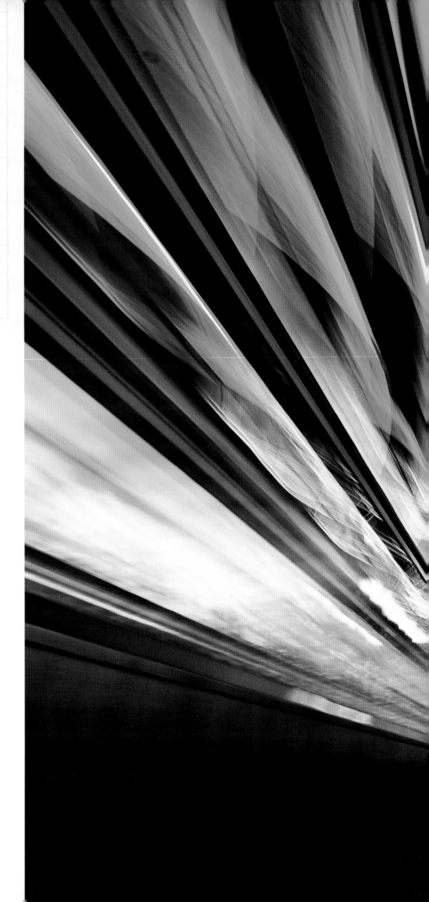

I've been through Chicago's O'Hare Airport many times, and I'm always amazed by the lights in this tunnel. I wanted to photograph it on a recent stopover with my fiancée, though we had only 30 minutes between flights. So I put my camera on a little tripod, stepped onto the moving walkway, set my camera for a 10-sec exposure, and shot the scene in one go.

—BYRON YU

141

MAKE POETRY WITH MOTION

Rolling along a moving walkway, Byron Yu used a tripod-mounted DSLR and a leisurely exposure—10 sec at f/4, ISO 100—to capture this kinetic neon ceiling sculpture and blur its lights into dynamic, converging diagonals.

Follow these rules to get great long exposures: Turn down ISO, since high ISOs generate more noise in your images. Select a small aperture to capture light trails—an f-stop as high as f/22 allows scant light to strike your sensor but still catches plenty of detailed motion. And for long exposures in daylight, bring a variable neutral-density filter, which you can set in stops to cut light entering the lens and enable longer shutter opening.

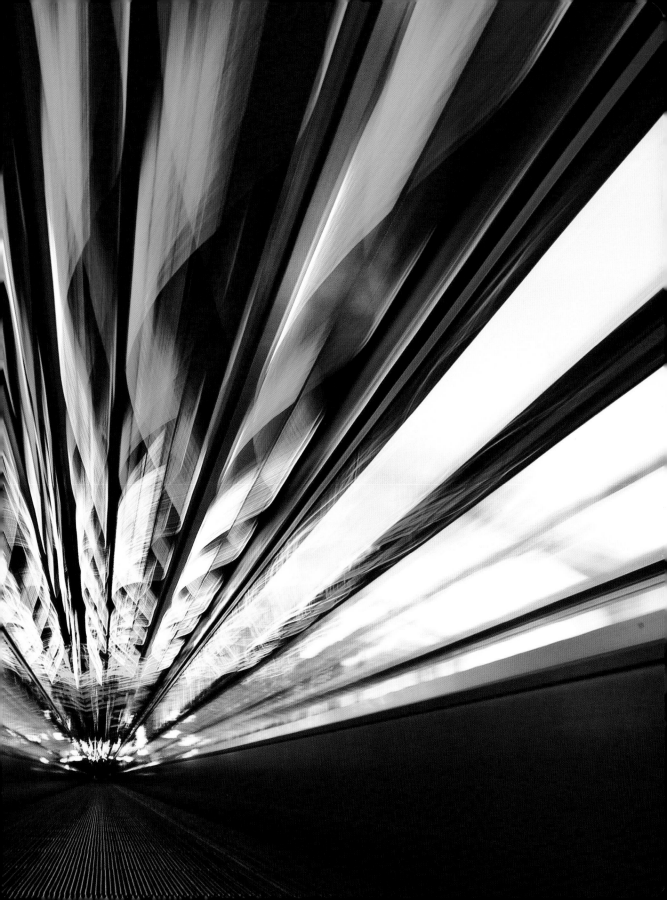

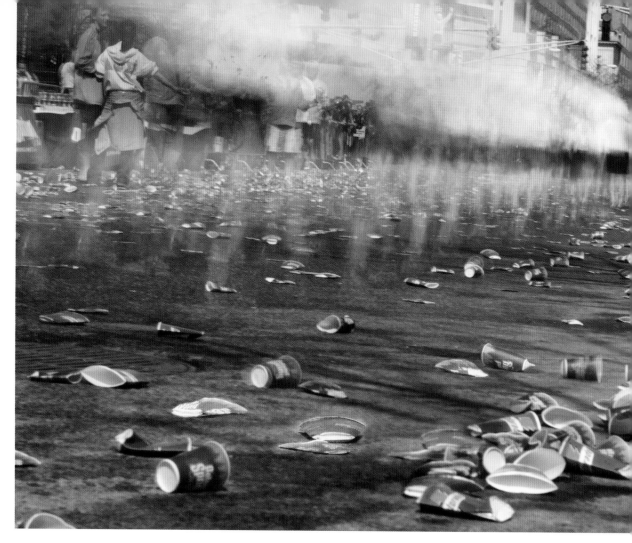

142 EXTEND EXPOSURE IN ACTION SHOTS

A long, carefully planned exposure is the key to this atypical photo of Boston Marathon runners—and the water cups left in their wake. Photographer Laura Barisonzi captured it with a 10-stop neutral-density (ND) filter that cut light and lengthened exposure time—a departure from the crisp shot of peak action that's typical of sports photography. To take your own unusual shot of an athletic event, follow these steps:

STEP ONE Plan a few creative images that focus on background (or in this case, foreground) as much as on the athletes. To get this shot, the photographer set up at a heavily used water stop, since that guaranteed there'd be a colorful array of discarded cups.

STEP TWO Gather gear. Since you'll need a generous shutter speed for this shot, use an ND filter and a tripod. Compose and focus before adding the filter.

STEP THREE Prep the site. For instance, the photographer rearranged these cups into an interesting pattern before she started shooting.

STEP FOUR Find the angle. To catch the foreground that's all-important to a photo like this, you'll have to lie down flat on the asphalt.

STEP FIVE Experiment with exposure. In this instance, holding the shutter open for 4 secs produced the dramatic line of runners, smudged but still recognizable.

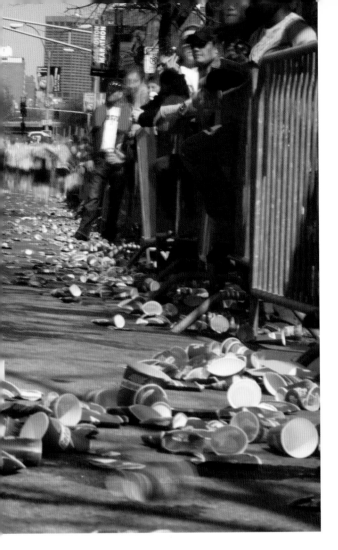

143 MAKE PEOPLE DISAPPEAR

It doesn't require a magic wand. All you need to make crowds vanish from congested landmarks and landscapes is a long exposure time and an overall ND filter: an often inexpensive, gray-tinted accessory that cuts light while preserving a scene's color. Your exposure must be long enough that anyone in the frame blurs completely away—which could take anywhere from 30 sec to several minutes—so you'll definitely need to use a tripod.

Set the smallest aperture (i.e., the largest f-number) that you can. Each 0.3 of density eats up 1 exposure stop, and each stop doubles exposure time. So, if a scene's correct exposure without an ND filter is 1 sec, a 3-stop reduction in light lets you shoot at 8 sec. Manufacturers make ND filters up to a staggering 3.0 density. That's 10 stops, which expands a 1-sec exposure to 17-plus minutes. Compose and focus with the filter off the lens, take a meter reading, and double exposure time for every stop of light your ND filter will gobble up.

144 BEAT MIRROR SHAKE

Even if it's on a tripod, your DSLR can shake due to "mirror slap": the vibration produced when the camera's mirror flips up and down. Another source of possible shake is your hand on the camera as you trip the shutter. You can lock up the mirror to fix the first problem, and fire with a remote or the self-timer to solve the second, but there's another solution. Most DSLRs feature a combined control with both mirror lockup and a two-second delayed release. You'll find it in the self-timer menu or drive-mode selection. The tool works without a tripod, too: Rest the camera or your elbows on a sturdy surface, and hold the camera firmly against your face. Breathe in, trip the shutter, and stay very still until the mirror drops down again.

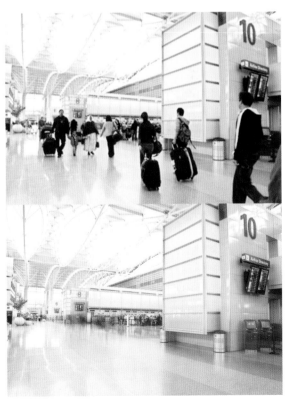

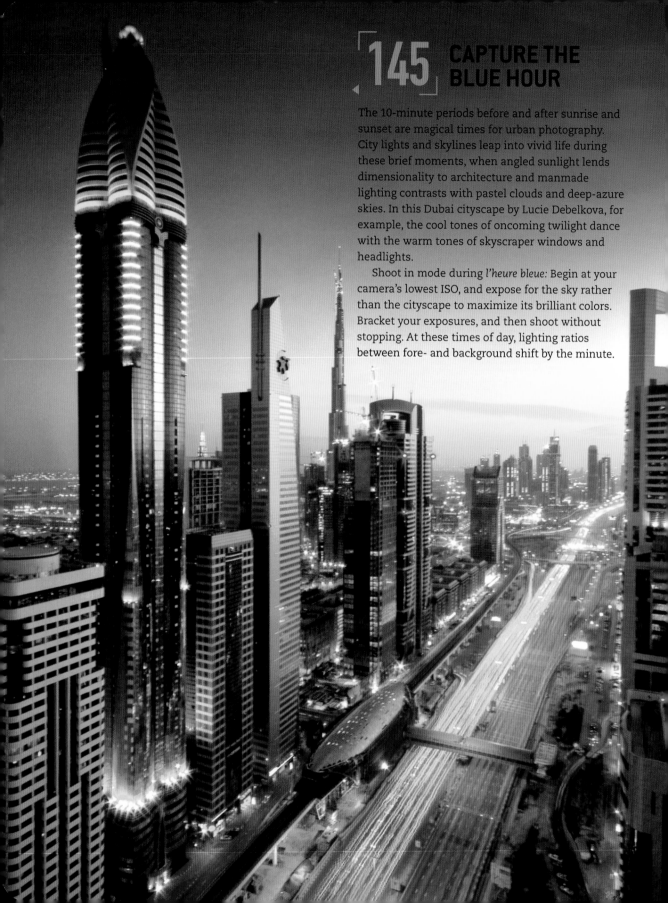

145 CAPTURE THE BLUE HOUR

The 10-minute periods before and after sunrise and sunset are magical times for urban photography. City lights and skylines leap into vivid life during these brief moments, when angled sunlight lends dimensionality to architecture and manmade lighting contrasts with pastel clouds and deep-azure skies. In this Dubai cityscape by Lucie Debelkova, for example, the cool tones of oncoming twilight dance with the warm tones of skyscraper windows and headlights.

Shoot in mode during *l'heure bleue:* Begin at your camera's lowest ISO, and expose for the sky rather than the cityscape to maximize its brilliant colors. Bracket your exposures, and then shoot without stopping. At these times of day, lighting ratios between fore- and background shift by the minute.

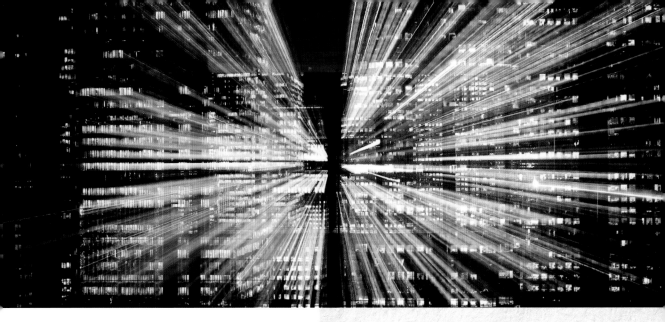

146

FAKE MOTION

Motion zoom—which means zooming in or out during an exposure—creates bright, colorful streaks that rush inward toward a vanishing point. This effect can be either cool or cheesy, so boost your odds with a few sure strategies.

Pick brightly hued and contrasty subjects (holiday lights are always a sure bet). Deepen the scene's natural colors by setting your DSLR to its top saturation level. Experiment with both long and short shutter speeds, too. Speeds of 1 sec or longer let you use the whole zoom range, and that produces brilliant abstracts that lack clearly identifiable subjects. Speeds under 1 sec preserve the subject but halo it in dreamy rays of color. Aperture is another motion-faking technique—small apertures generate narrow streaks, and large ones create broad smears. Structure can also produce an impression of motion: If you want straight streaks and physically powerful structure, bring a tripod. If you desire some creative chaos, handhold your camera. Shift it up, down, left, and right as you zoom. To shape your image into a vortex, twist the camera around as you work.

147

FACTOR IN BLUR

"Is the picture crisp?" "How sharp is that lens?" Photographers ask such questions all the time. But remember the alluring flip side of sharpness: softness, which is the perfect treatment for many subjects and moods. Apply blur to areas of your image—or brush it across the whole thing—with one of these methods:

☐ **MOVE THE CAMERA** Shift it at slow shutter speeds to produce blur in scenes with contrasting tonalities.

☐ **MOVE THE SUBJECT** Shooting a moving subject produces motion blur with long shutter speeds of 1/25 sec or more. This tactic charges your image with kinetic energy.

☐ **MOVE BOTH** Pan the camera in the direction opposite subject movement to produce a pure abstraction. Pan it in sync with subject motion to capture a sharp subject against a soft, blurred background.

☐ **CHANGE ZOOM SETTING** Zooming during exposure produces fascinating kaleidoscopic effects that work beautifully with colorful, high-contrast scenes.

☐ **USE SOFT-FOCUS FILTERS** Whether they're glass or digital, filters let you decide where and how much image softening you'll apply.

148 GET FAMILIAR WITH FILTERS

Once you've picked a lens, fine-tune its effect with filters and other add-ons. Filters screw or clamp on to the lens front so you can alter color, exposure, and other elements. Other task-specific accessories fit between the camera body and lens to add effects such as magnification.

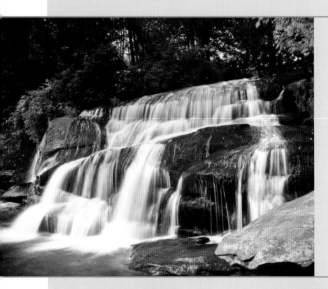

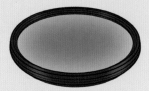

POLARIZING
Perfect for forest, sea, and sky shots, this option cuts glare and reflections and deepens greens and blues.

A polarizing filter helps you capture the true hues of brilliant foliage and sunny days.

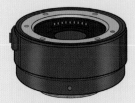

TELECONVERTER
This secondary lens, mounted between camera and lens, extends focal length.

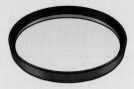

UV
This filter blocks ultraviolet sunlight and protects the lens front from scratches without affecting images.

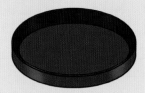

INFRARED
This intriguing option blocks visible light and passes only subspectrum light to create dreamlike, eerie images.

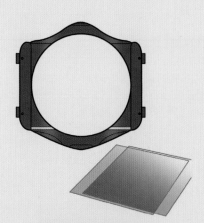

FILTERS AND HOLDER
Interchangeable special-effects filters fit into a single adjustable holder so you can use them with all sorts of lenses.

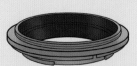

REVERSING RING
Use this ring to mount your lens to the camera backward so you can magnify without a macro lens.

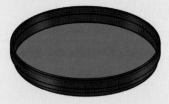

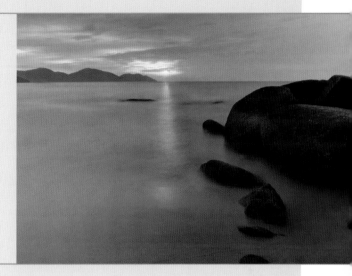

NEUTRAL DENSITY (ND)
This filter cuts the light passing
through your lens to allow you slow
shutter speeds or wide apertures.

A basic tool of landscape photography, light-limiting
ND filters are available in many different densities.

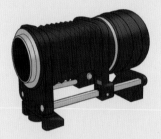

MACRO BELLOWS
This system allows intense
and precise magnification
even without a dedicated
macro lens.

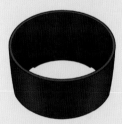

LENS HOOD
Attach this crucial accessory to the
front of the lens to shield it from light
and thwart glare and lens flare.

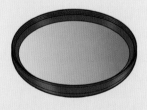

SPLIT NEUTRAL DENSITY
This handy filter applies the
ND's effect to just half the
image to balance a scene's
light and dark areas.

A split ND filter is the ideal tool when foreground
and background need different exposures.

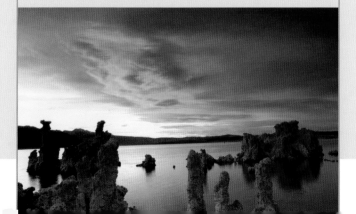

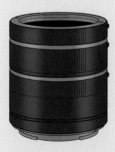

EXTENSION TUBE
This tube sits between the lens and
the camera body, increasing
magnification for close-up shots.

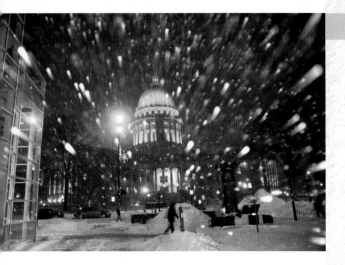

149 KEEP SNOW WHITE

It's a sad, familiar story: You spot a pristine snow scene and shoot it, only to discover later that your sparkling snow has turned into gray sand. The culprit: your light meter. It seeks medium gray and always underexposes snow. (The same problem occurs when you shoot pale beach sand.) Here are five tricks to solve the problem.

☐ **METER THE SNOW** Then manually set exposure 1.5 to 2 stops brighter than its reading.

☐ **CHOOSE YOUR STOPS** Set your exposure-compensation feature at +1.5 to +2 stops, and then lock it.

☐ **FIND SOMETHING NEUTRAL** Aim at a midtoned rock or gray card and lock the exposure.

☐ **CONSULT YOUR DSLR'S HISTOGRAM** If there's no gap between the image tones and pure white, your snowscape will blow out into blank white.

☐ **REMEMBER THE CLASSIC "SUNNY 16" RULE** On bright days, at f/16, set your shutter speed to 1/ISO. Moderately overcast? Increase this exposure by 1 stop. Heavy clouds? Increase by 2 stops. In shade, go up by 3 full stops.

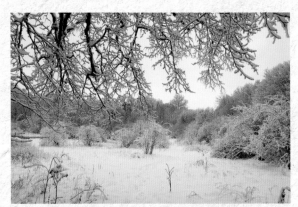

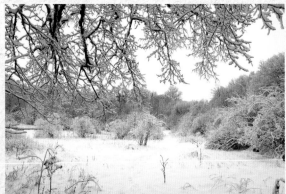

150 CATCH A FALLING SNOWFLAKE

Landscape photographers relish the gifts that snowstorms bring. They reduce visual clutter, hiding rocks and dirt. They isolate foreground subjects such as bare trees. Their wetness intensifies natural colors, and their flat light enables DSLRs to capture a full tonal range. Plus, nearly everyone else is hibernating indoors, so new snow is your own private canvas.

Midwinter yields the most snow and thus the most abstract, simplified shots. But "shoulder seasons" offer treats, too. Autumn snow contrasts beautifully with changing leaves, and spring snowfall with emerging buds and flowers. Whenever you venture out, use weather-sealed cameras and lenses, a lens hood, and a UV or skylight filter—and take an umbrella to protect your setup. Bring a wide-angle lens for shots with few visible snowflakes or a long lens to capture more of them, casting a lacy veil over your scene.

When snowflakes are falling, use slow shutter speeds to turn them into fanciful streaks, or quick ones—say, 1/250 to 1/500 sec—to freeze them in midair. Underexposed snow is a constant bugbear: See #149 for tips on avoiding it. And once you're indoors, you can expand any grayed-out shots' tonal range by using Photoshop's Curves, Brightness/Contrast, or Levels tools (see #318, #319, and #320).

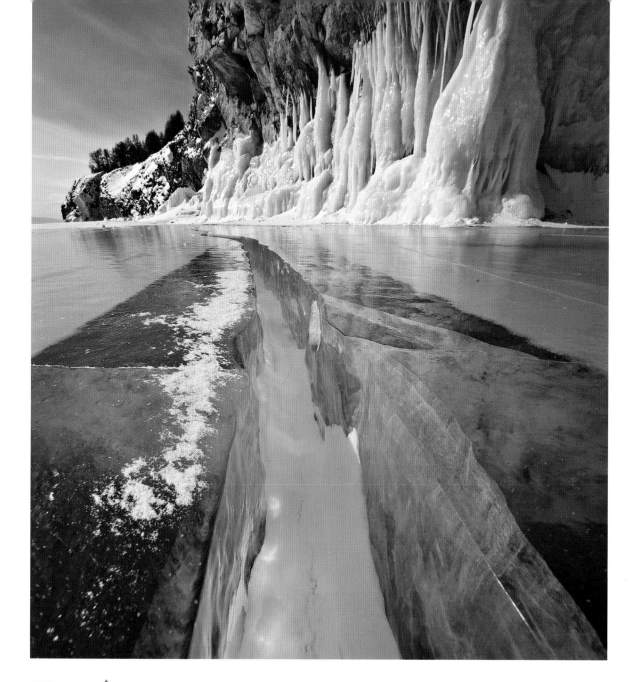

151 FIND NICE ICE

Ice is everywhere in winter. The trick is to find photogenic stuff, which can mean venturing off the beaten path. Waterfalls, streams, and frozen cliff seeps—often vividly hued by minerals in the rock—make ideal subjects. And look for the sculptures ice crystals make of branches and rocks. When shooting on open ice, search out naturally strong lines, such as the deep crack here, to lend structure to your composition. Shoot ice in the glowing backlight of dawn or dusk if you can. Pack along common sense: Check local forecasts, bring a friend, and don't venture out on ice less than 5 inches (12.5 cm) thick.

152
MAKE THE MOST OF FOG

Some landscape photographers who prize sharpness and saturated color pack up and head home when fog rolls in. They miss a lot.

Atmospheric conditions in which water droplets such as mist (or dry particles such as dust) are suspended in midair can conjure up mysterious, nuanced shots. Fog also provides an exaggerated sense of depth, since it looks darker as it recedes into the distance, accentuating a scene's dimensionality.

Low-contrast fog-blanketed landscapes are also easier to work with than those in strong sun because they diffuse light in pleasant ways. Plus, you can easily tweak shadows and midtones to find the right look for your fogscape. Finally, mist lends body and substance to light beams streaming through trees and clouds. Those diagonal beams, invisible in bright light, take on shape and, seemingly, life when shot in fog.

QUICK TIP

153
CAPTURE MIST IN B&W

Fog photos often reveal their deepest drama in black and white. Just remember: For best results, shoot in Raw color, then convert your image in software afterward (see #315).

154
FIND FOG

You're eager to make misty magic, but where's a fog bank when you need one? Cold-water coastal areas are your best bet. Here's the science bit: Salt particles from breaking waves form nuclei that attract tiny water droplets. When those build up, especially when hot inland weather coincides with a cold ocean current, thick sea fog will shroud vast stretches of coastline. Inland valleys at night—and virtually any place enjoying a chilly morning after nighttime rainfall—are also prime fog-stalking grounds.

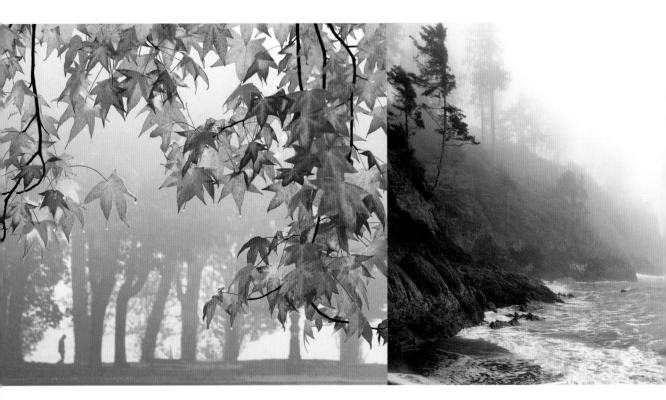

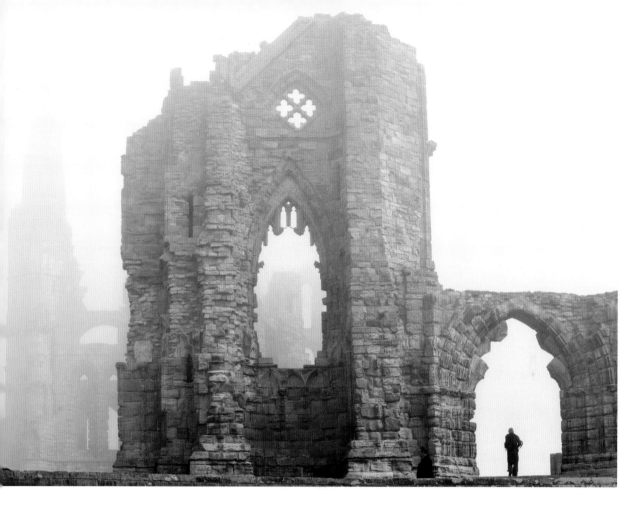

155 KEEP DRY IN THE DAMP

When you're deep in the mist, you need a moisture-sealed camera and lenses. And in truly thick fogs, condensation and drizzle are threats to the quality of your shots and the safety of your gear, so bring a plastic bag to shield the camera, an umbrella (and someone to hold it) to keep moisture off your rig, and a dry rag to wipe down everything both during and after the session.

On the plus side, there's definitely some gear that you can leave at home—fog frees you from the filters, including polarizers, that are an essential piece of equipment in almost every other kind of landscape photography.

156 MASTER THE MIST

Shooting a foggy scene can be tricky, so take these steps to capture misty majesty.

STEP ONE Select a strong subject. Fog dilutes color and masks shape. So only a defined subject, such as an isolated, emphatically contoured tree, can withstand that softening.

STEP TWO Get in close. The farther your subject is from the camera, the less impact it has, thanks to fog's blurring effect.

STEP THREE Avoid underexposure. Fog casts reflections, leading your meter to think that more light is available than is actually present. This can mean underexposure—photos that look like dingy gray smoke. To compensate, increase exposure above your camera's recommendation. If you have an exposure-compensation dial, add an extra stop with +1.

STEP FOUR Go long. A long focal length enhances fog's effect, compressing mist and subjects so detail blurs away.

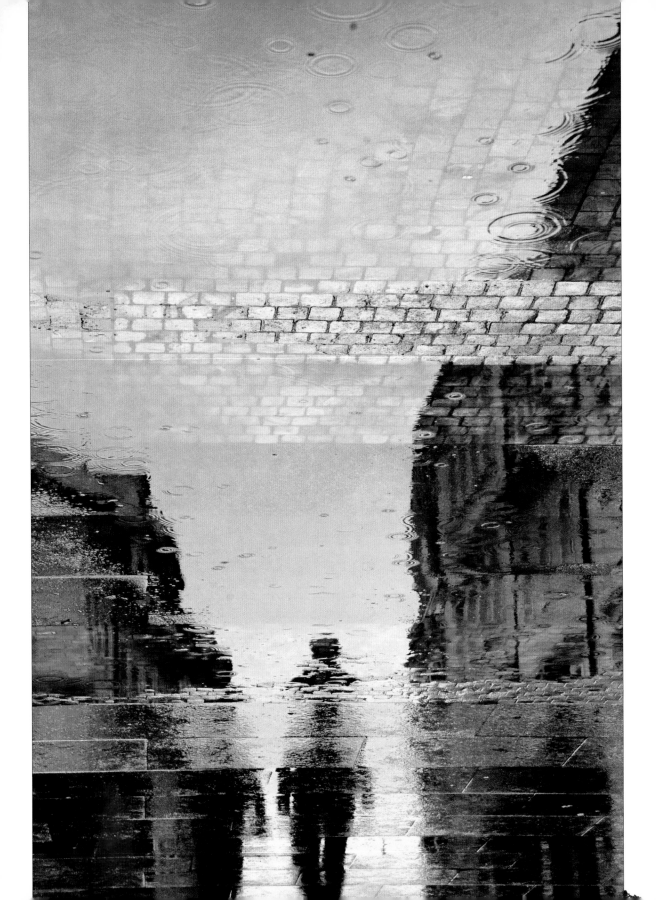

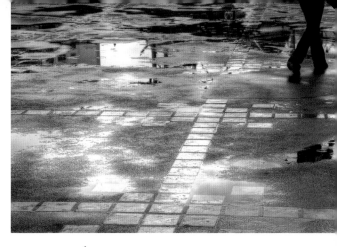

157 GO SHOOTING IN THE RAIN

Shooting during rainfall opens up creative doors that are locked tight in drier times. So venture into the wet to capture thunderstorms in the woods and reflections in urban puddles. Because mist and water droplets scatter light, rainscapes can be pleasingly pastel and soft-focus. Or, if you want to make bright colors really sing, shoot wet surfaces with a polarizing lens.

Remarkable light shows are another stormy gift, especially when the sun nears the horizon and paints clouds' undersides in Technicolor. If you're really lucky, you may even encounter a rainbow—a pot of gold to reward any soggy photographer.

159 CHASE RAINDROPS

Rain splashing into puddles lets you freeze water in motion, so play with shutter speed for varied looks. To record droplets as streaks, shoot against a dark background with the shutter set to about 1/30 sec, depending on lens focal length. (The longer the shutter speed, the longer the streak.) To home in on the drops themselves, take some macro close-ups at a shutter speed of 1/500 sec. Drops clinging to surfaces add glistening highlights to any subject.

158 CREATE YOUR OWN WEATHER

Hollywood cameramen call it the "wet down": soaking streets so that exterior shoots thrum with sheen and tonal life. When dry, asphalt is a wan gray, but wet it and you get a glistening black adorned with iridescent oil smears. Thanks to the visual drama of streetlamps and headlights, night is the classic time for a wet down, but the angled light of sunrise and sunset will lend your wet shots diffuse yet dramatic illumination.

Pros use water trucks to soak scenes, but an ordinary garden hose gives you the wet look, too. Soak a section of your street (tell the neighbors first!) to create reflections. You can also fake rainfall or mist as you shoot by getting an assistant to set a hose to spray in a wide fan, then aim it high above the scene.

160 HACK A RAIN HOOD

Costly rain gear—watertight yet breathable Gore-Tex rain sleeves, moisture-proof hard gear cases, even underwater housings—can keep your camera dry. But if you're caught without it, there are some cheap and cheerful ways to ward off raindrops, too.

Cut a hole large enough to fit snugly around your camera lens into the bottom of a clear plastic bag, then use a rubber band or gaffer's tape to make sure the seal is tight enough to keep out errant drops. Snip two more holes in the bag's sides to thread your camera strap through. Put your hands in through the open end of the bag to manipulate camera controls as you shoot.

Clear, elasticized shower caps are also decent gear covers. When you're shooting on vacation, you can pick them up for free in hotel rooms.

161 TACKLE SURF SAFELY

Wherever you find an awesome beach, you can get good distant surf shots from shore. But to get killer photos of towering waves, you must dive in. The greatest wave photographers carefully study their favorite breaks—sometimes for years. They scrutinize weather and surf reports to learn what's breaking where and how big it will be. To grab in-the-barrel shots without risking life and limb, take safety seriously. Start small if you're a surf novice— invest in a few lessons on the board, sans camera—and practice holding your body parallel to the tube when a wave breaks so you'll roll like a ball tumbling downhill. If you wind up perpendicular to the tube, the wave could hammer you end over end. Never let a wave break on top of you, and remember that practice makes perfect: Surf shots in the tube require you to be almost as good a surfer as your subject.

162

BRUSH UP ON SEA SHOOTING BASICS

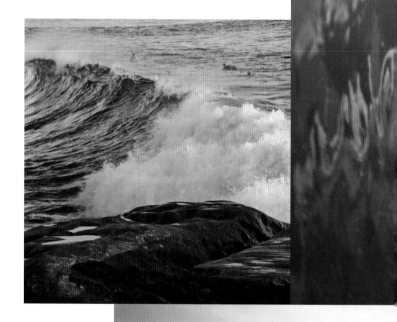

In surf, shoot wide, fast, and constantly. A fisheye lens enhances the drama of breakers and barrels. Use your fastest shutter speed for the lowest ISO possible, expose in shutter priority, and shoot in Continuous mode.

To freeze waves, set the shutter to at least 1/250 sec. For soft effects, go longer than 1 sec. Hold your camera close to the surface to enhance waves. And in big surf, do presets onshore so you don't have to fiddle with settings amid walls of water.

163 SOFTEN SURF

Opening up the shutter while shooting surf adds a painterly quality to seaside shots. Use a tripod and set shutter speed to 1 or 2 secs, with the aperture on the high side of the numeric scale. Use your camera's self-timer to minimize camera shake. Check results as you go, and experiment with settings so you can capture an artful blur that evokes the power and beauty of water on the move.

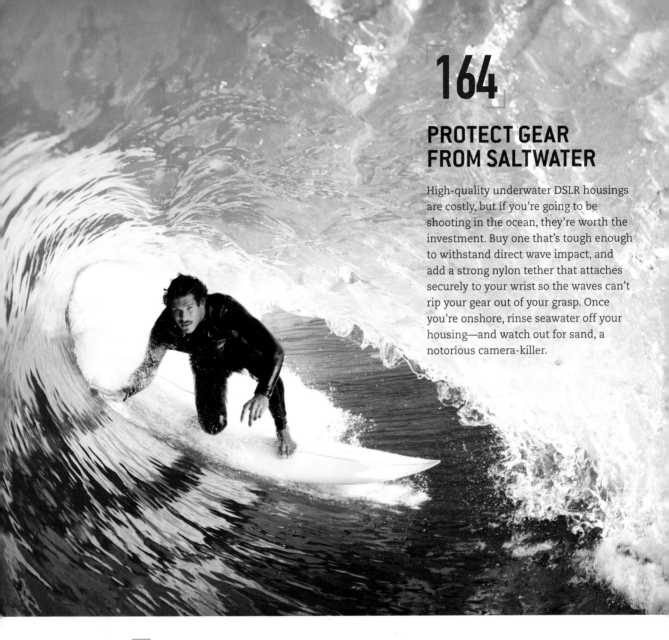

164

PROTECT GEAR FROM SALTWATER

High-quality underwater DSLR housings are costly, but if you're going to be shooting in the ocean, they're worth the investment. Buy one that's tough enough to withstand direct wave impact, and add a strong nylon tether that attaches securely to your wrist so the waves can't rip your gear out of your grasp. Once you're onshore, rinse seawater off your housing—and watch out for sand, a notorious camera-killer.

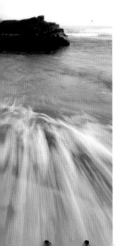

165

PLAY WITH TINY WAVES

A 30-foot (9-m) monster breaker is an inherently impressive thing—even a photographer with sloppy technique can make an awe-inspiring image from such a beast. But with the right tricks up your sleeve, you don't have to tangle with skyscraper waves to shoot imposing surf. A 6-inch (15-cm) breaker can do the job, too.

Search out sandbars or other natural rises where small waves break. Get as close as you can and extend your arm and camera into the waves' minibarrels as they crest and roll. A fisheye lens and low sunlight will amp the wee breaker's effect and, as with any wave, high-speed continuous shooting is the best choice. The result: a shot that evokes gnarly surf even if you snapped it close to the beach on the calmest day of summer.

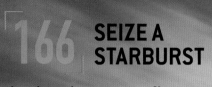

166 SEIZE A STARBURST

Thread a starburst accessory filter onto your lens to transform a light source into a many-rayed jewel. Or do things on the cheap: Shoot at your smallest aperture, using a lens made with a coating to suppress flare. Bracket exposure and take as many shots as possible.

Place your DSLR on a tripod to eliminate blur and limit the amount of light smacking into your lens. And pack along patience. If you're shooting the sunrise or sunset, your window of opportunity is measured in minutes—wait till the sun is just at the horizon, then snag yourself a snazzy starburst.

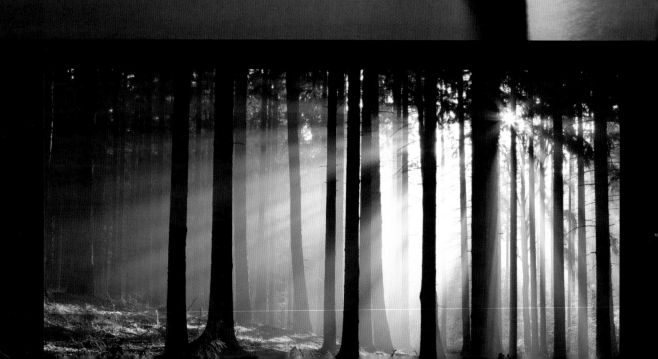

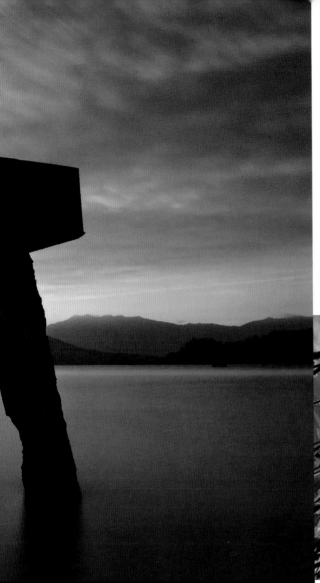

167 SHOOT INTO THE SUN

Using your camera's autoexposure with glaring sun in the frame leads to gross underexposure. So for starters, switch to manual. Then, with an aperture of f/16, set shutter speed to twice the ISO speed of your film. Then bracket, bracket, bracket. And remember, there's no single correct exposure for every shot. Try out a few exposures to find the one that appeals to you—and remember, you can produce high dynamic-range (HDR) composites while shooting or in the editing stage.

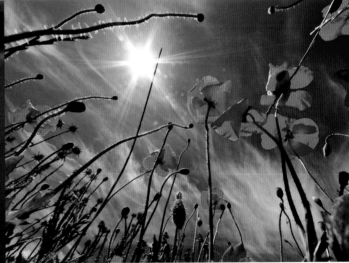

168 GRAB A "GOD RAY"

These ethereal light beams arrowing through clouds or treetops are also called crepuscular rays. Whichever term you favor, timing is all: Shoot in early A.M. or late afternoon, preferably when a storm is brewing or breaking. Fog, too, can produce romantic beams. Expose properly for the beams and check the histogram to ensure highlights aren't clipped. (Clipped areas are blown-out patches of maximum brightness.) If they are, dial down exposure compensation.

169 OUTRUN GHOSTS

Shooting in dazzling sunlight? Watch out for ghosts. Not unquiet spirits, but single or multiple phantom images, usually of the lens diaphragm itself.

Modern lenses' multicoating helps control ghosts and flare, especially if you choose your lens carefully. Single-focal-length lenses are best, but some modern zoom lenses ghostbust effectively, too. Don't want to buy a new lens? Hide part of the sun's disc behind a foreground boulder, tree, or, in the cold glare of winter, an intriguing ice formation.

170 CAPTURE THE CITY'S BUSTLE

Capturing the spirit of a metropolis—with its flashing lights, not to mention the endlessly moving people and vehicles—is an invigorating challenge. Tack-sharp photos that freeze the moment do the trick, but you can also paint impressionistic masterpieces by playing with the speed, light, and space that are the essence of a city.

Stalk your location and know the light. Sunrise and sunset are reliable standbys for fetching blends of ambient and artificial light, and storms add drama to cityscapes, too. Seek out motion wherever people rush in or out of structures (train stations are a good bet). Stay low-key with a handheld camera, and shoot slow and low to capture crowds' movement. Bracket exposures from about 1/30 to 1/8 sec to find the right balance between form and focus. Low ISOs need more light for exposure and enable long shutter speeds. Focus on each interesting figure who passes through your center autofocus point and keep snapping.

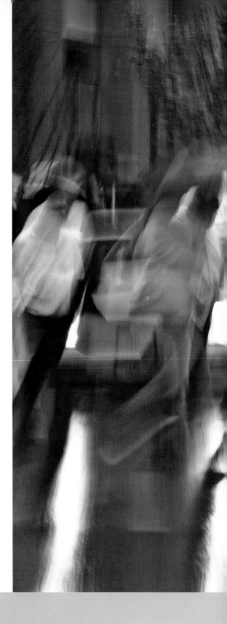

171 SHOOT A STRANGER

To ramp up your portraiture game, ask a stranger to pose. Some will say no, but a surprising number will agree, especially if you're polite. Talk to people before you take out a camera, and explain what you'll do with the photos.

Shoot in auto mode first, then finesse exposure as a comfortable rapport grows. People relax as they get used to the shutter's click, letting you capture character rather than wariness. Experiment with accessories, such as wireless lighting gear, remote triggers, and perhaps a cheerful, talkative assistant to hold strobes and extra gear.

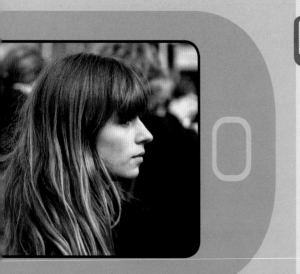

MOBILE TIP

172 SNEAK A SMARTPHONE SNAP

Too shy to ask strangers for a shot? Choose a subject, switch on your smartphone's camera, and pretend you're deep in conversation on your phone as you aim, frame, and fire. The trick is especially easy where subjects are seated, such as restaurants, bars, and subways.

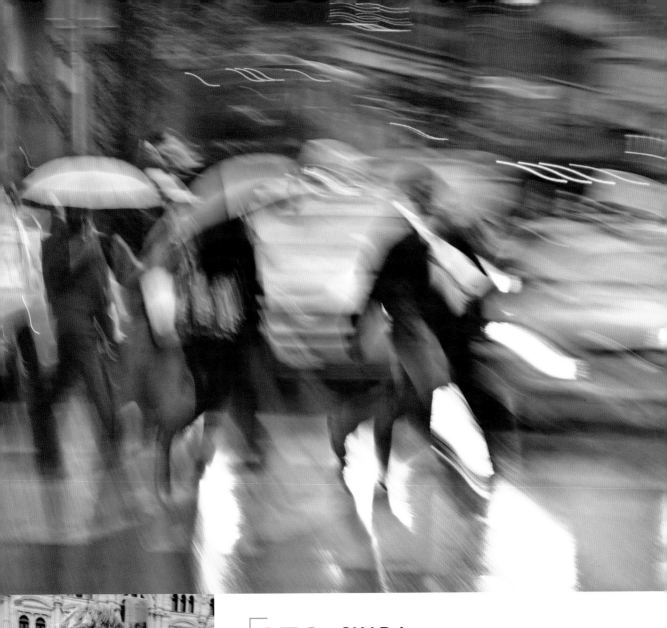

173 SNAP A CANDID

Whether you're an aspiring paparazzo or just grabbing unguarded moments among passersby, try the tricks that celebrity photographers use. Catch people by surprise by avoiding the viewfinder and prefocusing a 28 to 35mm lens at 8 feet (2.4 m) and firing away. Compose after the action—crop in postproduction. Pros often shoot at f/8 to f/11, settings that deliver sharpness with any lens. Use with a high ISO for a midrange aperture and fast shutter speed. Look for naturally illuminating pale ceilings or walls to avoid the scared-rabbit expression that direct flash produces. Finally, experiment with black-and-white for a spontaneous, graphic mood reminiscent of old newshound candids.

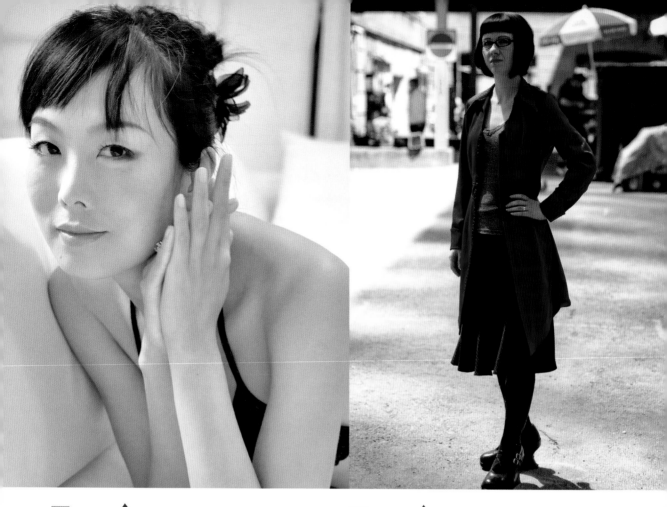

174 SMOOTH OUT SKIN

Problem skin doesn't require postprocessing labor in order to create a flattering portrait. As a matter of fact, you can fix most issues while you're shooting.

Lighting is essential. Fill lights cut down on unflattering shadows—don't exceed a 1:2 ratio between fill and main lights. Zap zits, scars, and wrinkles by positioning your main and fill lights just above your camera—one to its left, one to its right. Avoid side fill, which tends to "moonscape" a bumpy complexion. With older subjects, keeping lights at eye level will minimize crow's feet, laugh lines, and other hallmarks of age.

A pleasantly neutral but nonsmiling expression usually works best, and a subtle soft-focus filter will flatter any model, old or young. Overexposure can be your friend, so don't be afraid to push the histogram far to the right (see #014).

175 SLIM DOWN A MODEL

Be they heavy or wispy, all photographic subjects benefit from the defined silhouette that comes with perfect posture. When you shoot at full length, ask your model to turn slightly toward your camera and place most of her weight on one leg. This technique, called contrapposto, animates her posture and makes her seem slimmer by twisting her waist and hips. Fine-tune her stance by asking her to draw back her shoulders and lift her head and chest to elongate her frame. And maintain some space between her arms and torso so her form remains well defined.

Any face can sprout multiple chins if you shoot it from the wrong angle. To avoid that, photograph from slightly above face level, and ask the subject to lift her chin while looking up at your lens. Lights set as high as possible firm jawlines further by casting contrasting shadows beneath the chin.

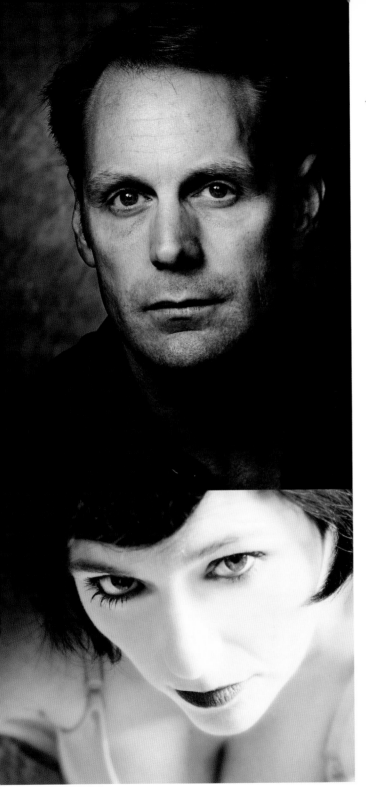

176 SCULPT A FACE

A clever lighting angle is a sure way to shape a face in a head-and-shoulder portrait. Several tactics are possible: Lift your camera to the model's eye level, and light his face exclusively so that his neck and body fade into shadow. Or set your main light at a 45-degree angle to your subject's face and turn him slightly into the light. His most prominent features—cheekbones, browbones, nose bridge—will be highlighted, but fleshier parts—such as lower cheeks—will darken as the light falls off. To downplay a feature such as a large nose, direct your subject's gaze straight into the lens and light his face so that his nose casts no shadow.

177 FLATTER WITH COLOR

Shoot against a background that will complement your model's eye, hair, and skin tones. To slim a subject and produce a cleanly defined photo, have her wear a single dark color from head to toe, then photograph her against a backdrop of the same hue.

178 PACK AWAY EYE BAGS

Most of us have them, even when we've gotten plenty of sleep. To hide them in a facial portrait, use only front lighting, set at eye level. Slightly lift your camera and encourage your model to turn her eyes up toward the lens while keeping her chin down. Men, women, and even kids all benefit from a little bit of concealing foundation makeup dabbed under the eyes.

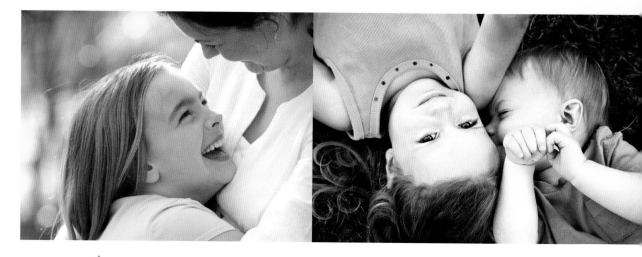

179 CATCH A FAMILY CANDID

It's easy for you to love photos of your loved ones; it's far more challenging to craft ones that others love, too. Those prime specimens tend to be candid shots that are taken on the fly with minimal gear—the best way to capture your family's personalities, moods, and interactions.

Sure, you'll have to fire off more frames to get a keeper than you would when shooting a posed portrait. But then again, the more you shoot, the more relaxed people will feel. Blend into the background at family events, be patient, and wait for moments when subjects aren't paying attention to you.

180 USE FAST LENSES FOR FAMILY

Fast glass is just the thing to capture your family at their unposed best. Prime lenses are ideal for natural light, and they're smaller than high-speed zooms. That means they're less intimidating, especially to little kids, and help you blend into the scene.

As for focal lengths, go wide—getting up close with a 35mm or wider lens ensures your dear ones will dominate the frame for the right intimate mood. Wide-angle lenses also let you layer background, midground, and foreground in intriguing ways—plus they're the best option for the speedy, from-the-hip shooting that generates the sweetest family images.

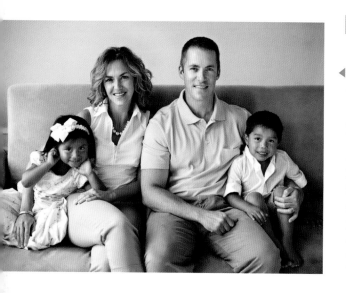

181 STAGE MANAGE YOUR CREW

While you don't want to pose people, a bit of staging is helpful. Search out your home's best light and coax your family into it (declutter those spots beforehand). It's also okay to make wardrobe suggestions. When everyone is dressed in similar or unified tones, shots look more coherent. If your framing captures lots of background, make sure it includes objects that say something about your relatives' character and personal stories. Build trust by occasionally showing off particularly nice shots on your LCD, and encourage connections by getting subjects to talk and touch. You'll get vivid interaction rather than nervous grins.

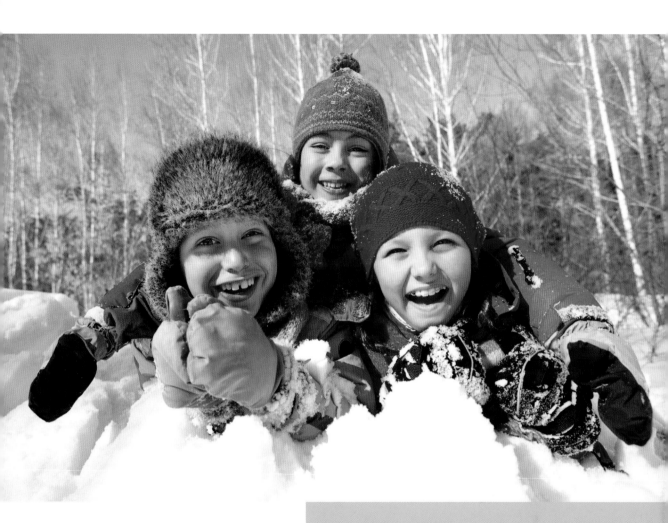

182 LIGHT YOUR KIN RIGHT

Keep lighting soft. Direct flash rarely works because it startles babies and reminds everyone that they're being photographed, thwarting the warmth, spontaneity, and ease that characterize good family photos. Instead, seek out diffuse window light or the angled, warm-toned rays of the setting sun. If you use any light gear, choose an unobtrusive large white reflector, which flatters older subjects by smoothing out wrinkles and adds a bit of glow to everyone's complexion.

183 TRY POSING PRIMERS

Models and shooters alike can be hit with posing block: Your subject wants some direction, but you're drawing a blank. The cure: Find about a dozen photos of pleasing poses, convert them to JPEGs, and add them to the memory card where you save your images. Refer to this cheat sheet via your camera's grid-view image playback. Share the poses with your subject and aim for ones you both like.

184 CATCH THE BAND OFFSTAGE

Shooting rock acts is a photographer's dream—performers hold still so you can work without the anarchy of a concert. To give subjects a commanding presence, have them pose with feet and shoulders squared off, leaving some space among them so they retain individuality but still cohere as a band. To make them look larger than life, crouch to shoot from their waist height, and keep the imaging plane parallel to your subjects. Backlighting separates figures from dark backgrounds and creates foreground shadows that can turn even Mick Jagger into a towering monolith. Bare bulbs or grids work well, especially if you hang them high and aim them down at the musicians. They'll look even taller and cooler than they do onstage.

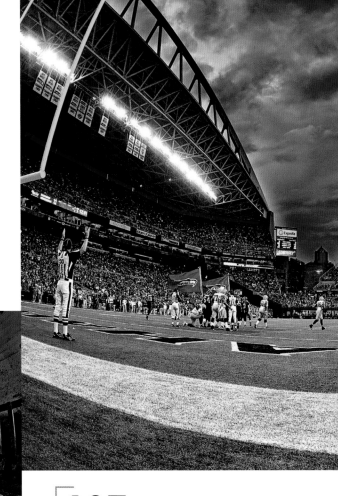

185 MAKE THE MOST OF BURST

Burst shooting captures action that occurs so swiftly it's tough to freeze. Start and end your burst as quickly before and after the action as possible to ensure there's enough room in your camera buffer should you need to shoot again before it has cleared. You'll get more shots per burst by shooting JPEGs rather than Raw, and more still by reducing JPEG quality (increasing compression) or the number of pixels you capture. Many DSLRs let you select burst speed. When shooting repetitive motion, such as jump-rope, set a burst rate slower than the camera's maximum to avoid grabbing almost identical shots.

186 SHOOT A DRESS REHEARSAL

Want to capture your kid singing and dancing her heart out in a recital or play? Ask if you can shoot at a dress rehearsal, not a performance, so you can move around the theater or backstage without disturbing an audience. Rehearsals also give you time to compose the best shots.

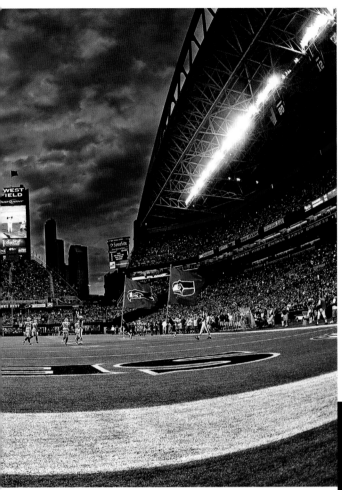

187 PICTURE A LIVE PERFORMANCE

A few essential rules win you great shots of live performance, whether it's a rock concert or your kid's football game. First, switch off flash. Venues usually forbid it, and flash will illuminate the heads of people in front of you, distracting from your true subject: the onstage or on-field action. Theater and stadium lighting is often mixed or dim, so use fast lenses and a camera that performs well at high ISOs, with the aperture wide open. Avoid auto white balance (WB), because changing lights can radically shift your camera's interpretation of the scene and produce inconsistent color. Set WB to Tungsten instead. To freeze action, set a fast shutter speed of at least 1/125 sec (and an ISO of 800 or 600 to allow that speed). If dim light forces you to shoot more slowly, time your shutter releases to the natural lulls between your subjects' movements.

188 GET IN THE GAME WITH BASIC GEAR

Shooting fast-paced sports is simple when you don't haul along much besides the camera itself. A small digicam is your best bet: Unless you're press, you can't pass the gates with a big telephoto bazooka mounted to a pro-level DSLR. Many small compact cameras have super-fast burst modes, image stabilization, good high-ISO performance, and great zoom options. Some are even water- (and beer-) proof.

Turn off the flash, set the camera to with a wide aperture, crank up the ISO, and let the digicam do the rest. If your images look too dark, push the exposure value setting up to +2/3 or so. Too hot? Dial back to –2/3. And enjoy touchdowns rather than trying to snag them: Quiet moments reveal the spirit of a game—and they're a lot easier to compose.

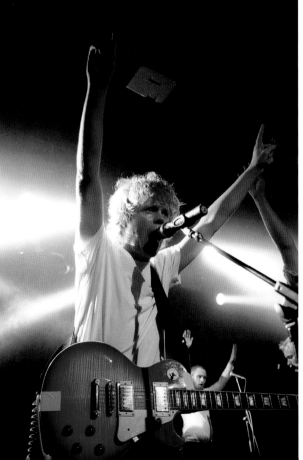

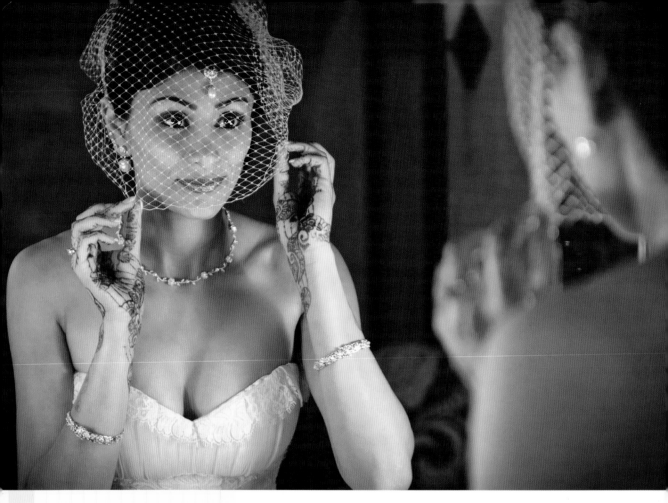

I took this during my first wedding shoot, right before the bride was about to leave the dressing area and walk down the aisle. This photo was totally unposed; I was photographing her bridesmaids when I saw the bride turning to her mirror. I focused on her just in time to capture the small, self-assuring smile that flickered across her mouth in the last moments before taking her vows.

—JEFFREY LING

189 SPOTLIGHT TRUE EMOTION

Although beautifully composed and posed portraits are key components of any wedding album, the images viewers linger over are often candids that showcase memorable exchanges and the implied narrative of the couple's love: unscripted kisses, misbehaving ringbearers, and quiet embraces are wedding-photography classics for good reason.

How to capture them? Think of yourself as one part friend, one part photojournalist. Show up early to chat with the couple to establish trust and an informal mood. During preceremony formal portraits, occasionally pull the couple aside to relax them and capture tender or silly interaction. Later, during the vows and reception, remain unobtrusive: Shoot quickly with a handheld camera and avoid mood-breaking flash whenever possible, relying instead on fast lenses so you can use available light. Follow the action and focus on the flow of unplanned moments that come together to compose an intimate story of a couple on a very special day.

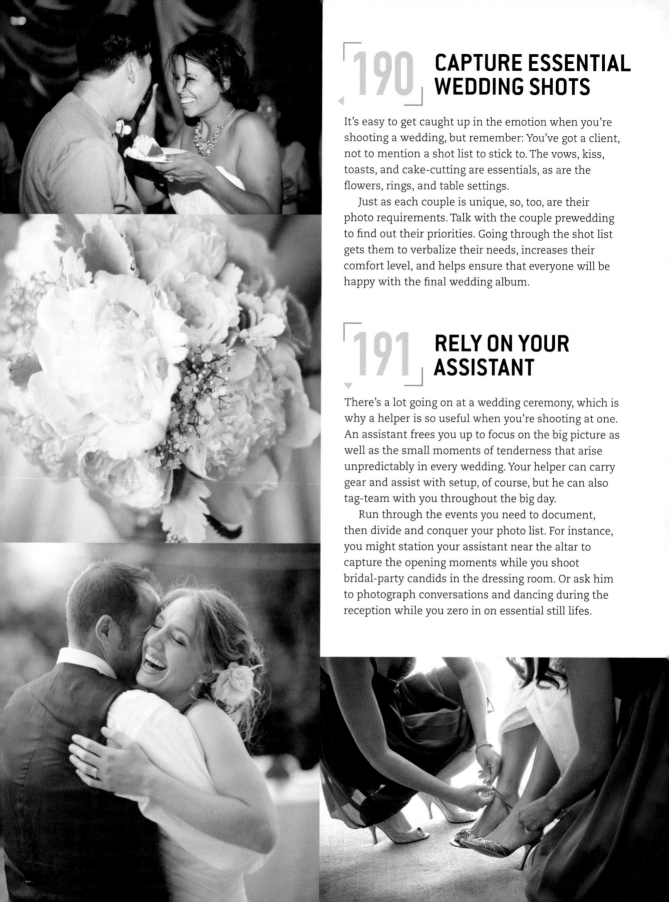

190 CAPTURE ESSENTIAL WEDDING SHOTS

It's easy to get caught up in the emotion when you're shooting a wedding, but remember: You've got a client, not to mention a shot list to stick to. The vows, kiss, toasts, and cake-cutting are essentials, as are the flowers, rings, and table settings.

Just as each couple is unique, so, too, are their photo requirements. Talk with the couple prewedding to find out their priorities. Going through the shot list gets them to verbalize their needs, increases their comfort level, and helps ensure that everyone will be happy with the final wedding album.

191 RELY ON YOUR ASSISTANT

There's a lot going on at a wedding ceremony, which is why a helper is so useful when you're shooting at one. An assistant frees you up to focus on the big picture as well as the small moments of tenderness that arise unpredictably in every wedding. Your helper can carry gear and assist with setup, of course, but he can also tag-team with you throughout the big day.

Run through the events you need to document, then divide and conquer your photo list. For instance, you might station your assistant near the altar to capture the opening moments while you shoot bridal-party candids in the dressing room. Or ask him to photograph conversations and dancing during the reception while you zero in on essential still lifes.

192 FOLLOW THE FIVE-SECOND RULE

Exposures of five seconds create unique effects—water morphs into mysterious mist and meadows transform into swirling abstracts. That exposure zone "paints" blur onto a photo's sharp canvas, keeping enough of moving subjects' outlines to create dreamlike effects. Five seconds, a tripod, and a polarizing filter on a 28–105mm f/3.5–4.5 lens are all it took for shooter Greg Tucker to capture the streak-and-swirl patterns of these camellia blossoms amid autumn leaves.

The five-second rule works with just about any camera; try it for yourself. Slow and steady gets you the best shot, so brace the camera or use a tripod, and trigger the shutter remotely so shaking fingers won't mess up shots. To reduce the noise that can intrude into long exposures, use a low ISO, set your camera's long-exposure noise reduction feature, and shoot in Raw so you can smooth out problems postshoot. Getting a good multisecond exposure is difficult: Try using an ND filter or polarizer to cut light and enhance blur.

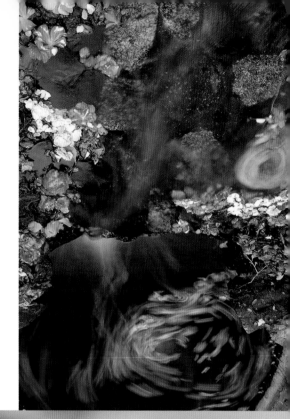

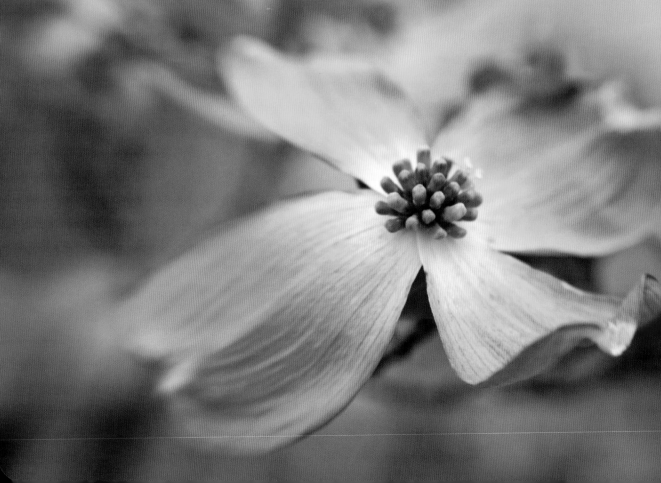

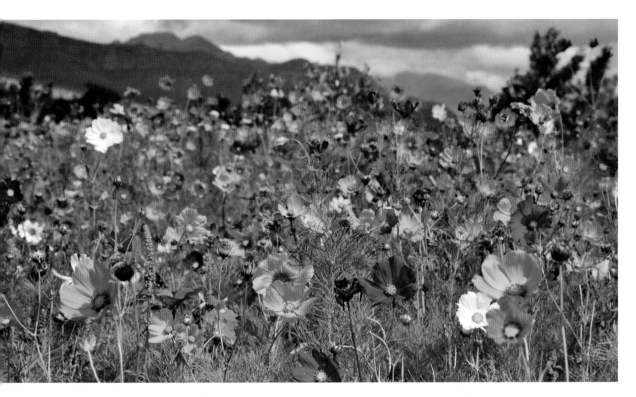

193 LIMIT FOCUS WITH A LENSBABY

If your nature shots feel the same, get your mojo back with Lensbaby selective-focus lenses, the swivel-barreled optics beloved for the funky effects they create. A Lensbaby Composer pivots at the barrel's central ball-and-socket joint (you set focus and exposure manually) to control which areas are sharp or blurred. It locks into position so you can play with depth of field, and its fine-focus adjustment is magical. You can easily shift the sweet spot of focus, zeroing in on a flower's heart while its petals blur. Broaden your palette with wide-angle and telephoto lens adapters, macro lenses, and creative aperture sets.

194

GO FOR BLOOMING BEAUTY

When spring fever hits, take your camera on a hike to capture new wildflowers—and heed these tips to bag the best blossoms. Do your research so you can target peak bloom season in your area of the country. It sounds perverse, but avoid perfect weather: The diffused sun of cloudy days reveals flowers in their best light.

Stabilize low-slung gear with beanbag supports, especially when you use long exposures to capture the pretty smudges created by breezes. Consider a tilt/shift lens, too (see #091), for maximum clarity and depth of field. Use a macro lens to capture bloom detail, and shoot from the flowers' height to maximize their form and fill your frame with their unfolding petals.

195 MAKE YOUR FLOWERS DANCE

Vertical flower stems can look dull if they parallel photo edges. Pitch your camera sideways and downward at the same time to make flowertops look larger than stems and lend the flora an offbeat zing.

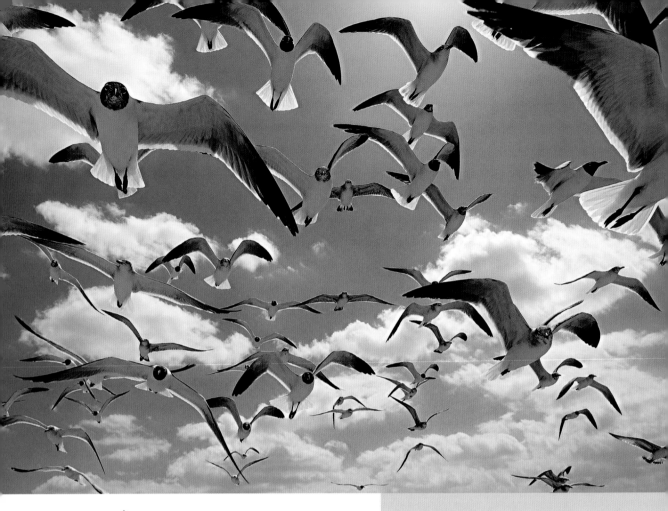

196 MASTER FLIGHT FUNDAMENTALS

You can't control a bird in flight, but you can fine-tune your own stance and settings to get the best shot. First, watch the bird's trajectory with your eyes before you look through the viewfinder—this provides a smooth transition from spotting to tracking a bird. Stand with your feet shoulder-width apart so you can move freely when you do begin to track through the viewfinder. With small, quick birds, you'll probably have to shoot handheld; try to maintain a secure but easy grasp on your camera. Keep motion smooth while panning, and follow through: Don't stop when the shutter releases. If your bird is very fast, aim slightly ahead of its path before you shoot. Manual exposure works best for birds on the wing, so use partial or evaluative metering to get a light reading. Shutter speed is vital to freeze motion: 1/1250 or faster, with an ISO of 320 to 400. Even when no bird is in sight, keep your camera on and in the "ready" position at your chest. A fly-by can happen at any moment.

QUICK TIP

197 FOOL THE BIRDIE

When you're shooting from behind a bird blind, bring a friend along. Birds have fantastic eyesight, so if these observant creatures spot you entering the blind, they'll wait until you leave before they emerge.

Try to trick them by asking your companion to depart first. The birds may assume you've left, too, and they'll come out to play. (This trick won't work on hawks, eagles, and falcons. They can count.)

198 TRY A MEDIUM-LENGTH LENS FOR BIRDLIFE

Wildlife photographers often depend on a 500 or 600mm lens as their tool of choice. But ultralong telephotos are bulky and expensive. Sometimes, shorter and wider lenses work best, especially with approachable birdlife. Moderate zoom allows you to quickly tailor your framing to the avian scene at hand, and handholding lenses in the 70 or 80 to 200mm class makes it easy to track and pan to follow birds, both in the air and on the water.

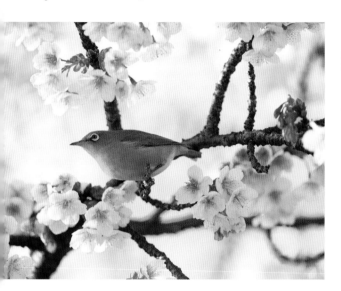

199 CREATE CATCHLIGHTS

Bird photos often work best if the subject's face is well lit and at least one eye displays a catchlight, or small reflection that distinguishes the eyes from surrounding feathers and shadows, animating your bird. The problem is that many birds have small, dark eyes that appear black and lifeless in images.

So create your own catchlight. Use a hot-shoe-mounted flash with an extender that lets the flash work with your telephoto lens. Extenders are typically used with lenses that go to 300mm or more. They increase the flash's reach by concentrating the light, resulting in up to a 2-stop aperture gain. Natural light can also produce catchlights, but you need to be patient. Position yourself between the bird and low, angled sunlight, and focus on its eyes. When it cocks its head into the light, shoot.

200 BACKGROUND YOUR BIRD

Sharply focused backgrounds can "fight" with delicately detailed birds, such as the Japanese white-eye above, spoiling an image. To emphasize a bird against its natural setting, experiment with background blur.

Shoot in manual, exposing for the bird itself, to make the background blow out slightly. Bright backgrounds are good choices, such as the cherry blossoms here. As you shoot, pay careful attention to the patterns that emerge in both the sharply focused foreground and the soft background bokeh (see #258).

If you don't get the background exactly right in the shoot, all is not lost. Postprocessing recropping and blurring can redeem clashing or overfocused backgrounds.

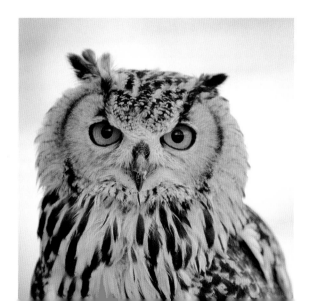

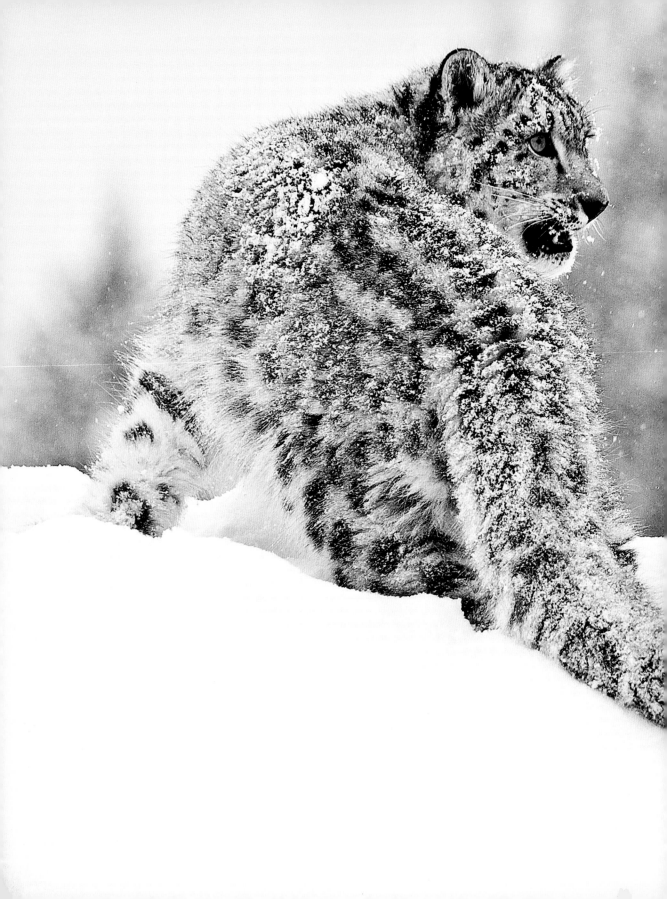

201 PHOTOGRAPH WILDLIFE SAFELY

Wildlife photos can be breathtaking, though taking them can be risky. First do your research so you know what you're getting into. If you're comfortable with risks, play it safe—or at least safer—by maintaining a distance between yourself and your fiercer subjects. (You can make your shots look more close up by shooting with a telephoto lens or cropping in later.) It's also wise to keep a can of pepper spray on hand. And with certain animals such as bears, make plenty of noise as you track them. If you startle them, you might put them on the defensive. And you definitely don't want to put a bear on the defensive.

Consider photographing at game farms. Purists turn up their noses at the idea, but the controlled conditions provide a safer way to get close to large predators such as mountain lions, bears, and tigers.

202 PLAY TO ANIMAL INSTINCTS

Trainers and handlers can teach you how to leverage an animal's natural inclinations to get the most out of a beastly photo shoot. So ask those in the know about the best way to approach and interact with wildlife.

Handlers can also engage your subjects while the shoot's going on. For instance, two trainers coaxed out the wowing over-the-shoulder glance captured here by tossing a snowball back and forth, drawing and holding the snow leopard's attention while the photographer clicked away.

203

ZERO IN ON ZOO CREATURES

You needn't jet to exotic locales to bag wildlife—just bring your camera to the local zoo. Follow these fundamentals to capture the beauty of wild creatures in close confines.

DO YOUR RESEARCH Review zoo websites to learn about feeding times, mating seasons (which often bring bright feathers and big antlers), and inhabitants with photogenic new offspring.

TIME IT RIGHT Schedule a trip for opening or closing hours in early autumn or late spring, when crowds are sparse and heat-sensitive creatures most energetic.

BE SELECTIVE Choose only a few sites to shoot each day. Look for enclosures with direct natural light, clear glass (not bars or cement enclosures), and natural rocks and plants.

PLAY WITH FOREGROUND AND BACKGROUND Settings with a deep foreground let you use lenses with a long, flattering focal length. And ones with a deep background are good because you can blur it to eliminate that "zooey" look.

PREP FOR ACTION Preset your camera so you'll be ready when the perfect shot roars into view. That means Continuous firing mode, a high enough ISO to let you use a motion-freezing shutter speed of 1/500 sec or faster, automatic white balance, and center-weighted metering.

DO NOT DISTURB Avoid flash when you can. It scares away the very animals you want to draw near, and many zoos frown on or prohibit it outright.

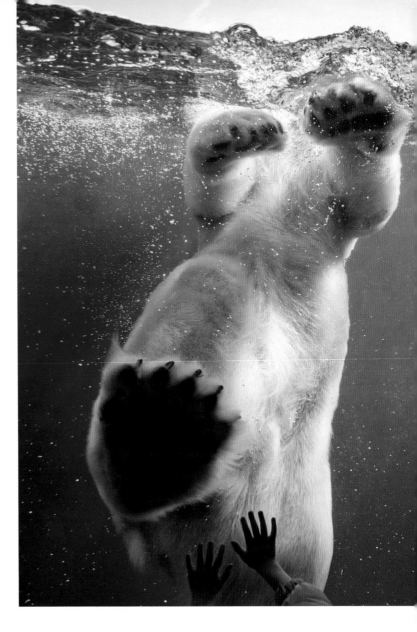

204 SEE EYE TO EYE

Sometimes the best vantage point on wildlife is the animal's own eye level. With small and slow creatures, huddle down and wait until the animal looks at you, and then take your shot. Bring a foam pad to protect your knees during long low-angle sessions.

But how do you get eye to eye with big, bad animals such as the 1,700-pound (770-kg) hippo here? Search out glassed-in enclosures that get you close to animals at their natural eye level. Place a zoom lens against the glass and await eye contact. Be patient—to grab this hippo's soulful glance, Gerardo Soria spent a half-hour at the window.

205 LURE ANIMALS TO YOUR LENS

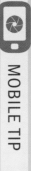

An eternal frustration of the zoo photographer—animals that won't come close enough—was solved by Mark Rober, who concocted a nifty way to get close-up monkey footage with a mirror and his iPhone. Make a hole in a small mirror with a carbide-tipped drill. Tape weather-stripping around the mirror's edges to make it easy to handle. Turn the mirror to its back side, align your phone's camera with the hole, and outline the phone with marker. Tape on more weather-stripping around the outline. At the zoo, place the mirror's reflective side against an enclosure, align your camera in its outline on the back side, and wait for an animal to approach and check out its own reflection.

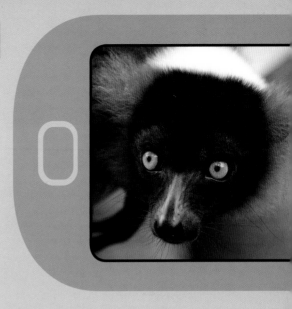

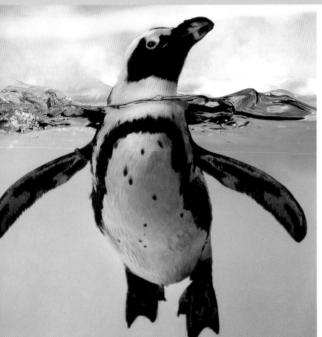

206 DELVE INTO DETAIL

Weary of animal-as-statue shots? Home in on a tiny detail that's intriguing or downright weird—eyeballs, paws, textured hide, whiskers, or feathers all work well—and fill your frame with a macro shot of it. With big animals, zoom in on your chosen part, then open your aperture wide if you want to blur out distracting background. Small-creature details are best captured up close with a wide-angle lens.

Remember: The closer you get to your subject, the shallower your depth of field. A small aperture (f/16 or smaller) keeps things in focus. If you're leaning in to catch a wee detail, you'll probably cast a shadow, so use a reflector to redirect the natural or strobe light. And as always, a tripod or focusing rail prevents slight movements from shaking up your photo.

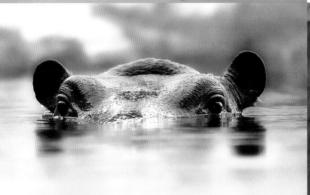

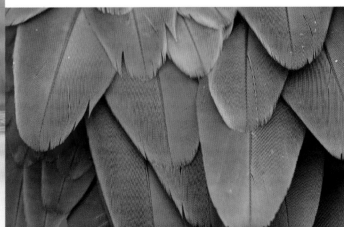

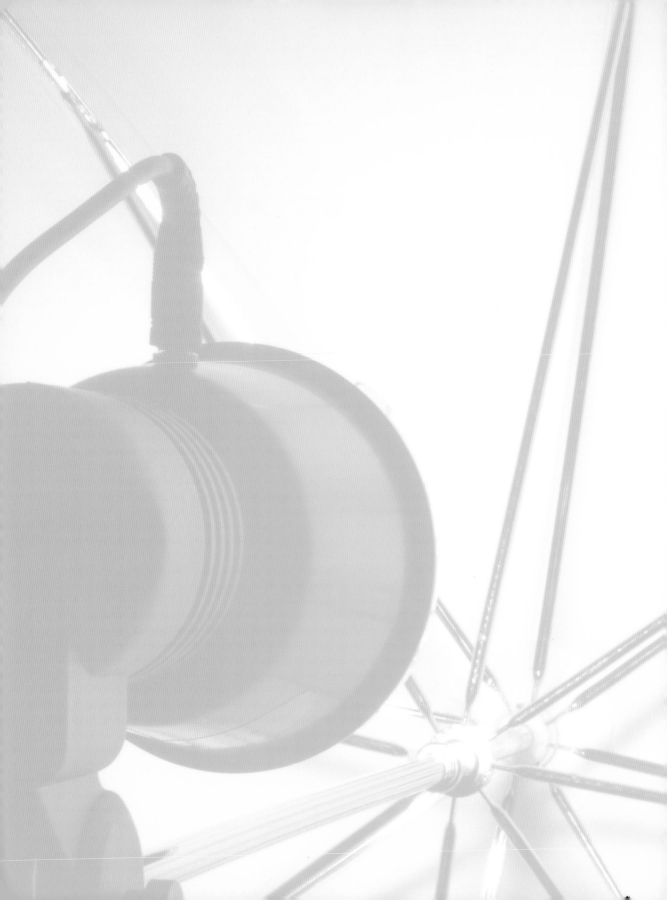

GEAR &
SETUP

207 KNOW YOUR LIGHTING GEAR

Photography is painting with light, so consider expanding your palette. Here are some lighting options that will help you flatter your subject's face, focus underwater, and flash in sync with action, as well as equipment that will help your lighting choices stay juiced and secure on the shoot.

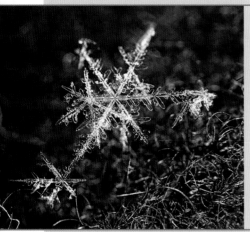

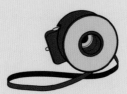

MACRO RING FLASH
A great choice for close work, this provides flash in all directions around the lens to soften shadows.

The macro ring flash's all-over light is great at capturing the shimmer of miniscule snowflakes.

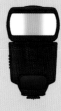

ACCESSORY FLASH
This flash, used remotely or slotted into your camera's hot shoe, syncs with your shutter release.

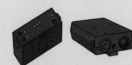

ACCESSORY FLASH POWER PACK
This power source fits on your belt or in your bag and ensures your flash is ready to go whenever you need it.

STUDIO STROBE BATTERY PACK
A key accessory, the strobe battery pack powers full-size studio lights when you're away from conventional power sources.

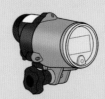

UNDERWATER STROBE
This light's waterproof casing permits you to use it for aquatic photography.

Place underwater strobes to the sides of your camera to prevent backscatter and preserve vibrant colors.

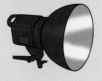

HOT LIGHT
These continuous-output, nonflashing lights are lighter and cheaper than strobes.

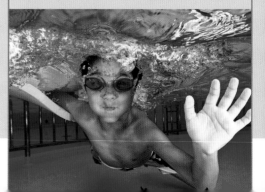

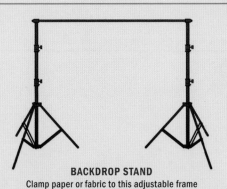

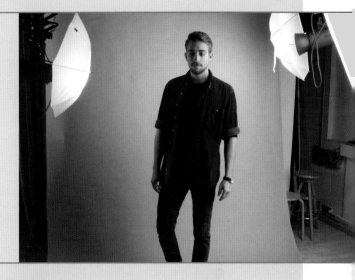

BACKDROP STAND
Clamp paper or fabric to this adjustable frame
for a smoothly hanging background.

Backdrops—paper, canvas, or fabric—focus attention
on a subject and eliminate distracting background.

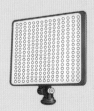

LED PANEL
Get continuous light for
video or "what you see
is what you get" stills—
all without the heat
of a hot light.

STROBE
A standard studio flash bursts off and on
when triggered and can be synced to fire
when you release the shutter.

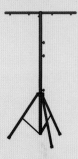

BOOM STAND
This support grants you versatile
positioning and can support a
strobe head and diffuser.

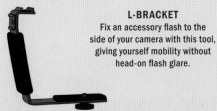

L-BRACKET
Fix an accessory flash to the
side of your camera with this tool,
giving yourself mobility without
head-on flash glare.

An L-bracketed flash lets you cast natural-looking
light onto one side of your subject.

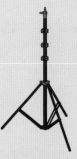

LIGHT STAND
This device gives you sturdy support and varied
setups for studio lights and modifiers, such as
diffusers and reflectors.

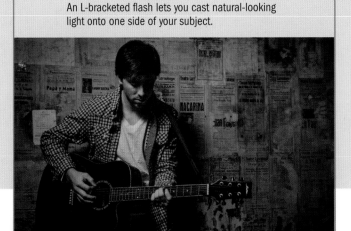

208 PAN LIKE A PRO

Panning is the ace in the hole of many sports shooters: It foregrounds a focused subject against vibrant horizontal blur that expresses swift motion for a gripping action shot. To pan, shift the camera in sync with a moving subject while the shutter stays open.

Sounds simple, but first you must figure out a few things. One is the background: High-contrast, colorful ones produce the zippiest streaks; monochromatic backgrounds make dull blurs instead. As for subjects, it's tempting to start out at auto races or airplane shows, but first try tracking a moving object you can direct, such a friend running past a wall of graffiti. Ask her to start slowly while you learn the art of the pan.

To do that, keep panning's three key elements—subject movement, camera movement, and shutter speed—in balance as you practice. Short shutter speeds produce sharp subjects, but if your speed is too short, you can't capture sufficient motion blur. Start with 1/15 to 1/8 sec, and experiment until your pan is perfect.

Now you're off to the races—where you can't control subject speed. Start following a subject's movement a good distance before your exposure point, and pan until after the shutter closes. Be ready for action by manually prefocusing on the place you'll be aiming when you open your shutter. For motion blur that's parallel to your frame edges, bring a ball-head tripod.

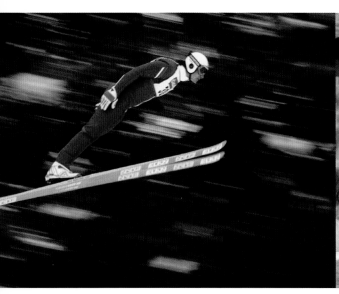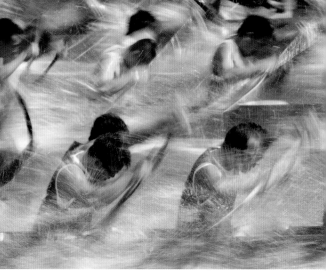

209 SHOW MOTION WITH FLASH

When you shoot flash photos with a slow shutter speed, moving subjects appear as sharp images amid blur in a phenomenon called ghosting. Useful in creating dynamic images of motion, ghosting has one glitch: Sometimes it appears in front of a subject rather than behind it. Since flash synchronization occurs at the start of an exposure, forward motion seems to travel backward, extending the blur in the wrong direction. Luckily, there's an easy remedy.

Set your flash to trailing sync (also called second-curtain sync), which fires the flash near the end of the exposure and blows ghosting out behind your subject. Experiment with 1/8- to 1/30-sec shutter speeds: The faster your subject, the longer his blur trail. Slow shutter speeds also elongate ghosts. To capture truly frenetic action, pan with your subject at a speed slightly slower than his own speed, and a streaky, smeared background will appear.

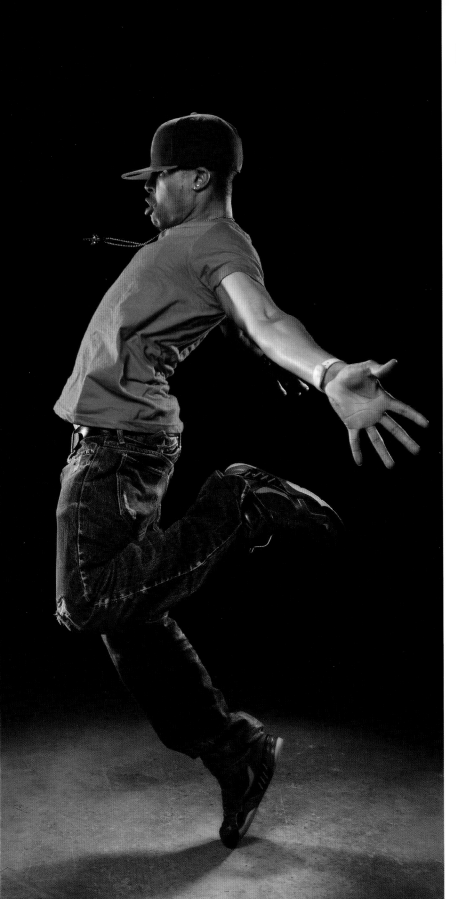

FREEZE MOTION WITH FLASH

Jacking up shutter speed isn't the only way to freeze action. Your flash—the built-in unit or, even better, an accessory shoe-mount unit—can do it, too. Plus, it's the go-to choice in low light (indoors or out) when you don't have the luxury of using high shutter speeds. This is the way to go for motion-stopping exposures of dance, gymnastics, and other indoor action.

The key concept here is that the lower the power you set your flash to, the briefer the duration—accessory units can fire at 1/50,000 sec or even faster. To get the fastest possible flash bursts, turn up your ISO as far as you think reasonable, and position your flash as close as possible to your subject—a remote trigger with an off-camera flash will permit you to do this. If you have sufficient space and time (and, of course, permission), set up a multi-flash arrangement for more three-dimensional lighting.

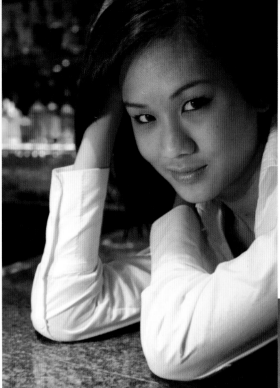

211 FINESSE FLASH EXPOSURE

Accessory flash units automate exposure by reading the bounce-back of a speedy preflash through the lens—that's why they're called through-the-lens (TTL) metering flashes. The camera and flash then adjust flash exposure by making its burst shorter for low light, longer for more light. A typical accessory unit on the market today has an astounding range: from 1/1000 to 1/50,000 sec. To take matters into your own hands, manually adjust flash power by changing duration, expressed in fractions: full power, 1/2, 1/4, and on down to 1/64 power for the briefest flash duration.

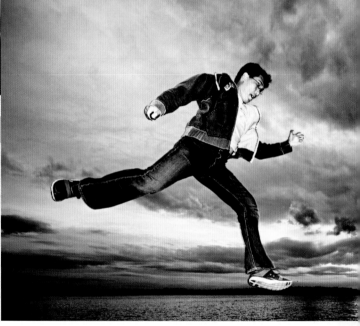

CHECKLIST

212 WORK YOUR SHOE MOUNT

Most DSLRs and ILCs accept shoe-mount flash units, which provide helpful lighting boosts. On-camera flash can produce harsh, flat, or blown-out snapshot-style light, but a few savvy shoe-mount flash techniques will let you skirt this danger to get subtly lit shots.

- ☐ **ADD A SHOE-MOUNT ACCESSORY FLASH**—there are dozens on the market—so you can lift your flash off the camera to generate off-axis directional lighting.

- ☐ **BOUNCE FLASH OUTPUT** off the ceiling or walls in interior shots. Don't aim on-camera flash directly at a subject.

- ☐ **SOFTEN LIGHT** with shoe-mount diffusers.

- ☐ **EXPERIMENT WITH APERTURES** to adjust the flash's output on a foregrounded subject.

- ☐ **ALTER SHUTTER SPEED TO CONTROL** how much background appears in your photo. A long shutter speed captures more background. A slow one shows less of the scene.

213 USE A FLASHMETER

Indispensable for elaborate setups and studio shots, a flashmeter provides exposure readings, determines the relative proportion of individual flashes in the setup, and takes readings of multipop exposures. Some even allow narrow spot flash metering, and you can switch them to ambient readings to balance a range of exposures.

214 MAKE THE BEST OF PHONE FLASH

To navigate your smartphone's flash options, tap the lightning-bolt icon on your phone screen's top left corner. Choose auto if you want the phone to determine when flash is needed, or set the mode to On if you want every photo flashed regardless of the amount of ambient light. If you'd like to diffuse your flash, simply tear off a piece of paper from a tissue, napkin, or even a coffee filter and tape it over your smartphone's flash.

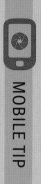

MOBILE TIP

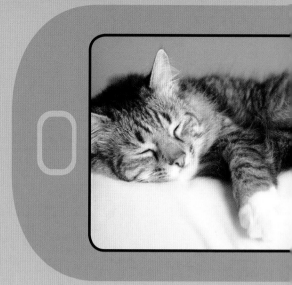

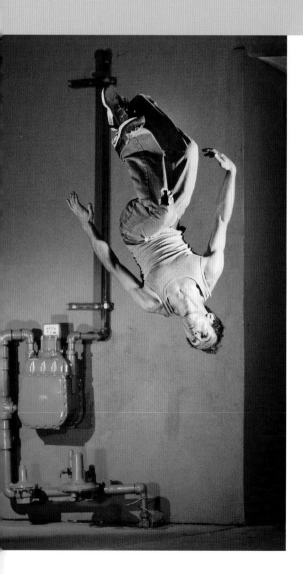

215 TURN ON TTL FLASH

A through-the-lens metering flash is basically lightning in a bottle. It can freeze action, tame tough midday sunlight, mimic studio lighting, balance or skew colors, and produce wild effects. As noted, it fires a quick preflash, then uses the bounce-back, plus information from the camera's meter, to determine how much light to emit when you shoot. So once you set your flash to TTL, you're free to set your camera to manual and play with ISO, shutter speed, and other variables until you capture the perfect background. In the meantime, TTL flash will take care of the foreground subject for you. Let's get started.

STEP ONE Set your camera to manual and its meter to evaluative mode.

STEP TWO Set white balance to Flash. Choose an ISO, aperture, and shutter speed. (Each camera has a maximum speed that its shutter can match, or "sync," with the flash. You can set your camera slower, but not faster, than the sync speed. Don't know your max speed? Start with 1/125 sec.) If you get confused, use the program, shutter, or aperture-priority modes as a guide, and dial the mode to manual.

STEP THREE Take a background shot. If you like it, you're ready to go. If you don't, alter the shutter speed or aperture.

STEP FOUR Turn on the flash. Most flashes default to TTL, but if yours does not, push the Mode button until TTL appears.

STEP FIVE Fire away! The evaluative meter will locate your foreground subject, the flash will expose for it, and the background will look just as you planned.

216

SMOOTH SKIN WITH A CLAMSHELL

To get the most flawless possible skin in portraits, try a clamshell. Not one from the mollusk: We're talking about a light-over-light setup, with two softboxes set at angles so their diffusion panels nearly touch, like an open shell. It's very effective in 1:1 lighting ratios. (Standard portrait lighting uses a 1:2 ratio with two frontlights, a main one and a softer fill. It creates pretty shadows but can also emphasize skin flaws.)

Set the main light in a softbox on a boom above your subject, aiming it down at her. Place the fill light below her, under a translucent umbrella, and angle it upward. Dial up the fill until it matches the main light—now you've got shadowless 1:1 lighting for a flaw-free face. For an even brighter look, strip the diffusion panels off silver-lined softboxes before you arrange your clamshell. Your model will glow like the moon.

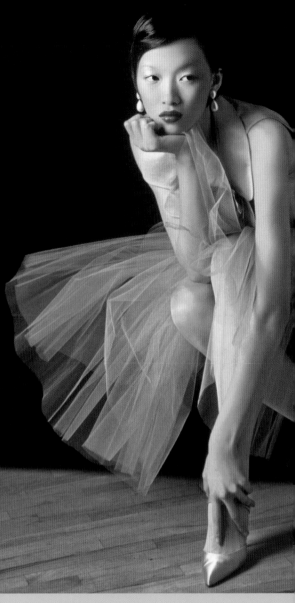

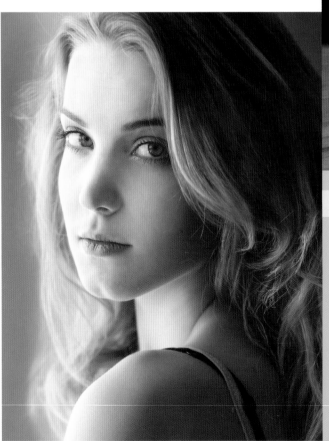

QUICK TIP

217 USE CLOTHES AS REFLECTORS

The world's simplest reflector? A white T-shirt. It bounces light onto subjects almost as well as the real thing. (Make sure it's clean!) To absorb excess light, wear a black one while you shoot.

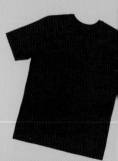

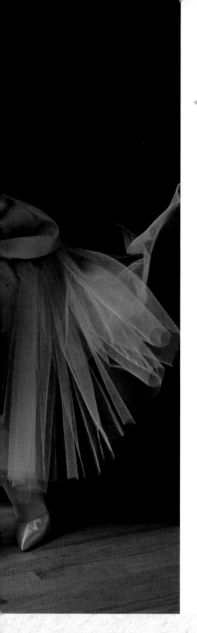

218 TURN A ROOM INTO A PORTRAIT STUDIO

Transform your little-used guest room into a much-appreciated studio with a setup that's ideal for stunning portraiture. There are many great things about having a home studio. For starters, you can invest in heavy, solid equipment that lasts a lifetime, rather than compromising on the modular gear a portable kit requires. Your lights are immediately on hand, so you needn't dedicate eons to setup and breakdown, and you have plenty of room to compose, shoot, and simply dream up inventive portraits. And because you control the room, you can place lights and stands wherever you choose, paint walls white or gray for diffused light (or black for high-contrast looks), then switch things up with frames to hold flattering backdrops, from paper rolls to patterned fabric.

The dreamy dancer here was shot by photographer Carol Weinberg in her home studio. After lighting the scene with a mix of window light and bounced strobe, she placed her model in front of a swatch of black velvet, which hid the chair the model was sitting on, contributing to the dramatic—and slightly surreal—effect.

219 GO WITH A SINGLE LIGHT SOURCE

The allure of the one-light portrait is obvious: It reveals striking shadows, and its setup is almost criminally easy. Place a strobe on a stand slightly to one side of your camera, raise it above your seated subject, and point it downward at a 45-degree angle to illuminate his face (single-source is more flattering if the light is "feathered" to one side of the subject rather than glaring straight at him). Play with position to ensure nothing looks funky (such as a big shadow under his nose) and to get a catchlight (see #199) in his eyes. Now position a reflector—a sheet of white cardboard will do—to reflect light onto your model's other side and brighten shadows. No cardboard? Seat your subject next to a white wall.

220 LET THERE BE LIGHT

Lighting kits can cost anywhere from a few hundred to several thousand dollars. As you shop, consider these five options, which all work well for portraiture. All but the tungsten can be daylight-balanced.

- ☐ **FLUORESCENT LIGHTS** are cool-operating and have long-lasting bulbs.

- ☐ **HMI** (hydrargyrum medium-arc iodide—try saying that three times fast) lights are soft and need little power.

- ☐ **LED LIGHTS** are cool-running and long-lived, but they're generally too dim to freeze action.

- ☐ **STROBE LIGHTS**, which flash at set speeds, are your go-to on shoots with high-speed action.

- ☐ **TUNGSTEN LIGHTS** offer continuous output and run very hot—buy ones with mesh bulb protectors.

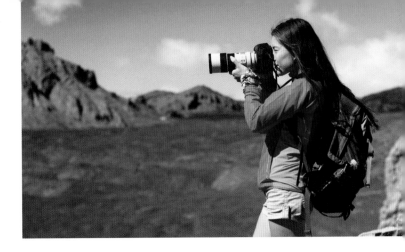

221

CARRY A LIGHTING SETUP IN YOUR BACKPACK

Location lighting kits can fit in any space, from large to small. When you carry lighting on your back for field shooting, though, you need compact, easy-to-schlep, bombproof gear and light-modifying accessories with as many features (and almost as much juice) as their studio-bound brethren. And all of it should be battery-powered. Sound impossible? It's not. Backpack lighting kits contain setups full of double-duty gear—tripods that also serve as light stands and reflector holders; LED flashlights that both illuminate the trail and act as dual-power fill lights. Most compact, battery-operated lighting setups will pack in the glow for prices from about $700 to $3,000.

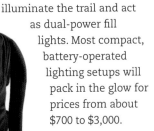

222

MOVE ON UP TO CAR KITS

Traveling by car or truck? Great: Now you can bring sophisticated gear that will expand your lighting options. Dozens of available location strobe kits all fit easily into your car's trunk (the most popular and flexible brands include a strobe, portable battery, trolley, umbrella/softbox, and stand in a compact case). Whichever one you buy, make sure it includes these accessories:

- ☐ **SOFTBOXES IN SEVERAL SIZES AND SHAPES** should be part of the package. The larger your subject, the larger a softbox must be.
- ☐ **SOFTBOX AND REFLECTOR ACCESSORIES** from grids to diffuser socks help you finesse and fine-tune your light.
- ☐ **A RANGE OF REFLECTORS,** from big ones for groups to beauty dishes for portraits, are essential for your kit, too.
- ☐ **SNOOTS AND BARN DOORS** help you direct and narrow strobe ouput.
- ☐ **A BUILT-IN WIRELESS FLASH TRIGGER** that couples with your on-camera transmitter via radio signal is indispensable.
- ☐ **FOAM PADDING,** to line your kit, ensures your gear won't smash when you hit a pothole.

223

CREATE A CLOSET LIGHTING CACHE

If you lack space for a full-size home studio, seek a modular lighting option to stash in a closet. Collapsible products are a must, and almost every lighting tool on the market comes in a foldable version. Fold-down beauty dishes? Inflatable, weather-resistant studios for backyard shoots? You'll find them and more for sale, plus hard-sided cases for easy stacking. As for the lights themselves, base purchases on the subjects you shoot most. For still lifes and product shooting, cool-running, easily stowed LED lights offer continuous output so you can evaluate lighting as you work. Instantaneous studio strobes are your best bet if you shoot speedy subjects such as pets and kids. To hold lights, choose space-optimizing accessories, such as wall-mounted holders that can grasp many stands at once or tripod stand organizers. Other niceties for closet-stored gear: tacky wax to anchor objects to tabletops, flat-folding product shooting tents, and looking-glass paint that turns glass squares into mirror reflectors.

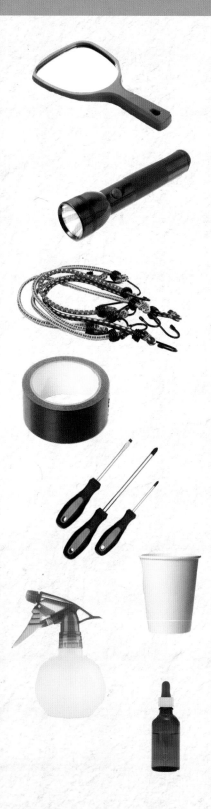

224 BRING EVERYDAY ESSENTIALS

We photographers love our gear. We dream of bags brimming with the latest, priciest gizmos. But gear needn't cost a mortgage payment—sometimes the right tool is in your junk drawer. Open it up and grab these 11 essential gear-bag items.

☐ **A SMALL MIRROR** is an excellent reflector for outdoor shots: It can open deeply shadowed areas or create bold fill. A cheap acrylic one won't shatter in the field.

☐ **GARBAGE BAGS** protect gear when the sky opens, and they keep you dry, too (tear three holes and you've got a poncho). Use them in lighting setups—white bags as reflectors, black ones as light-blocking flags.

☐ **A FLASHLIGHT** is a no-brainer. You need one when you're fumbling with teeny camera controls in twilight. They're aesthetic tools, too: Create delicate light paintings with a penlight, or dramatic background pattern with a wide-beamed light (see #266). Don't want to hold a light? Get an LED headlamp.

☐ **ZIPPER BAGS** are perfect impromptu weather housings (poke a hole and rubber-band it around your lens), and they keep dust off lenses and backup bodies in your bag.

☐ **MINI BUNGEE CORDS** lash up tripod legs and fix snapped camera straps. Bring lots so you can daisy-chain them into longer straps.

☐ **GAFFER'S TAPE** will save those sessions when everything from your hiking-boot soles to your focusing ring falls apart at once.

☐ **MICRO SCREWDRIVER SETS** can help you fix your tripod head, as well as your eyeglasses, on chaotic days.

☐ **WHITE PAPER CUPS** make fantastic impromptu snoots if you cut out their bottoms, or you can line them with black tape and mount them as backup lens shades.

☐ **A WHITE PAPER PLATE** is the poor photographer's ring light. Cut a hole in it and tape it to your lens as a reflector for backlit close-ups and facial portraits. Or tape some foil, shiny side out, to the plate to make an extra-bouncy reflector.

☐ **A SMALL SPRAY BOTTLE** can fake morning dew on foliage and flowers when Mother Nature hasn't done her job, and puts sheen on models' faces and skin.

☐ **AN EYEDROPPER AND GLYCERIN** give you "droplet control"—place drops of glycerin precisely where you want them (on a petal or twig, perhaps), and the sticky globs will wait while you compose and focus.

225 | LEARN ABOUT LIGHT FALLOFF

The farther a light source sits from a subject, the more its light falls off, or grows dimmer. Light falls off as the square of its distance: When you move a light twice as far from a subject as its original distance, only one-quarter of the original light reaches the subject. (Or skip the math and just bear in mind that light dims quickly when you move it away.)

You can use falloff to your advantage—to contrast a subject with its background, for example. Placing a light close to a subject makes the falloff from subject to background more pronounced. Move the light away, and the background grows relatively brighter. The same is true for sidelighting. Keep light close to your subject's side for dramatic light falloff across the frame, or pull it back for subtle falloff.

BACKSTORY

This image of a springing dancer, captured by Jason Petersen, combines flash and flour to produce an arresting image of emotion in motion. On a cold, dark night, with an outdoor black backdrop and two strobes (one facing the backdrop, one just behind and to the left of it), Petersen shot dancers as they leaped and arched. The dreamlike aura? Handfuls of strobe-lit flour tossed on the models by assistants. "I dreamed up something with a modern-art feel," he says. "I locked focus and tracked them until they hit the peak."

226 | PUNCH IT UP WITH HARD LIGHT

Hard light is one rough character, but it's also useful. For maximum contrast, unroll a black backdrop as a foil to a hard-lit figure, as Matthew Hanlon did for the shot below. He also used a light for every angle he wanted to highlight.

If you're following suit, think about texture: Hard light picks out every blemish and flaw. But flattery might not be your goal. Check out the highlighted scar on the boxer's right eyebrow and his callused knuckles—they make him look even tougher.

Want to pull your punch? A single soft source tempers hard light. Hanlon set a softbox behind his camera for fill that retained detail in shadows—a clever feint that produced a powerful portrait.

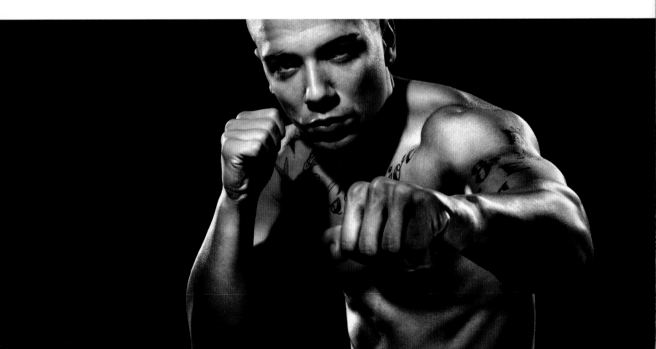

227 TAKE A LEAP IN THE DARK

Jason Petersen used a tripod-mounted DSLR, exposing for 1/250 sec at f/22, with a ISO of 200, and amped up the crescent shape of this dancer's body with trailing clouds of flour. If you want to dramatize human movement, borrow some of his techniques.

A black backdrop and a well-positioned flash or strobe are essential; so, too, is the patience for multiple shots until your subject and the substance are moving in tandem. Sugar, glitter, and fine sand all extend and emphasize movement or blur a body into clouds of light. A helper can sprinkle the substance on your subject as she moves, or the subject herself can toss handfuls in midmotion. See #210 for other pointers on capturing action shots.

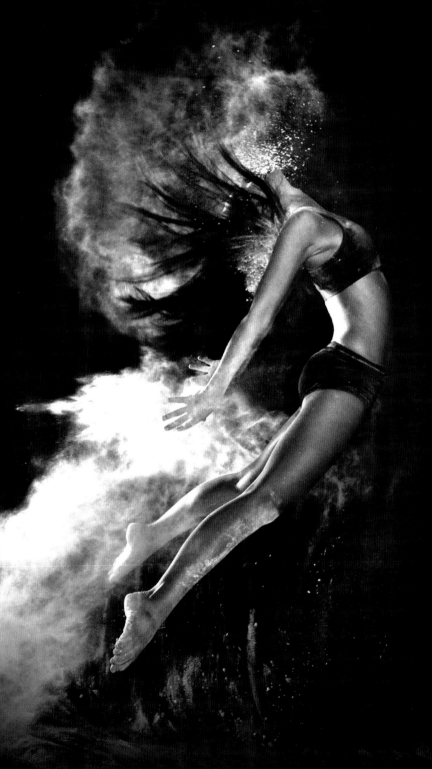

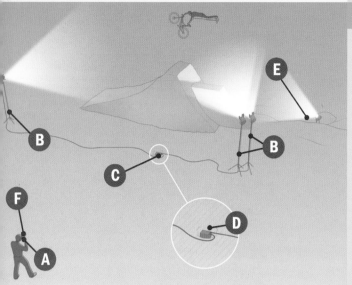

228 SOAR WITH STROBE POWER

Strobe lighting illuminates, sure. But it can also suggest shape and dimension, pull viewer attention to specific details, freeze action, and make a subject seem to leap straight out of the background.

In this can-you-believe-it action shot, strobes perform all these tasks. Professional mountain biker

229 AMP UP THE ACTION

Here are four principles for top-flight high-speed action shots:

☐ **FOCUS ATTENTION** For instance, here the track and the ramp are vividly illuminated while the foreground and the background are heavily shadowed, a feat achieved by focusing the strobe heads' output through narrow 50-degree reflectors. Using these, photographer Scott Markewitz selectively lit key areas, such as the parabolic approach ramp.

☐ **SEPARATE SUBJECT AND BACKGROUND** Markewitz fired up his lights for an output brighter than the cloudy ambient daylight, and set an exposure that rendered the ground and sky dim and the athlete brilliant.

☐ **DEFINE SHAPE** Thanks to Markewitz's crafty backlight position, the rocky ramp looms larger than life and its sharply delineated curves make the biker's horizontal flight all the more breathtaking.

☐ **TRY A SUPERSHORT FLASH-DURATION STROBE HEAD** It's pricey top-flight gear, but it kills the faint but visible motion blur produced by ordinary, slower heads.

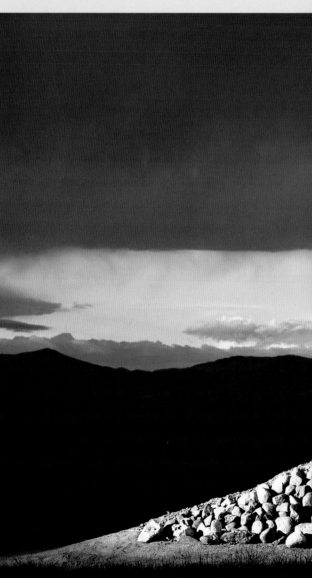

Paul Basagoitia, airborne in an outrageous "Superman Seat Grab" maneuver, is a spectacular subject by anyone's lights. And action-adventure photographer Scott Markewitz's strobe savvy turned the stunt into an object lesson in how to compose and capture a thrilling trajectory.

He chose an unusual belowground locale for his batteries and lights, and mounted a 70–200mm f/2.8 lens with image stabilization onto his camera (A). Then he set two short-duration strobe lights (B), with zippy minimum durations of 1/5120 sec, at the ramp's approach and another strobe to its left—all juiced with battery packs (C). The foreground pack intruded into the frame, so Markewitz got creative and dug a shallow pit in which to conceal it (D). He positioned his right backlight (E) belowground, too, so its output would not reach his lens and produce flare. Balancing this radical symphony of light sources with a high-end flashmeter (F), Markewitz cued the athlete and bagged his soaring Superman.

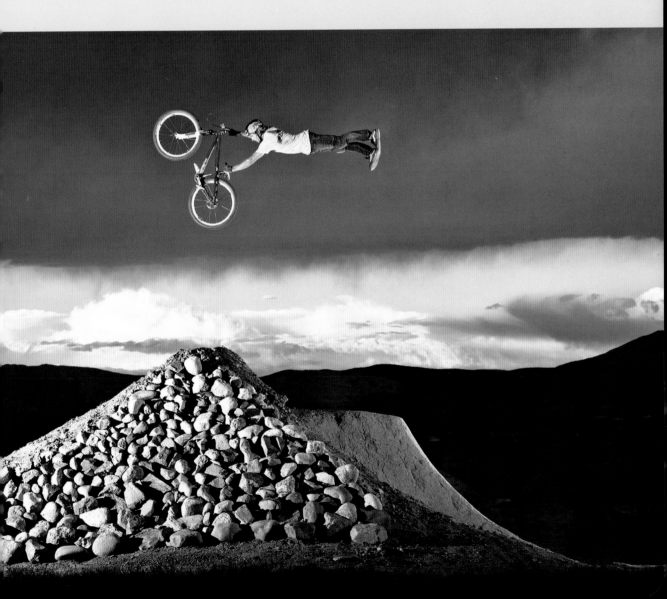

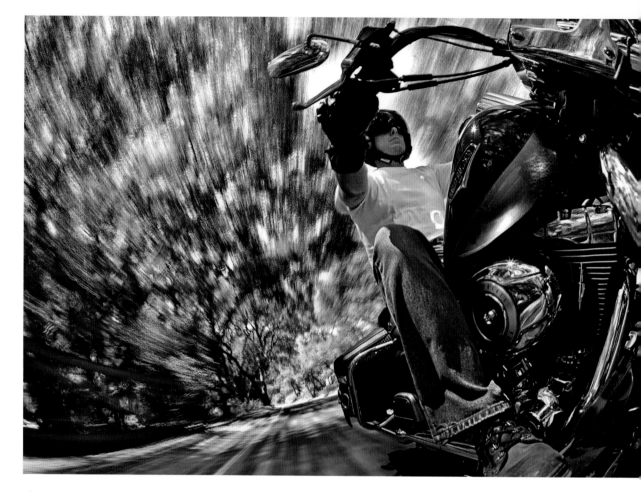

230 SHOOT AN EASY RIDER

For a photo that conveys the scene the way a motorcycle rider sees it—as zooming streaks of color and light—clamp a camera to the bike itself.

For the widest possible sweep of road and bike, your best rig is a DSLR or interchangeable-lens compact with a full-field fisheye lens, but you've got to secure it first. Attach two heavy-duty clamps to the bike's front fender rail. Fasten an elbow-hinged arm—one that's made to grip lights and cameras with a locking lever control at its pivot—to your camera base, and use a Super Clamp to secure a metal stud in its hot shoe. Strap the rig to the cycle with safety cables so it won't bite the dirt.

Now cue the rider to drive slowly: Speeds of 5 to 10 miles per hour (8–16 km/h) are safe but generate thrilling motion blur. Get ahead of the bike—a pickup bed is a good spot to sit—and trigger the shutter remotely. Shoot like crazy, playing with shutter speeds between 1/10 and 1/30 sec for optimal motion blur.

231 SYNC AT HIGH SPEED

Most deluxe accessory flashes offer high-speed syncing, liberating you from your camera's slower sync. Shooting flash at speeds of 1/1000 sec or faster, you can use wide apertures to create beautifully defocused backgrounds, thus spotlighting brightly flash-lit foreground subjects. Or darken or saturate background colors by underexposing with superhigh shutter speed. High-speed sync is often dimmer than conventional flash, but you can beat that problem by adding extra flash units.

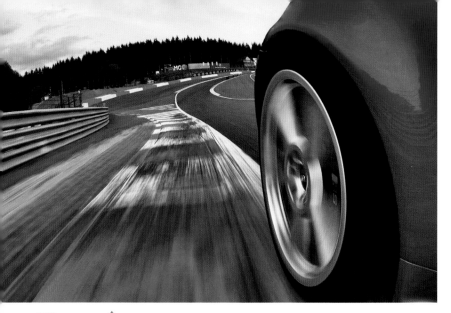

232
FIRE UP A FLASH PARTY

Using a few off-camera flashes? Why not 20, or 100? Round up a pack of photographer friends, ask each to bring along an accessory flash, and head out into the country to illuminate incredible shots. Fantastic for shooting nighttime action—a BMX bike race, or a four-wheeler rally in the desert— "flash mobs" can light a subject from a wide range of angles.

Keep things organized via careful stage direction. Divide your "flashers" into groups and assign them to provide lighting from the sides, from behind, or above and below, then trigger their flashes with optical and/or radio slaves. Move your friends and their flashes around until you capture the rip-roaring action in the dazzling light you envisioned.

233 CATCH SPEED FROM THE PASSENGER SEAT

Ever snapped a shot while riding in a speeding car? For the shot above, pro racing shooter Regis Lefebure handheld his DSLR, strap wrapped around his arm, as he leaned out of the window of an Audi driven at 80 miles per hour (145 km/h) by Formula 1 racing star Allan McNish. If you're after a similar shot, halve the driving speed and secure the camera to the car with a strong window or suction-cup mount. Finessing the composition is impossible, so use an ultrawide lens set to its hyperfocal distance using the depth-of-field scale on the lens barrel. To imply a hurtling pace, you need motion blur: Set your camera to 1/60 sec or slower in shutter-priority mode, and adjust your ISO so that your aperture will be set at about f/11 for depth of field. Shoot in high-speed Continuous mode to snag frames in dizzying succession.

234 FREE YOURSELF WITH WIRELESS FLASH

Today's sophisticated accessory flashes let you take lighting off-camera and trigger it wirelessly. Why? To produce intriguing light and shadow that harsh on-camera flash just can't. The setup is simple—a master (or "commander") controller attaches to your camera's hot shoe and uses infrared pulses or radio signals to tell your accessory flash (or "slave") to fire. No wires connect controller to accessory, so there's nothing to trip over or clone out in post-production. You can position an accessory flash anywhere in your scene, hold it, ask a friend to hold it, or stick it on a light stand. Wireless shooting allows you to control the output and firing mode of remote flash units from your camera—perfect when flashes are in hard-to-reach positions. Flash units are compact, light, and battery-powered, unlike costly studio strobes.

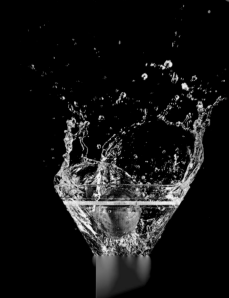

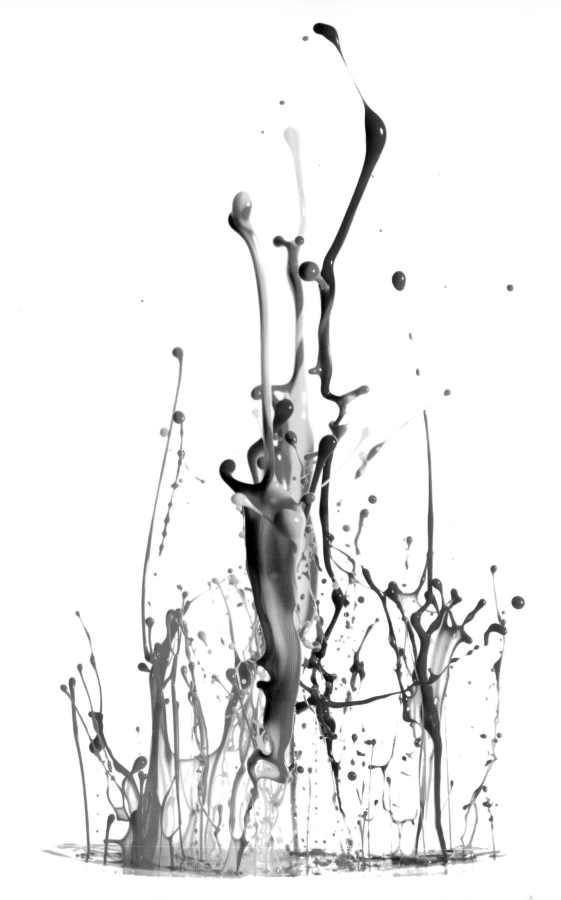

235 CAPTURE DANCING PAINT

How in the world do you get paint to leap up like this—much less catch a photo of it in midair? With a little creative setup, that's how.

Ryan Taylor of Cedar Rapids, Iowa, used sound to activate both his subject and his camera's flash. After stretching a white balloon over an everyday stereo speaker and pouring paint onto it, he rigged an audio trigger that would vibrate and launch the brightly colored globs into the air—and set off his camera at the same time. Here's how he pulled it off.

To generate the low-frequency pulse that sent the paint flying, Taylor downloaded a program that let him create a repetitive oscillation called a sine wave. He played it through a laptop (A) connected to an amplifier (B) and the speaker (C) with the paint-covered balloon (D).

To illuminate the set, he put a light-stand-mounted strobe fitted with a softbox (E) to the front right of the speaker. A second flash (F) to the left of the speaker lit both the subject and the backdrop (G).

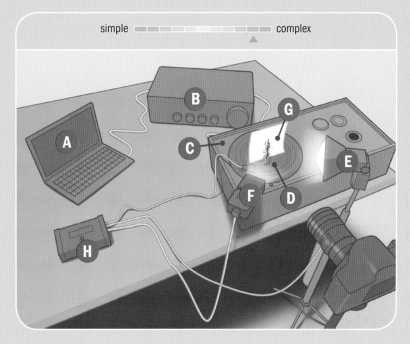

simple ▬▬▬▬▬▬▬▬▬▬▬▬▬ complex

Taylor fired the strobes with a multipurpose flash/camera trigger (H), which fires either when it detects a sound or when its infrared beam is broken. He set a delay of 50 millisec to ensure that the droplets reached maximum height. To render his active subject sharply, he set the strobes to extremely short flashes of about 1/20,000 sec.

He dimmed the room lights, opened the camera's shutter, and hit Play on the laptop. The sound blasted, the paint jumped, the flash popped, and the picture was his.

236 EXPERIMENT WITH AN AUDIO TRIGGER

Let's face it: We don't move at the speed of sound. That can be a problem when you need to push the shutter button quickly to capture a superfast, noisy action. That's where an audio trigger comes in handy. This specialized gadget can be used to open the shutter when it's triggered by sound. Paired with a high-speed strobe, it initiates an intense but brief burst of light that freezes fast action—such as a paintball hitting a wall or a glass breaking.

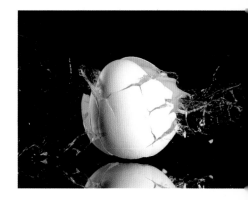

237 ACQUAINT YOURSELF WITH LIGHT ACCESSORIES

Beyond your camera's built-in flash (if it has one), there are endless types of lights and accessories available to help you control the color, intensity, distribution, and directionality of light in your images. Use them alone or in combination to create photos that capture any mood you desire.

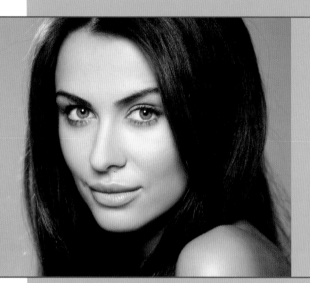

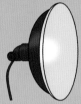

BEAUTY DISH
This accessory's bowl shape gathers light toward a focal point to create an effect like that of a paired softbox and direct flash.

With their dramatic, skin-flattering light, beauty dishes are beloved by fashion photographers.

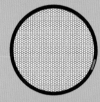

GRID
To crisply define and direct light toward a subject, fit this honeycomb-patterned disk over your light source.

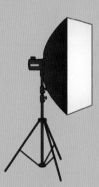

SOFTBOX
This accessory fits around a light; its reflective walls and the diffusing material at its front broaden and soften the light's beam.

BARN DOORS
This device's four metal doors open and close around an attached light source to control the light's spill.

Barn doors allow you to artfully control the amount and angle of the light on your subject.

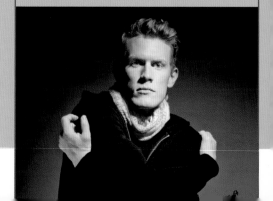

ACETATE SHEETS
These colored gels are attached to a light source so that you can tint and shade light in rainbow tones.

Gels can play up the natural hues of a scene or, as shown here, create wild effects.

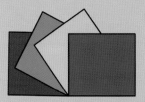

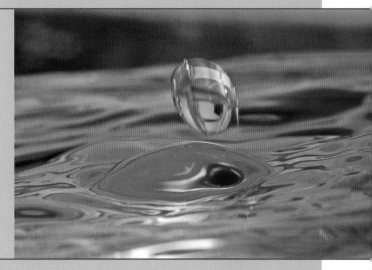

LIGHT TENT
A simple box covered in fabric diffuses external light through its walls, evenly distributing illumination across an object placed inside it.

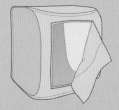

UMBRELLA
Position this diffuser before a light pointed away from your subject—it'll bounce and diffuse the glow to flattering effect.

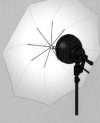

SNOOT
This snout-shaped shield focuses light into a narrow beam for dramatic illumination and maximum light-and-dark contrast.

An arrow-sharp snoot light precisely defines your subject and keeps flash where you want it.

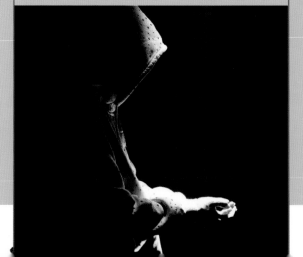

BAFFLE/REFLECTOR
Sometimes two-faced is a good thing: This versatile tool has a reflective side and a light-blocking one. Hold it, or clip it to your light stand.

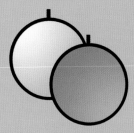

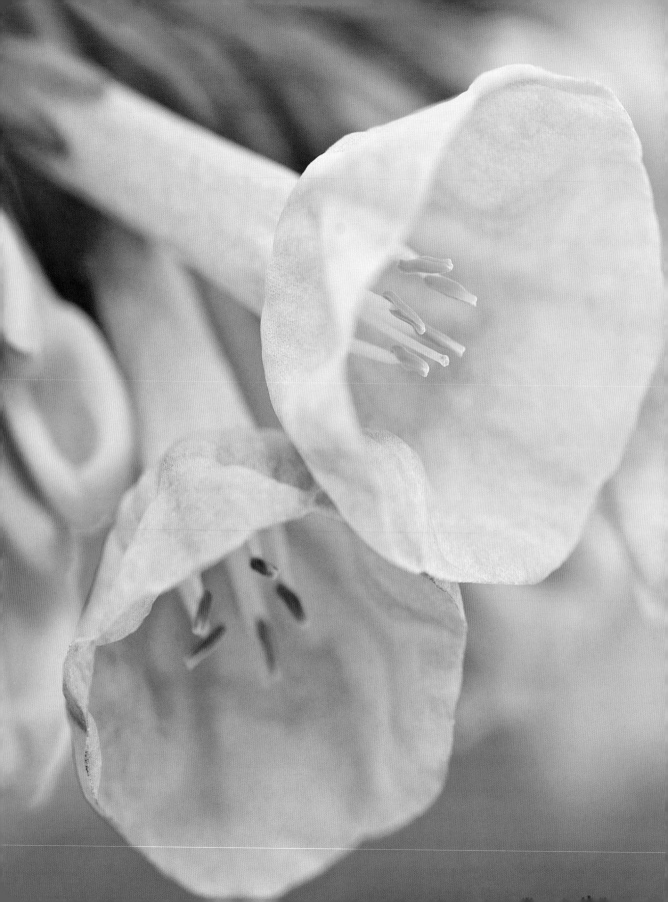

238 SHOOT FLOWERS IN A LIGHT TENT

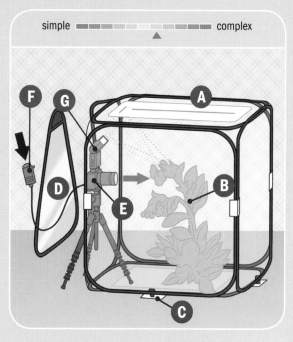

simple ▬▬▬▬▬▬ ▲ ▬▬▬▬▬ complex

When photographing wildflowers, you want certain conditions. The ideal illumination is the flat, neutral light of an overcast afternoon, when the sky acts as a giant softbox and burnishes the petals' subtle textures and colors. Taming wind is just as important as diffusing light—flowers stir in the gentlest breeze, making it hard to get a sharp photo.

So how do you shoot wildflowers when it's sunny or windy outside? First, buy a lightweight photography tent (A). In the field, choose your bloom (B) and select the best angle from which to frame it. Position your tent over the plant, making sure that the bottom edges are flush with the ground so you can push stakes through grommets (C) in the fabric to secure it. Remove your tent's zipper panel (D) and insert your gear (E), including flash, through your tent's front zipper to increase bounced light. Use a cable release (F) outside the tent to trip your shutter without shaking the tent or the flower.

Consider the backdrop that you'd like to shoot against. To turn your light tent's wall into a pure white background, slightly overexpose the image to blow out the detail in the fabric. Do you want to include a natural background? Shoot from the side: Position the midsize opening around the flower and keep the two larger portals on either side of the tent open, giving you a window to reveal nature in the distance.

For stronger lighting, use flash (G). Bounce its output inside the tent, away from the blossom. Or attach a card to your flash head, sending more of the light onto the flower to replicate bright overcast conditions. Another option: Use an off-camera flash outside the tent, experimenting with different angles.

To reproduce the flower's colors accurately, set a custom white balance if your camera allows it. Do this inside the tent, using one of its walls as your target (if not, use the Cloudy setting).

239 PROTECT YOUR KNEES DURING FIELDWORK

Your knees can really take a beating during long sessions of outdoor setup and shooting. Protect them by spreading out a yoga or gardening mat before you go to work. Hardware stores also sell mats—ones that are stiffer, sturdier, and designed for construction work.

Consider some add-ons as well. If the ground is wet, set a garbage bag or small tarp under the pad. Kneeling on rocky or really hard ground? Use sports knee pads, such as those made for skateboarding. They're highly durable and protective but allow you a full range of motion.

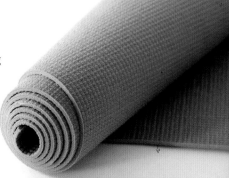

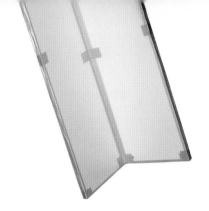

240 CRAFT A V-CARD REFLECTOR

Build yourself a sturdy, light, and versatile V-card reflector out of white foam core, available at art-supply stores. Lash together two sheets, both about ½ inch (1.25 cm) in thickness, at one edge with horizontal strips of strong duct or gaffer's tape. (Cut the sheets tall or short, depending on the size of your intended subject.) This adaptable tool can do it all. Use it to narrow or broaden light by opening or closing its V. Or control contrast by moving your lights toward or away from the apex of the V. You can even shelve your softbox and use your V-card to produce a glow that is broader and smoother than the light that pricier gear can generate. When you're not using your V-card, stow it by closing it up like a book.

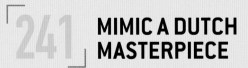

simple ▬▬▬▬▬▬▬▬▬▬▬▬▬▬ complex
▲

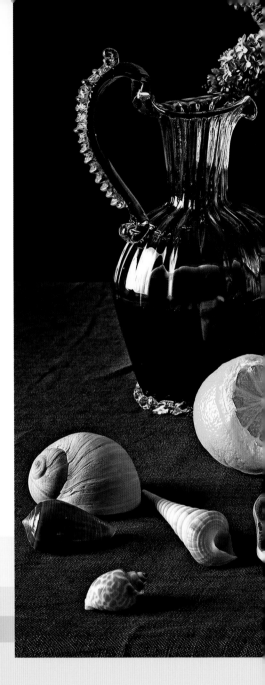

[BIG PROJECT]

241 MIMIC A DUTCH MASTERPIECE

If you make them yourself, lighting reflectors aren't a drain on your savings account. Photographer Skip Caplan arranged this Dutch Masters–style still life using his homemade V-card reflector (the materials cost $106) to mimic natural window light. Consisting of two foam-core panels and some gaffer's tape, a big V-card

reflects soft light, but it's far more economical than gear such as a softbox or beauty dish.

Here's how Caplan snagged the shot. He aimed two strobe heads (A) on stands into a large V-card (B), and propped up a black gobo (C) so the main light would not illuminate the dark background. A white reflector (D) opened up the set's shadowed right side. Then Caplan fine-tuned his light just as a painter would: A little mirror on armature wire (E) bounced light onto the sliced lemon at the left of the composition, popping it

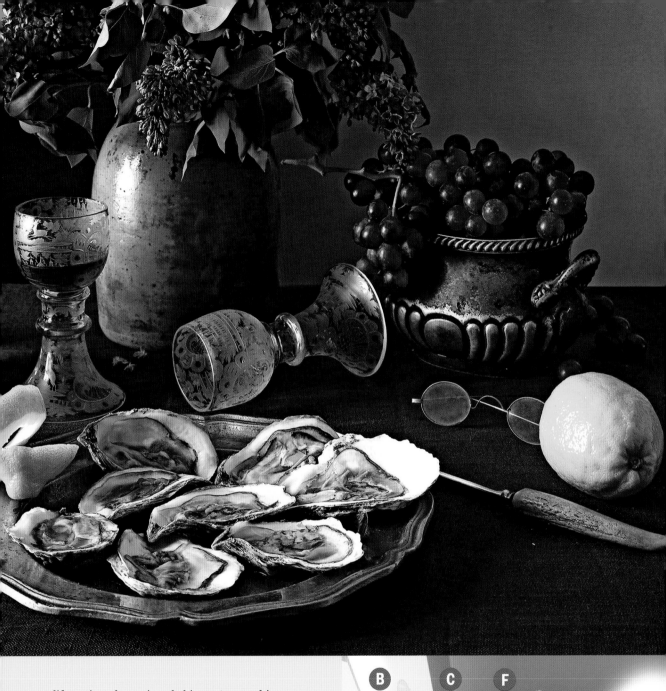

to life against the antiqued objects. A wee white reflector (F) behind the goblet amped the wine's color, and a third strobe head and a softbox (G) provided overall depth and glow to the composition. His tripod-mounted camera (H) sat close to the table edge, centered before the platter of oysters, while Caplan shot the feast at 1/125 sec at f/22 with an ISO of 80.

Why not simply use his studio's real window light? "It took me six hours to arrange everything," Caplan says. "Window light would have changed too much."

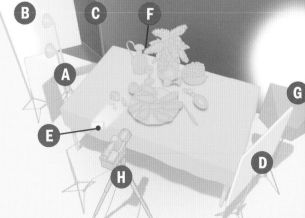

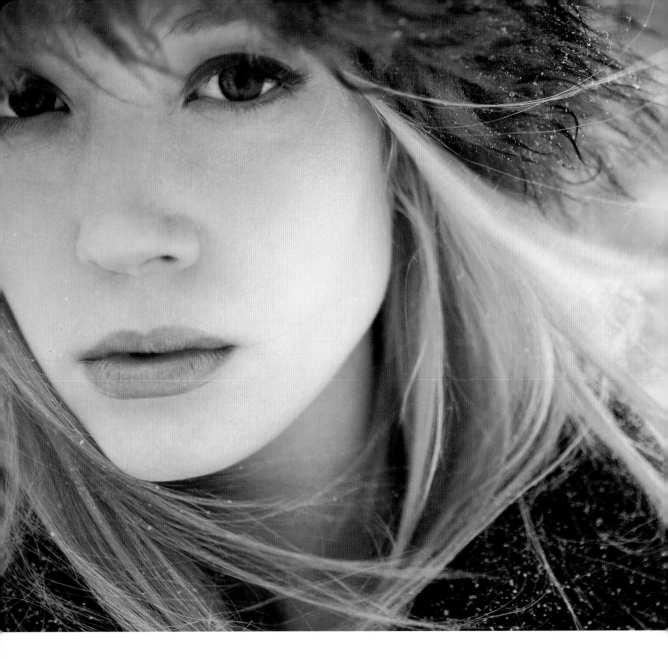

242 | USE WET-WEATHER REFLECTORS

When you're photographing in snow or rain—or around water in any form—non-electrical reflectors are the best, safest, and sometimes the only lighting tool you'll want to have on hand. Battery packs can short out in the damp, and light stands and artificial light sources are a lot of trouble in nasty weather, even with a willing assistant.

Craft your own reflector from foam or poster board (for an example, see #240). Or turn on your creative faculties and search out objects onsite that can serve as ready-made reflectors. For instance, a pale-colored wall or smooth, brilliantly reflective ice on a pond can bounce light onto your subject almost as well as high-priced gear can.

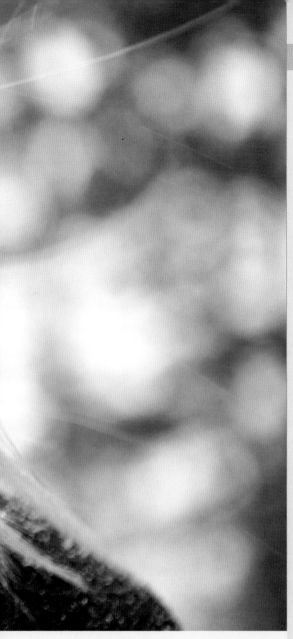

243

SHOOT IN SNOW LIGHT

Like any other art, great lighting doesn't call attention to itself. But it makes all the difference, as demonstrated by the seemingly effortless beauty of this wintertime portrait. It was achieved through a simple yet clever combination of reflectors and ambient light sources. You can work similar magic by following the four-stage setup used by Buffalo, New York, photographer Rhea Anna.

She did not want to lug extra gear such as stands or artificial lights across the knee-deep snow of the farm pasture where she staged this portrait. So instead she used the overcast sky itself (A) as her primary light source. It provided a softbox-like light—large, bright, and very diffuse. The freshly fallen snow (B) served as another broad panel of light. It radiated gentle fill light from below, illuminating the model's lower face and canceling out the shadows that otherwise would be cast by her browbones, nose, chin, and hat.

Then Anna employed two cheap, portable reflectors to really make her subject glow. To add punch and directionality to the dispersed natural light of sky and snow, one assistant held up a 3½-by-6-foot (1-by-1.8-m) white reflector (C) to the model's right. And to balance the inherently blue, chilly tones of snow light, a second helper held a 2¾-foot (82-cm) soft, nonmetallic gold reflector disc (D) to the model's left, which goosed up the subject's strawberry-blond hair for a nice counterpoint of color. Exposing at 1/60 sec at f/2.8, with an ISO of 100, Anna handheld her camera (E) and shot. The model's face and hair dramatically contrasted with the cool background: a no-muss, no-fuss picture of wintry perfection.

The best thing about that setup? The non-electrical reflectors were easy to use. "We had an ambitious shot list that day," Anna says. "I handed my assistant and stylist each a reflector, and in less than 15 minutes, we were done and on to the next shot."

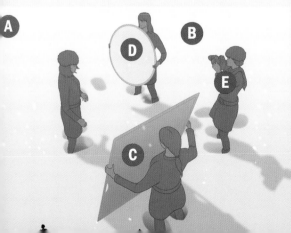

simple ▰▰▰▰▰▰▰▰▰▰▰▰ complex

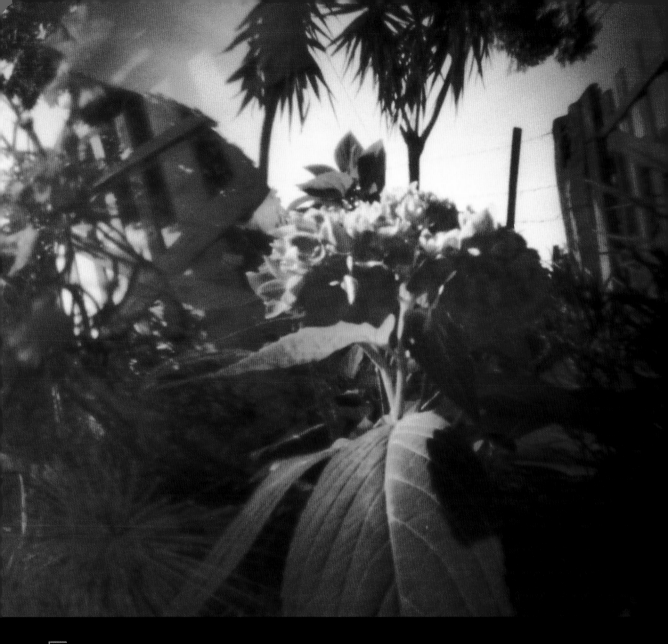

244 CAPTURE COOL PINHOLE SHOTS

Once you've built a pinhole camera, what can you shoot with it? Anything you like, and you can print photos in endless ways to vary and effect. Reminders: Pinhole pics are soft and dreamy, not tack-sharp, and the bigger the camera, the more light will fall off as it travels through the camera to the photo paper. Check out these shots for inspiration.

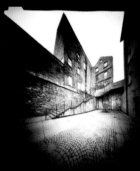

■ Print on different papers. Try a paper negative instead of a cellulose one (such as the shot at left), or try fancy silver gelatin.

■ Put your pinhole camera in motion. At near right, it sits on a seesaw's fulcrum.

■ Create tiny abstracts. Rotate a matchbox pinhole over a flower for a shot such as the one at center right.

■ Play with ghosts. The far-right image's blur is the photographer

245 BUILD A PINHOLE CAMERA

You don't need a lens to take a picture. A box, photo paper, and a teeny hole do the job very well. This ancient technique produces simple shots with virtually limitless depth of field—and you can make a "camera" out of any opaque container, from a matchbox to a trashcan to a whole room.

STEP ONE Find a cardboard box with flat sides. Gather matte black paint, black duct tape, a no. 10 needle, a thin metal square (cut it from a can or thin brass shim stock), sandpaper, a craft knife, heavy black paper, and photographic paper.

STEP TWO Paint the box's interior black to prevent reflection. If any light leaks in, cover holes with tape.

STEP THREE Poke a hole through the metal square with the needle. Sandpaper the hole's edges smooth. The smoother the edges, the sharper your photograph.

STEP FOUR Cut a small square in one side of the box.

STEP FIVE Tape the metal square into the box, lining up the pinhole with the square hole's center. If the metal shows through the outside of the box, cover everything but the pinhole with more tape.

STEP SIX Cut a small square of black paper. Tape one edge above the pinhole on the box's exterior. This is your "shutter."

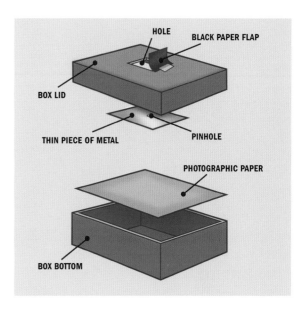

STEP SEVEN Load your photo paper in total darkness. Try a closet, windowless bathroom, or changing bag (see #248). Tape the paper inside the box, opposite the pinhole, with its shiny side outward. Close the box and hold down the shutter. Now you're ready to "shoot."

STEP EIGHT Lift the shutter flap for 30 sec to 4 minutes, depending on lighting conditions. To keep the box perfectly still, tape it down.

STEP NINE In the darkroom, untape and remove the photo paper. Process it in the usual fashion (see #336). Make a contact print from your paper negative with its emulsion side facing the printing paper's shiny side.

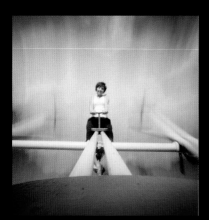
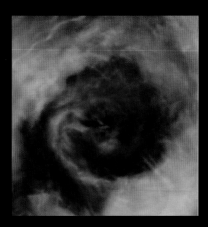
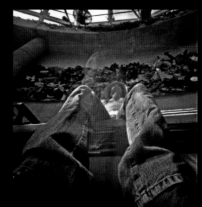

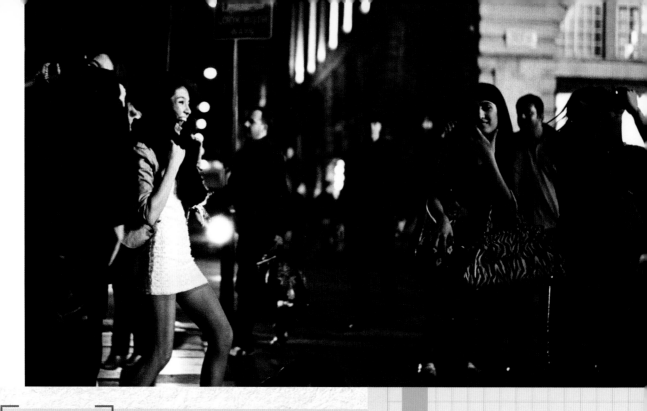

246 LEARN THE BENEFITS OF FILM

Digital photography has taken over the world, but film is the elder statesman—distinguished and a bit finicky. You might want to go with it for numerous reasons:

☐ **ULTIMATE IMAGE DETAIL** is film's greatest gift, as long as you shoot in large-format with a 4-by-5 or 8-by-10 view camera. And a medium-format camera with interchangeable backs lets you shoot digital and film with the same body to compare them for yourself.

☐ **IT'S GOT OLD-SCHOOL APPEAL** There's something truly magical about watching an image emerge from a chemical bath in the darkroom (see #336). In B&W, you'll experience this directly; most color printers use a machine that keeps these more toxic chemicals away from your skin.

☐ **YOU CAN USE OLD CAMERAS AND LENSES** High-quality gear that you inherit or buy second-hand connects you with photography's past and may also offer fabulous image quality at a much lower price than the digital version of the same camera.

☐ **IT MAY HELP YOU LEARN THE BASICS** Working with film requires more planning and careful attention to each exposure—after all, you're paying for each frame you shoot and print.

☐ **YOU CAN GET UNPREDICTABLY FUNKY LOOKS** such as blur and irregular color that are trendy now when you use a cheapo vintage-style film camera (see #256).

These are my sons, Milo and Seth. It was Saturday morning, and they were just doing what they usually do, though it was a lucky coincidence that they were wearing those PJs while playing with a paper airplane. I really like the simple mechanical feel of having a Leica in my hands, so that's what I used for this shot. Learning how to develop my own film and do lots of experimenting without sending it out made it easier, too. I thought I'd be using digital by now, out of convenience. But I don't feel any real need to switch. This is just for pleasure, and the Leica is what I feel like using.

—BUD GREEN

247 | KNOW YOUR FILM

Manufacturers don't make much film these days (even old king Kodachrome finished its 75-year run back in 2009). Online retailers and labs are now your best sources for all film types, as well as for processing if you lack a darkroom (see 333). Before you shop, learn which kind of film your camera takes, and how to load it.

The standard is 35mm, sold in 24- and 36-exposure rolls in cylindrical cases. Load it in daylight, but rewind it before opening the camera so you don't expose it. (This isn't a problem with disposable film cameras.) Stick it in the fridge until you're ready to develop it.

Medium-format film is usually two to six times larger than 35mm film. Most is sold in 6cm 120 and 220 sizes. Medium-format cameras wind film from one spool to another as you shoot, so you can open the camera to unload it yourself. Use its little tape tab to keep it spooled.

Most large-format view cameras shoot 4-by-5-inch (10-by-12.5-cm) images—that's 13 times the area of a 35mm film frame. Load each sheet of film into the holder on the camera back in complete darkness.

QUICK TIP

248

HAVE FILM IN THE BAG

Changing bags are wearable darkrooms: lighproof, double-sleeved pouches. Insert your arms to remove film from a canister or load or unload sheet film holders. They're zippered and roomy enough to hold your camera, gear, and tools.

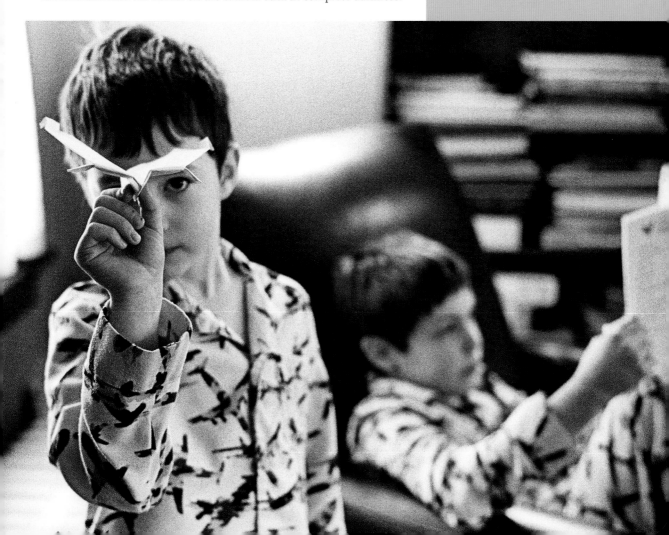

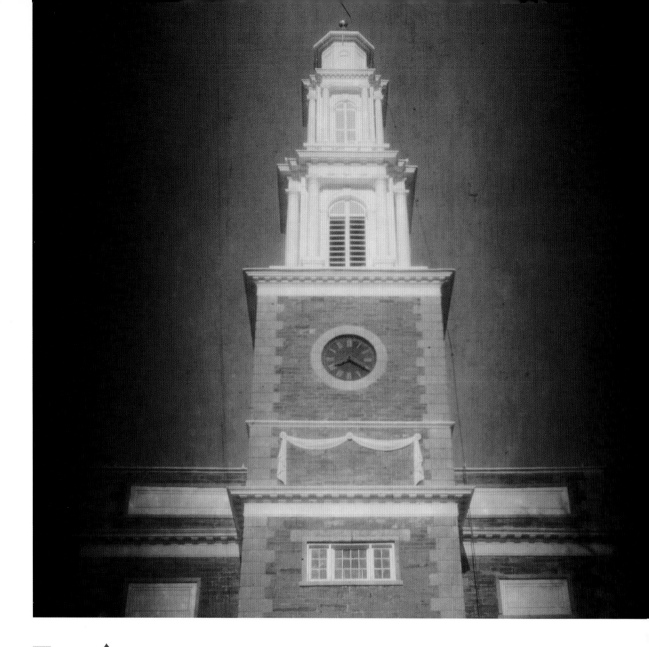

249 EXPLORE OUT-OF-DATE FILM

So you're cleaning the attic and discover rolls of unexposed film marked with ancient "use-by" dates. Don't toss them out—instead, use those antiques to create breathtaking nostalgic shots.

Photographer Chuck Miller used a roll of Kodak Super-XX 120 high-speed panchromatic film—which expired in May 1959—in a Rolleiflex to get the image above. The film's lightproofing was too weak to keep ambient light and radiation seepage out of the film wrapping over the decades, so light leaks painted on intense fogging and vignetting before any photos were shot. Those effects imitate the natural aging process of an old print, but here the film is aged, not the paper. Shots on old film resemble lomography (see #257), and there's a satisfying randomness to old-film shots that digital retro-photo applications can't quite capture.

250 SHOOT WITH A FILM CAMERA

If you've been shooting with a DSLR and would like to try (or get back to) the film experience, there are many options available. Recent and current film SLRs have autofocus, autoexposure, autowind and rewind, and auto setting of ISO—everything a DSLR has, except the instant gratification of seeing your photos on the spot.

On the spectrum's other end are vintage and modern-classic film cameras that are strictly manual focus and exposure. Try one (whether new or a used-market find) for the experience of making all settings yourself, rather than leaving it to an electronic brain.

Start with color-print films, which give the most leeway and are forgiving of errors of up to several

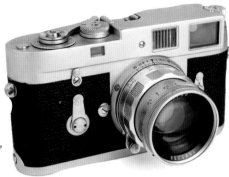

stops. They also allow you to scan them to a digital file that you can share, edit, and print. B&W films give good latitude, too, while color-slide (or reversal) films offer the least latitude, but capture crystal-sharp images and rich saturation. Frame carefully, and monitor depth of field—there's no LCD to check your work after the shot.

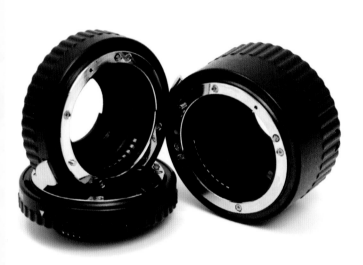

251 MANUALLY FOCUS YOUR CAMERA

Virtually all digital cameras, and many film cameras, sport autofocus. But when you're shooting some subjects—such as dark ones in low light—manual focus is your friend.

Many film SLRs, and a few digital SLRs, have split-image focusing that breaks your viewfinder's image in half. You adjust the focus until the two halves line up perfectly. Most DSLR focusing screens today have matte screens; with these, shift the focus until the image looks sharpest. But don't do it slowly—instead, quickly turn the lens's focusing ring until you are roughly in focus, then slow down to make it sharp. Practice helps, as does diopter correction. The latter is correction adjustable to suit your eyesight; it allows eyeglass wearers to shoot without their specs. Look through the viewfinder and adjust the diopter (a small knurled wheel adjacent to the viewfinder eyepiece) until f-stop settings and other text in the finder are sharpest.

252 USE OLD LENSES ON YOUR DSLR

Got old film-camera lenses but a new digital SLR? If they're the same brand, the old lenses will likely fit on the digital camera. Depending on their age, they may not have full functionality, such as autofocus. Different brand of lenses? Try to find an adapter, but shoot in all-manual mode if your DSLR can't "talk" to your lens.

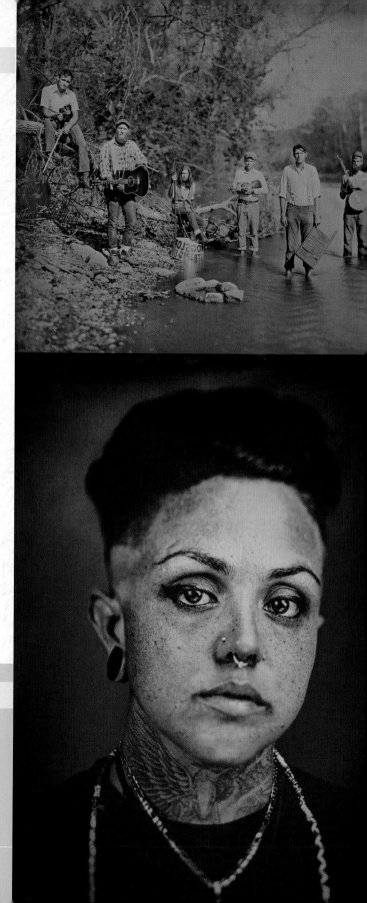

253 TURN BACK TIME WITH TINTYPES

These days, we produce and immediately forget photos, so it's no wonder that some of the most interesting photographers today are slowing down—way down. Enter tintype, a wet-plate process whereby chemicals are applied to metal and then an image is exposed directly onto the metal and developed on the spot. The dreamy, silvery results harken back to Civil War–era images. To try it yourself, gear up for a process that, while fun, is laborious.

☐ **SOURCE A VINTAGE CAMERA** Tintypes are usually made with antique view cameras (large-format models with bellows between a lens and a plate holder).

☐ **CUT YOUR PLATES** Modern tintype artists buy or cut black-enamel-backed aluminum sheets in their camera's format (commonly 4-by-5 or 8-by-10. When it's time for collodion, peel off the protective layer.

☐ **FIND THE CHEMICALS** This process requires a collodion solution, a silver-nitrate sensitizing solution, a developer bath, and a fixing solution, plus a protective varnish. There are a number of wet-plate kits on the market. Keep in mind that these chemicals are dangerous—some are poisonous and flammable.

☐ **WEAR PROTECTIVE GEAR** You need a cheap but effective respirator mask and a pair of black nitrile gloves to protect from stains.

☐ **FIND A DARKROOM** Since you'll be working with light-sensitive plates, you'll need access to a light-tight room in which to treat and develop your plate.

254 PICK TINTYPE SUBJECTS

While old-timey subjects feel like apt fodder for tintypes, seek out contemporary scenes and portrait opportunities—the contrast can make for a unique (if not even spookier) result.

255 EXPOSE USING THE COLLOIDAL PROCESS

Once you've obtained the proper gear, the tintype process works more or less like this:

STEP ONE Working in a dark room with good ventilation (and the lights can be on at this stage), first clean your plate with collodion. Pour the solution into the center of the plate and move the plate from side to side, up and down, to coat it thoroughly and smoothly. Let the collodion sit for about 15 to 30 seconds so it can form a slick surface. (If you purchased a kit with precoated plates, you can skip this step.)

STEP TWO Turn off the lights in your workspace and immerse the plate in a silver nitrate bath for between 3 and 5 minutes, which will make it sensitive to light for your exposure. Then insert the plate into a plate holder to make it light-tight for transit to your set. Move quickly, as you've only got about 15 minutes before the chemicals dry out.

STEP THREE Transport the plate to your shoot space, insert it into your camera, and prepare for your exposure. When your scene is set, remove the dark slide from the plate holder to reveal the plate, then remove your lens cap to start the exposure.

STEP FOUR Leave the camera be during your exposure, which will likely take between 10 and 15 seconds (depending on how much light is in your scene). To end the exposure, simply screw the lens cap back on. Put the dark slide back in place and remove the plate holder from the camera, then take it back to the darkroom for development.

STEP FIVE Take the plate out of the plate holder and coat it in a bin filled with developer chemicals, swishing it back and forth for 15 seconds or until the darkest areas of your image begins to appear. Rinse well with water to stop the development—this is your negative.

STEP SIX Next up, you'll need to lock in your proper exposure with a fixing solution, which will transform the negative into a positive image. Let the plate dry for several hours, as it'll be fragile.

STEP SEVEN To protect the image and enhance its old-timey look, coat it in varnish.

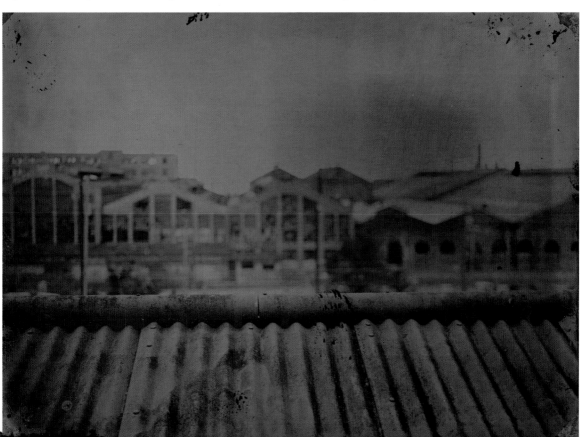

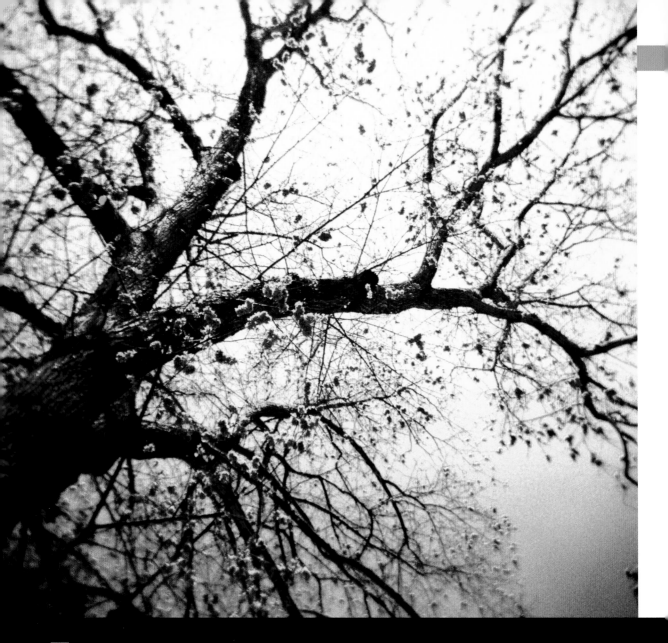

256 GET THE LO-FI LOWDOWN

Lomography, another term for lo-fi film shooting, is mostly a process of happy accidents. But a few tips come in handy as you make your way through the wild world of lo-fi. For starters, shoot in color to exaggerate the bright hues of flowers, neon, and storm-lit skies. Cross-processing slide film (getting it developed in the wrong solution) further distorts color and heightens oddball contrasts. Color effects vary among films: Cross-processing Fujichrome Astia or

Sensia gives you a red effect, Provia and Velvia, a green one. Konica films give you yellow, and Kodak, blue.

Have fun and be sure to shake things up as you shoot—unlike with your fancy DSLR, feel free to vibrate the camera, hold it over your head, or lie on the floor. Remember, it's the serendipitous "flaws"— such as the double exposure in the portrait at near right, the light leaks in the center image, and the color shift at far right—that make lomo images so arresting.

257 TRY A RETRO LO-FI CAMERA

Lo-fi film photography is the ultimate in retro chic. Its unpredictable, intentionally poor-quality aesthetics—light leaks, weirdly rendered colors, blurs—are best produced by cheap cameras old and new, including toys and pinhole creations (see #245).

One lo-fi staple is the Holga, a medium-format toy camera invented in Hong Kong in the 1960s. It's a simple beast with two light settings, two shutter speeds, and four focusing modes. Shooting with its plastic 60mm f/8 lens, you'll get images with soft focus, blurred or trailing colors, and heavy vignetting.

Or try a similar gadget, the Diana. Another plastic roll-film snapper, the Diana fell out of production in the 1970s, but it has been resurrected as the Diana Mini-35mm and the Diana +. The latter boasts a panorama mode and can even be turned into a pinhole camera.

For modern takes on retro photography, check out plastic cameras such as the Blackbird Fly 35mm. Or you might want to look into apps like Instagram for smartphones.

Professional photographers love to modify cheap cameras for uniquely peculiar or pretty results. "The more you beat up a Holga, the better the pictures," says lo-fi expert Liad Cohen. "Don't be afraid to drop the camera a few times."

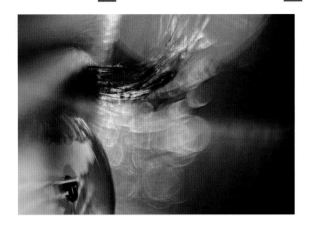

258 GO FOR BOKEH

Most photographers obsess about sharpness, but there's an equally passionate subset concerned about unsharpness. Its holy grail? Beautiful *bokeh*. This Japanese word translates roughly as "the quality of blur or haze," and it refers to defocused areas in front of or behind a sharp subject, usually formed from defocused points of light. Desirable bokeh shows these circular highlights as creamy soft and smooth-edged.

To get a bokeh effect, find a subject dotted with small light sources, then screw on a lens with an aperture made up of many blades. Put your camera on a tripod, set a large aperture, and opt for shallow depth of field to render your subject sharply. It will contrast nicely with the heavenly blurry background.

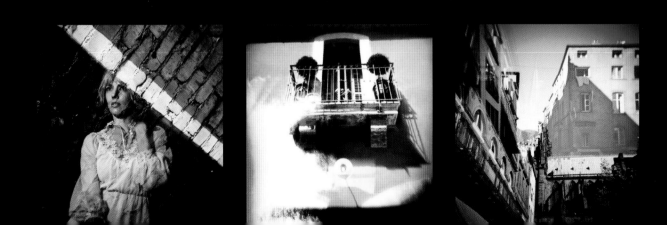

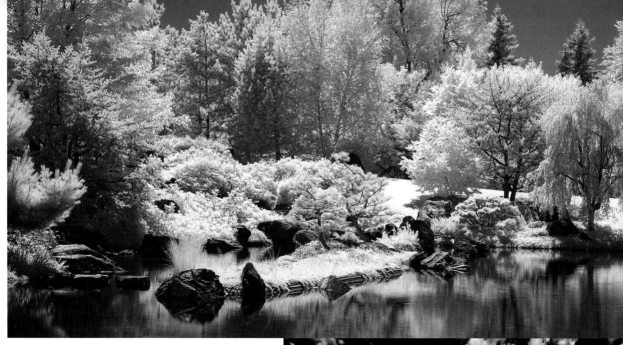

259

CONSIDER THE REALM OF INFRARED

Infrared (IR) light falls outside the narrow band of the light spectrum visible to human eyes, but some digital cameras, especially older ones, can detect it. IR photos reveal a dreamlike alternative reality of dark daytime skies, snow-white foliage, and ice-colored grass.

If you want to explore the mysteries of IR, you'll need special gear. Most camera sensors have IR-blocking filters, but some older models' filters are weak or nonexistent. Unsure if your camera has one? Aim a TV remote control at your camera and click the shutter while you press one of the remote's buttons. If the remote's signal light appears in the picture, you're set to shoot in IR. If not, buy a cheap used digital camera with a wimpy IR-blocking filter. If you shoot with that filter in place, dribbles of infrared will make it through to your sensor. To let more IR light in, get an IR-pass filter for your lens: It blocks visible light so only IR strikes the camera sensor. You can also use an IR-filter removal service for a few hundred dollars.

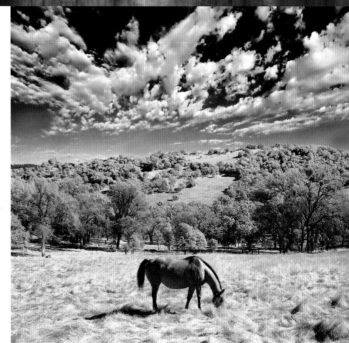

260

SHOOT WITH IR FILM

Yes, it's still on the market, and beloved by many for its eerie vintage look. Each brand has a particular level of sensitivity to IR as well as visible and ultraviolet light. In general, it is more sensitive than other film, so use a changing bag to load and unload it, and never put it through airport X-ray machines.

261 SET UP THE IDEAL IR SHOT

Landscapes are perfect for infrared shots. Because of the contrast between what we expect to see in the natural world and what the camera actually "sees," landscapes make the strongest IR subjects.

STEP ONE Ponder your composition. Set your camera on a tripod, as your exposures will be lengthy ones—1/2 to 30 sec or longer at about f/5.6, depending on your camera. (Don't add the IR-pass filter yet. It's dark, so you can't focus through it.) Compose per standard landscape-photo rules: Employ the Rule of Thirds (see #060), ensure you have strong leading lines, and choose a potent focal point. Now you can thread the IR-pass filter onto your lens.

STEP TWO Set manual white balance. For phantom-pale foliage, set it using a green target, such as grass.

STEP THREE Set exposure. Meter in evaluative mode (see #016), erring toward underexposure. Use a midrange aperture and low ISO. High ISO will make shots noisy.

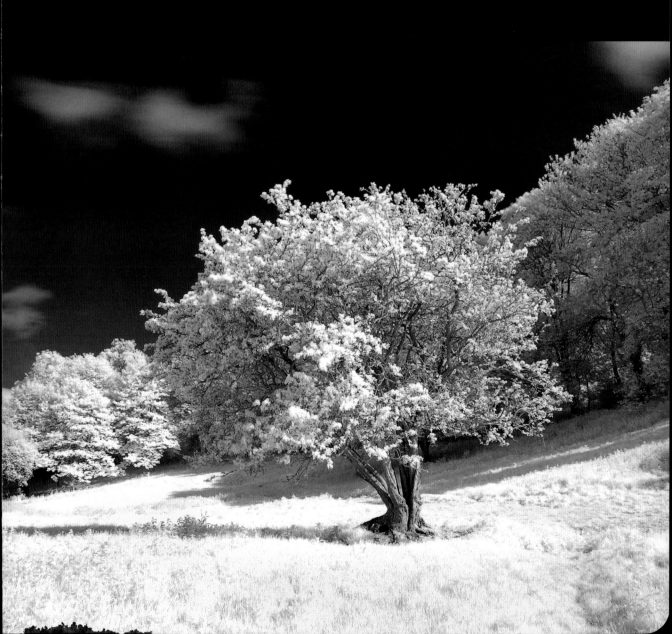

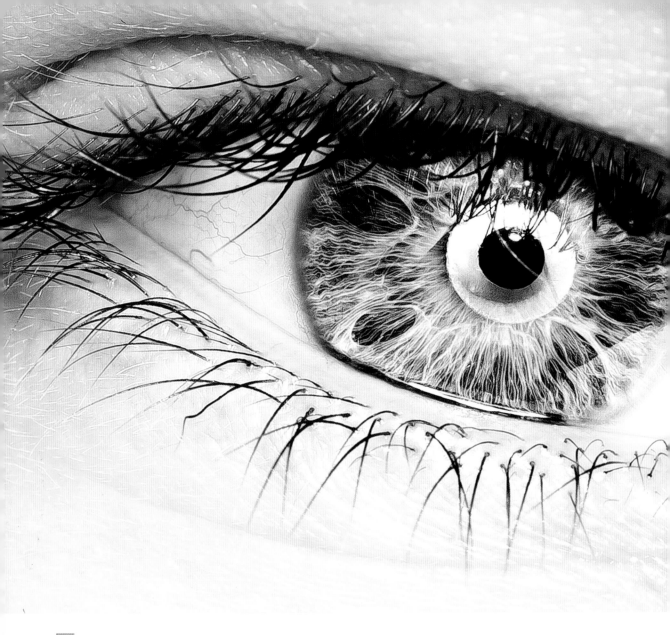

262 PRESERVE PUPILS

Eyes are often the first features we notice in portraits, and, subliminally, they strongly influence our emotional reactions. But as important as the eye is overall, the pupil is the real power player. In fact, a science called pupilometrics demonstrates that our pupils dilate to mimic the pupil diameter of anyone we see in person or in photos. Tests also show that people prefer photos—whether of animal or human eyes—in which pupils are dilated.

So if you're after a pleasing portrait, avoid bright, pupil-contracting lights. Instead, try sidelighting or place your lights above or below your subject, which both produces a subtler, more flattering portrait and protects the alluring look of a widely dilated pupil. Of course, you can always adjust the diameter of a pupil, or emphasize the pupil-to-iris contrast, in post-processing work (see #356), but it's less work to preserve attractive pupils while you're shooting.

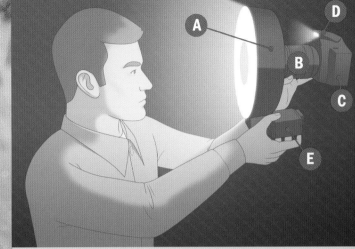

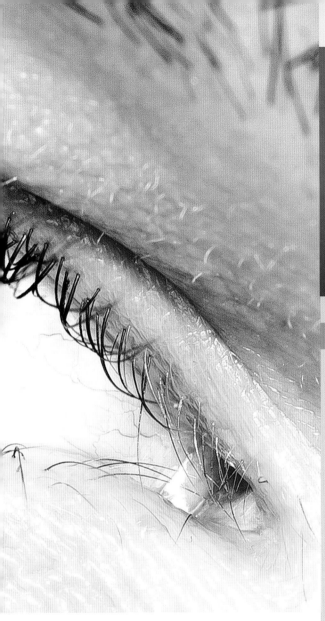

263 MAKE YOUR OWN RING FLASH

The foundation of your photography—your eye—can also make for a compelling subject. For excellent eye shots, a macro ring flash may be your best choice: Mounted around the lens, it evenly illuminates the eye so every detail is bright and shadow-free. But ring flashes can be pricey, so resolutely self-reliant photographer David Becker crafted a homemade one that cost less than US$10 to make—and produced this awesome portrait of his own blue iris.

To immortalize your peepers, follow his lead. Becker lined an angel-food cake pan (A) with tinfoil, and then taped wax paper over the pan's front for diffusion. The hole in the pan's center was big enough to admit the macro lens (B) on his DSLR (C), which had a built-in pop-up flash (D). Using tin snips, he cut a hole in the pan's side, lined it with duct tape, and poked a shoe-mount flash head (E) through the hole. When he was set up and ready to shoot, the camera's pop-up flash triggered the flash head's optical slave to illuminate the ring light. He shot at 1/60 sec at f/13, ISO 200. Patience was key: Becker took dozens of autofocused test shots to position the circular catchlight on his pupil. Afterward, he worked in Adobe Lightroom to enhance contrast, adjust cropping, and finesse the image.

264 AVOID RED-EYE

Many cameras use a flickering flash (the anti-red-eye function) to control the way flash tends to turn human eyes demonic. But the flash can be more annoying than useful. If you must use it, keep it off camera and as far away from the lens as possible. The closer a flash is to a lens's optical axis, the more likely red-eye is to occur. Another tip that may help: Ask your model to look slightly to the left or right of the lens, not directly into it.

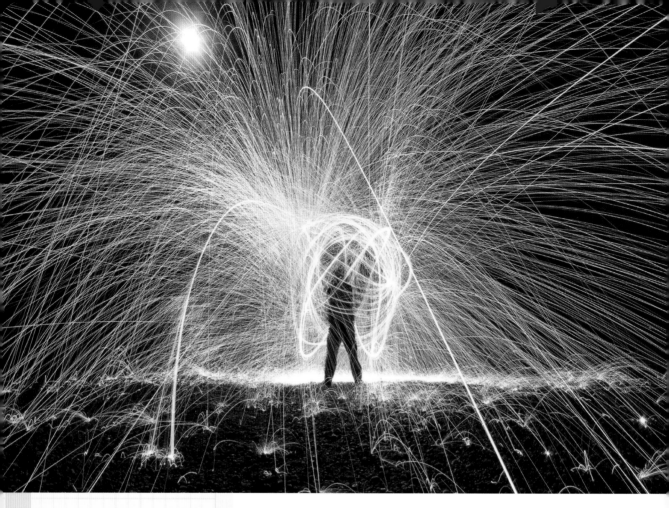

We drove for hours to Deception Pass, hoping to capture a beautiful sunset. The weather began to go south, so we switched gears. This was the first time any of us had tried "spinning"—the biggest challenge was not catching on fire. A ball of flaming steel wool came flying at me and set the backpack next to me on fire. I focused on the shot while my friend stomped out the blaze.

—LISA MOORE

265 PAINT WITH LIGHT

Cook up phantasmagoric light paintings with simple ingredients: a ball of superfine (grade 0 or lower) steel wool, a kitchen whisk, a long but lightweight chain, and a nine-volt battery—plus a bit of bravery. Choose a calm, dark night and an isolated spot free of flammable litter, leaves, and bystanders. Lacking that, stand on a wet tarp or even in shallow water. If you're feeling adventuresome, try an abandoned tunnel for maximum spark bounce and glow. Don a protective brimmed hat, long sleeves, and gloves, and turn your attention to your camera.

Set it on a tripod and start with a slow shutter speed—try 30 sec—an aperture of about f/8, and an ISO of 200 (play around with effects as you work). Use an LED or flashlight as your stand-in so you can focus on its light. Then switch the camera to its manual setting, stuff the wool inside the whisk, and hook the whisk's handle to the chain end. Rub the wool with the battery, and watch sparks erupt. Now it's show time, so hit the spot you prefocused on. Spin the chain around your head, carve flaming circles in the air, or experiment with angular and curving movements. When you're done, put out errant sparks.

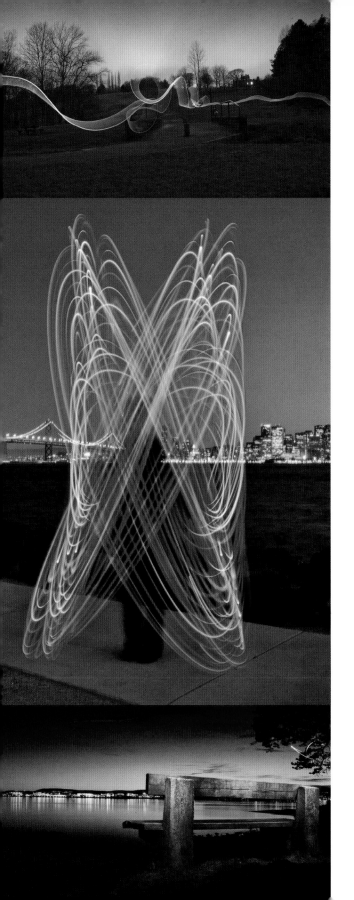

266 DRAW WITH A FLASHLIGHT

To create scintillating tapestries of lights such as the ones shown here, you need a tripod-mounted camera, a flashlight, and a dark spot where passersby won't blunder into your long-exposure shot. (If you're inside, turn off the lights and draw the drapes tightly to stop light leak.)

First focus on your subject, then stop down to a medium aperture in manual exposure. Shine the flashlight on the subject and check the meter reading for a rough exposure time, then set your camera to Bulb or 30 sec. More time produces brighter lights; less makes for darker ones. Now trip the shutter and go wild.

Run your flashlight over your subject, "painting" it with lines and loops of light. Moving quickly produces a brushlike streak, while going slowly or revisiting a spot produces interestingly blown-out blur. You can even draw on your sensor by aiming the flashlight directly at your lens, tracing shapes in the air or spelling out words. Make like a kid with a sparkler and have big fun with light!

267 KNOW YOUR LIGHTBRUSHES

Various flashlights generate different colors of light. Mix and match them, or tape colored gels over their lights if you hanker for a hue a flashlight can't produce. (Or seek out one of the marketplace's several wands or tools designed specifically for lightpainting adventures.)

Once you've got the hang of light painting, experiment with LEDs instead of flashlights: Wire them onto a moving model, or tie them to strings that an assistant can swing in smooth, painterly arcs in front of your camera. You can also play with your locations: Try running your lightbrush around the inside of a tunnel, "write" a caption over a landmark such as a skyscraper or bridge, or paint a colored glow on stationary objects such as the bench at left.

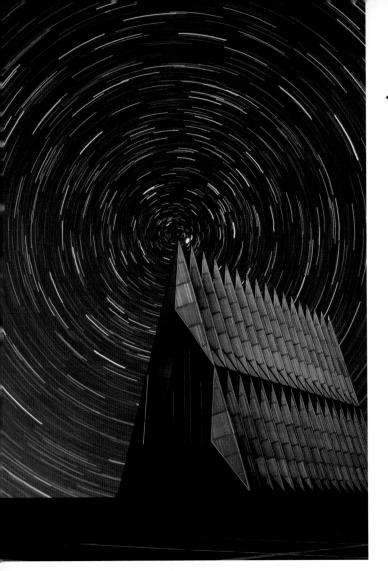

268 PHOTOGRAPH STAR TRAILS

If you use a sufficiently long exposure, the rotation of the earth makes stars, planets, and the moon seem to spin in the sky. To capture the celestial ballet of star trails, you need a dark, clear night far from city lights. You also need a camera capable of long exposure (one with a B, or Bulb, setting, or long exposure settings from 30 sec to several hours). Bring new or freshly charged batteries—keeping shutters open for hours sucks batteries dry.

Then head out into the night. Set your camera on a fixed tripod that you secure in place to defend against squiggly star trails. A wide-angle lens produces the best results. To show scale, compose a shot that includes a foreground element such as a barn or tree, and set ISO between 400 and 800—high enough to record dim stars, but low enough to prevent noise. Choose a medium aperture, f/5.6 to f/11; smaller ones reduce "sky glow" from nearby towns. Use a remote release, set focus manually, focus on infinity (put a bit of masking tape on the lens's focus ring to hold it in place), and open the shutter. Leave it open as long as you like. Remember: Long exposures produce long star trails, but also pick up more sky glow.

269 SHOOT THE MOON

Planning is everything when it comes to great moon shots—of both the NASA and the photographic kind. Start off by picking the phase that beguiles you most. Are you after an artful crescent? Or the wow factor of the full monty? Do some research to pick a night with the kind of moon you seek.

While you're at it, check the sun, too. The best time to capture the moon is 10 to 20 minutes before sunrise or after sunset. The moon is distinct if it is visible at all then, but there's still enough light to capture detail in the foreground. Not sure in which direction you should orient your gear? A full moon will be opposite the sun (in the east at dusk and the west at dawn).

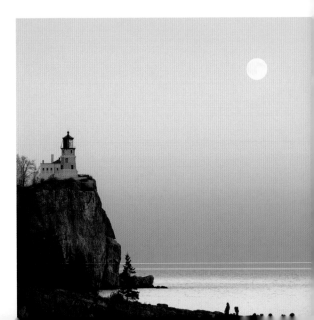

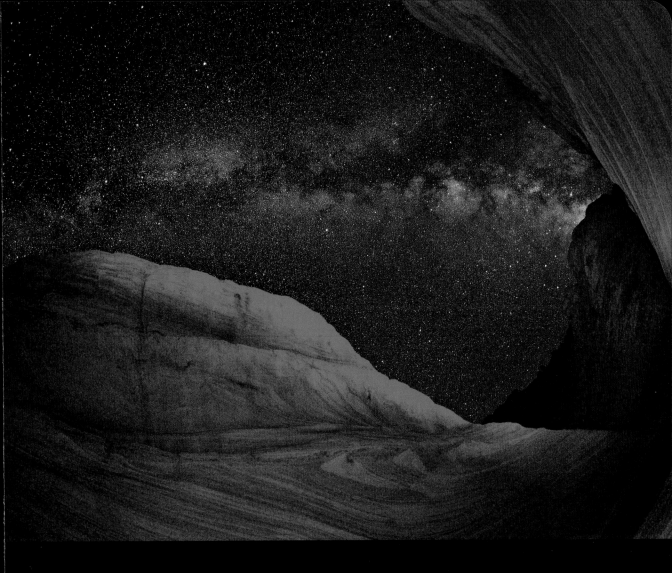

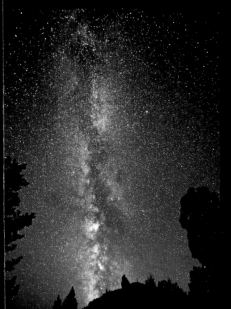

270 CAPTURE STARS WITHOUT TRAILS

Sometimes you'll want to take an image of stars as we actually see them in the sky, without any trails. To do so, use a fast lens, one with a large (f/1.4, f/1.8, f/2, or f/2.8) maximum aperture. As with star-trail images, include an intriguing landform or structure in the foreground for scale and contrast. The same setup rules apply, too: Use a sturdy tripod, a remote release, and an ISO of 400 to 800. For the best illumination of your foreground, shoot when the full (or nearly full) moon is just beginning to rise in the east. Aim your camera west, away from the moon, so the moonlight will light up foreground objects without washing out the brilliant stars.

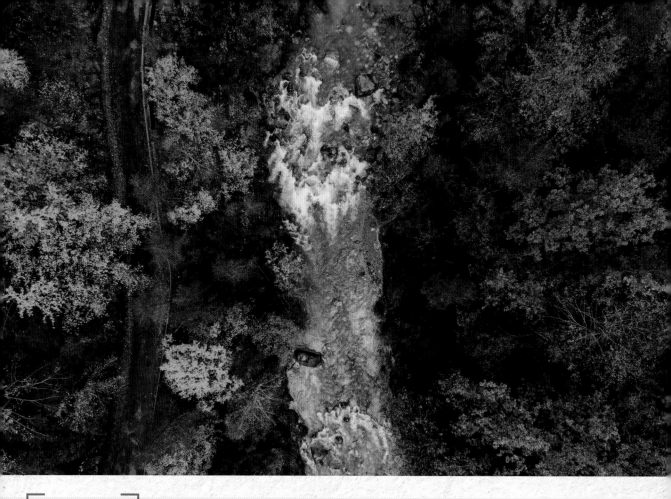

271 PREPARE FOR TAKEOFF

One of the most exciting recent developments in photography has been the surge in affordable, entry-level-use drones. Whether you buy or rent a model with a built-in camera or one robust enough to safely carry your DSLR onboard, heed this advice before your first liftoff.

☐ **KNOW THE LOCAL LAWS** Be they for recreational or professional use, unmanned aerial vehicles are currently the focus of rapidly changing legislation; much of what you can and can't do depends on where you live. It's likely there are height restrictions and no-fly zones around airports, military bases, and even some parks or wildlife preserves near you, as well as rules protecting the privacy and safety of those on the ground. Check your national and local aviation authorities to understand your legal parameters and obligations, and always keep an eye of sight on your drone.

☐ **PRACTICE YOUR PILOTING** It's crucial that you practice taking off, maneuvering, and landing your drone before attempting to shoot photos with it. Start outside in a wide, open space far from people, bodies of water, and electrical lines. If you sense a crash coming, kill the throttle immediately to reduce the chance of damage.

☐ **CHECK THE WEATHER REPORT** No taking your drone out into high wind or thunderstorms—unless you want its last photo to be one of its own demise.

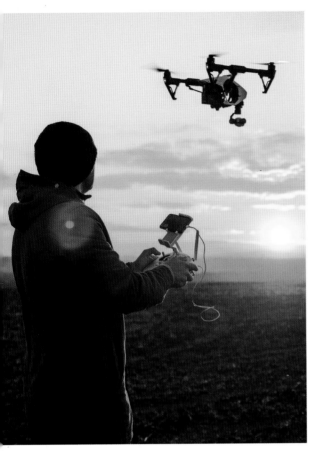

272 AUGMENT YOUR AERIAL PHOTOGRAPHY KIT

Your drone will likely come equipped with a handheld transmitter that commands altitude, rotation, and horizontal motion; it may also allow for remote control of auto or manual exposure, Raw capture, time lapse, and more. Some of these stream video or link up with a smartphone app to give you a glimpse of the ground from above, letting you tweak composition. (If you aren't working with a built-in camera, you'll likely need to purchase a separate transmitter that feeds footage to a smartphone app or portable monitor.) For those interested in nighttime aerial photography, there are lightweight spotlights and landing lights to help illuminate the scene below.

One important (though expensive) addition you can make to your setup is a gimbal: a stabilization system that pivots to keep the camera level as the aircraft moves, eliminating shake and blur. Another practical purchase is a set of propeller guards, which prevent the delicate blades from hitting the ground while still spinning.

Above all, it's wise to invest in multiple batteries, as even short flights can deplete power rapidly. (Seek out a drone that automatically returns to you when power dips dangerously low, rather than just dropping out of the sky.)

273 SNAG THE BEST DRONE SHOTS

Once you're airborne, how do you capture arresting images? Start by screwing on a short lens, as long lenses can unbalance the drone or shoot its landing gear. You'll need to set your focal length while the camera is on the ground, so a fast prime works nicely. Wide apertures will be able to focus on a large swath of landscape, while shutter speeds of 1/500 sec or faster will freeze the scene as your machine buzzes above.

The most dramatic shots tend to be bird's-eye-view captures (instead of three-quarter angles, which can often look as if they were taken from land). Learning to hover your drone is key to these photos—try GPS or loiter mode, which lets you go hands-free while the drone maintains position over a subject.

As for subjects, sweeping landscapes or graphic urban views are crowdpleasers—they compress nicely into graphic studies of form and color. But don't forget the quotidian scenes that might be happening in your backyard. Even a view of life pool- or grill-side from a mere 10 feet (3 m) might prove compelling drone fodder.

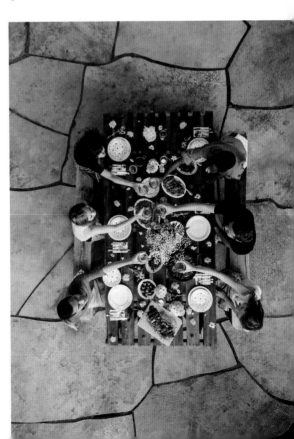

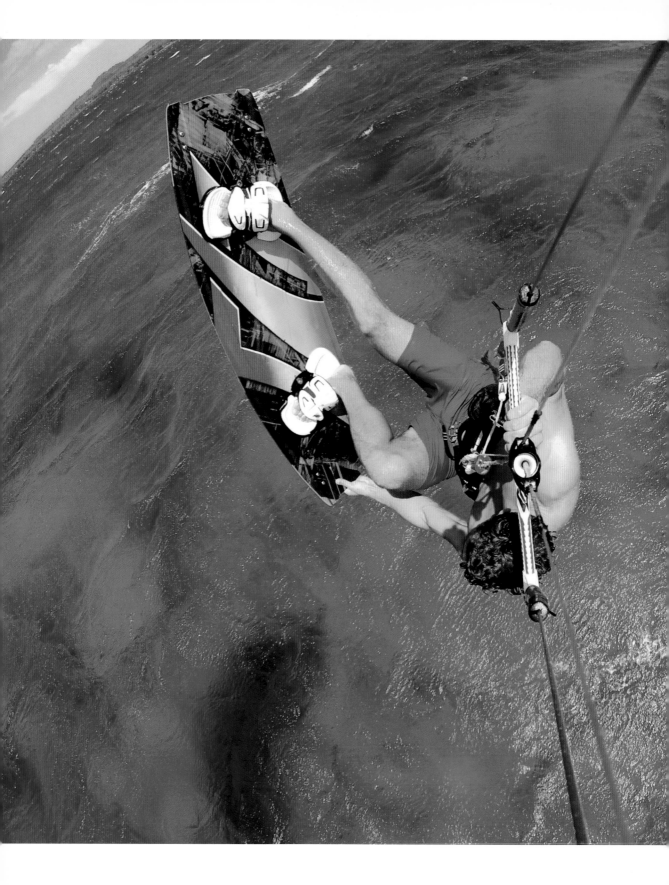

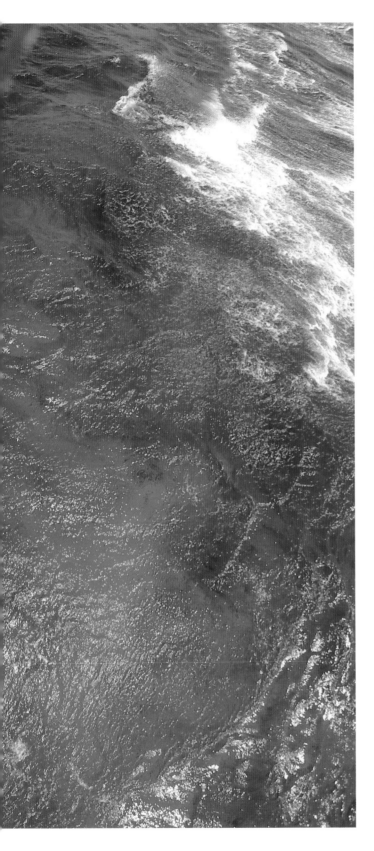

274 ROCK OUT WITH AN ACTION CAM

These incredibly portable, lightweight yet rugged little cameras took the extreme sports world by storm, and since then have won over amateur and pro photographers of all tastes. Typically outfitted with a ½-inch (1.25-cm) sensor, a fixed lens of a short focal length, and several field of view options, today's action cams can generate single and burst-mode stills at a resolution of about 12 megapixels, plus smooth timelapses and 4K video at frame per second rates above 100. Some action cams come complete with fancy yet miniaturized LCD and menu displays; others are no frills affairs with a dead simple viewfinder and a single button for all functions. Most have wireless capability for easy sharing and remote control and viewing, too.

Specifications aside, the fun with these gizmos is all in the mounts and surprising angles that they afford. You can strap one to a helmet to document gnarly snowboard feats or to your handlebars to chronicle an epic mountain biking session, or suction-cup one to a car window for a timelapse of your road trip. Even pets can get in on the fun with action cams clipped to their collars. (So *that's* what Fido does all day.) Since most models come housed in a waterproof casing, you can also take them surfing, kayaking, or just splashing around in the pool. These cameras' small sizes also allow you to position them in out-of-the-way vantage points where you couldn't fit a standard camera—like on the undercarriage of a kiteboard rig, as shown here.

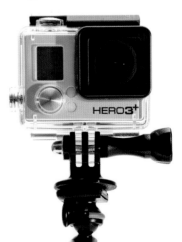

275

SEE THINGS IN BLACK AND WHITE

Photographers revere B&W because it emphasizes form and heightens drama. Today's cameras can produce digital monochromes as beautiful as those created in wet darkrooms—but first you must shoot the right subjects.

Learn to "see" in monochrome by visualizing tones, or degrees of brightness, rather than colors. Even contrasting hues—red flowers against green leaves, for example—might be the same gray when they're rendered in B&W. With practice, you'll be able to anticipate how the elements of your composition will appear relative to one another once the color is removed. Photographers describe tonal ranges in terms of separation and contrast. If one element is significantly brighter or darker than another, contrast is high and the elements will be well separated when rendered in B&W. When contrast is low and elements are similarly toned, they'll mesh together in B&W. Search, too, for compelling elements such as lines, curves, and patterns.

A contradictory-sounding B&W rule is that you get the best images by shooting in color. So ignore the camera's B&W mode and shoot in Raw. Raw files contain all the data from the image sensor, and they let you (not the camera) decide on brightness, contrast, and tone. With all that original color data, you can create tonal separations and make edits such as darkening blue skies or softening skin tones.

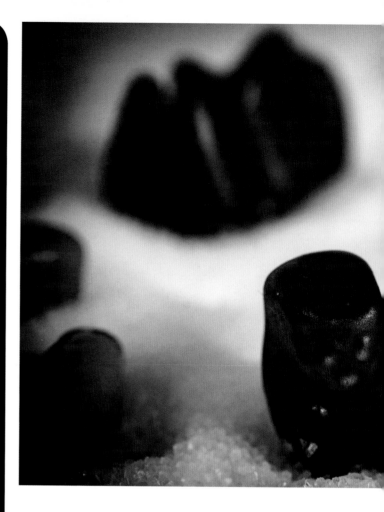

276 TETHER YOUR CAMERA TO YOUR COMPUTER

Tethered photography—shooting with a DSLR hooked to a computer—is a versatile way to preview, save, and tweak photos as you work. You need a camera that you can connect to a computer via USB cable, plus compatible software such as Adobe Photoshop Lightroom. Onscreen you'll see a true preview of color and tone (if your monitor is color-corrected), and because the screen is bigger than any camera's LCD, you'll have a broad canvas to check focus and ensure you've properly captured your subject. Tethering also lets you save photos to both hard drive and memory card as you shoot, so you're instantly backed up. Better still, you can process all Raw files in real time. First try tethered shooting with a simple setup at home. Later, you can venture into the field, where accessories from laptop-supporting tripod mounts to daylight-cutting screen hoods are real boons.

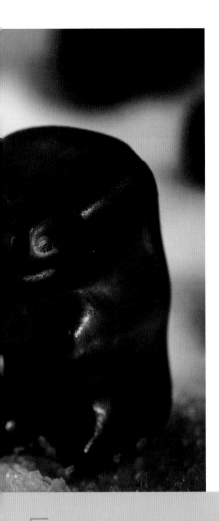

277 TRY A TETHERED STILL LIFE

Tethering allows you to view labor-intensive compositions, such as the eerie gummy-bear picnic at left, on your computer screen as you shoot.

STEP ONE Hook your DSLR to a computer with a USB cable. Launch Adobe Lightroom. Go to File > Tethered Capture > Start Tethered Capture. Fill in the session name and destination and choose a metadata template. Add keywords to tag shots, and click OK. The tethered toolbar will appear first.

STEP TWO Click the toolbar's shutter button (not the camera's), and the image zips into Lightroom on the computer. (The toolbar also shows exposure and white balance settings, but change them only on camera.)

STEP THREE Shoot until your exposure settings and lighting look right. Don't worry about composition yet; just develop an image that will help you create the final product. Now click to select the last properly exposed photo you've shot, and switch to the Development module. Process the image as you would a Raw file—pump up vibrancy, tweak white balance, or add vignette. Hide the tethered toolbar as you work via Ctrl + T.

STEP FOUR Create a preset with your current settings: Click the plus sign at the Presets panel's top right, then Check All so all adjustments you made to your image will apply to subsequent ones. Name and save the preset.

STEP FIVE Type E to go into Loupe View in the Library. Ctrl + T restores the tethered toolbar. In Develop Settings, pick presets via the pulldown menu. Lightroom applies these settings to any new images, so you'll easily see how framing and lighting alterations will affect your final, ideal photo.

278 BUILD A SMARTPHONE TRIPOD MOUNT

MOBILE TIP

You can buy a zillion tabletop and pocket tripod accessories, including mounts and adapters, to steady a smartphone for clear shots. Many let you clip your phone to just about any tripod out there. But making your own versatile mount is easy and fun, via DIY tricks that range from simple to complex. One basic method involves cutting two 1-inch (2.5-cm) notches on either side of a paper cup, then tearing away the narrow flap of paper between them on both sides. The resulting slots provides a place to rest your phone. Another simple method just requires two binder clips: Fasten both binder clips to one of your phone's longer edges, then fold back the metal loops and balance the phone on their legs. What else do you have lying around that could make a good ad hoc tripod?

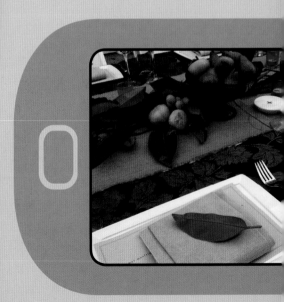

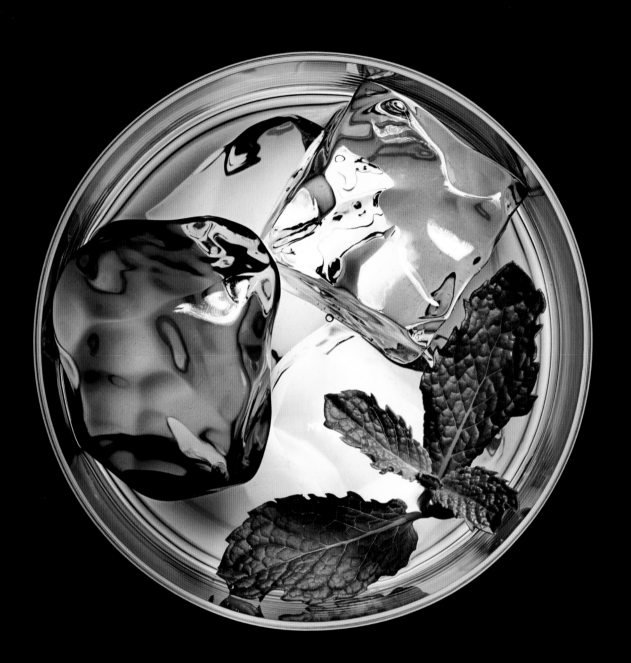

279 MIX UP A DRINK SHOT

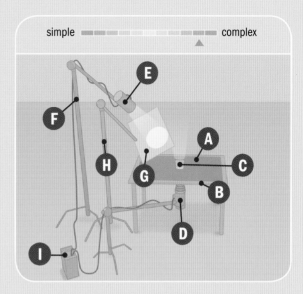

simple ▬▬▬▬▬▬▬▬▬▬ complex

This whiskey smash, shot by liquids specialist Teru Onishi, looks good enough to sip, doesn't it? And this photograph is even more intoxicating when you know that he styled and shot it—one of 25 he photographed for a magazine cocktail roundup—in under seven minutes. (The whole shoot took just five hours.) As a kicker, he did almost no postprocessing work.

Two-light simplicity helped Onishi hold his liquor—and turn it into an artful shot. First, he sliced a tumbler-sized hole in a sheet of black cardboard (A) with a craft knife and placed it on a table topped with translucent acrylic (B). Setting the tumbler (C) on the hole, he put a strobe (D) under the table, almost touching it, to emphasize the brilliantly hued beverage. Then he adjusted the strobe's angle until he captured an appetizing yellow-to-amber color gradation. Left of the table, he attached a top strobe (E) to a light stand (F) and positioned another translucent acrylic square (G) on a second light stand (H) just below that strobe. To minimize flare and produce the shortest possible flash duration, he dialed in the lowest output on the power pack (I) fueling both strobes.

Onishi carefully studied the distance between the cocktail and the diffusion panel above it, tweaking position for nicely sized reflections in the ice cubes, as well as the distance between the panel and the strobe over it to adjust the intensity of light falling on the drink. Finally, he angled the top strobe to cast hard light on the cubes and generate strong reflections.

Want to try some light mixology at home? Aim for straight-up success by carefully observing how a light's placement affects your subject, and then adjusting its position patiently and methodically. Cheers!

280 FAKE ICE CUBES

Most of us can't whip up a drink shot as fast as Teru Onishi. One of the pitfalls: Ice cubes melt quickly under hot lights, especially when a complex setup takes time to construct.

That's where fake ice comes in. You'll find acrylic cubes in stores, but making your own is far cheaper. Buy clear plastic beads from a craft store and pour them into a metal (not plastic) ice-cube mold until each slot is three-quarters full. Ensure that no beads slop from one to the next. Melt the beads for 15 to 20 minutes in a preheated 375°F (190°C) oven. Remove the tray and let it cool. Pop the cubes free, scrape off unsightly edges, and plop them in a drink.

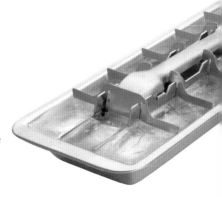

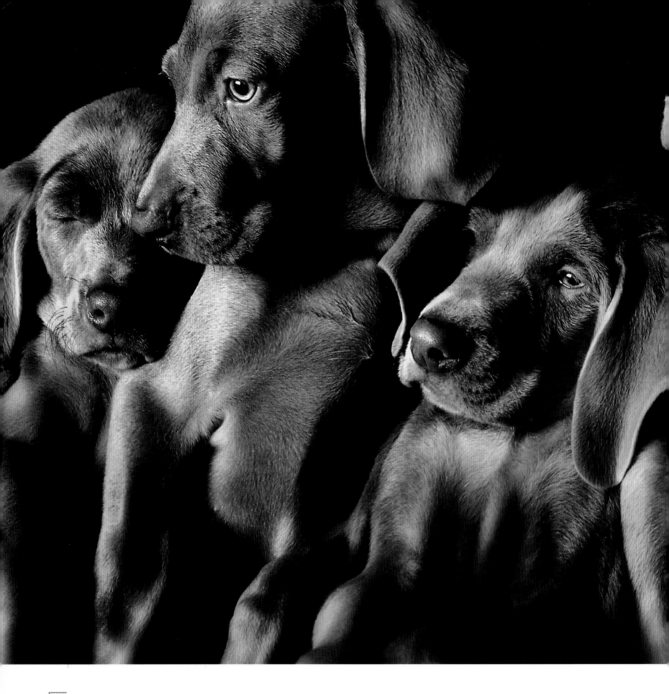

281 USE TREATS TO PHOTOGRAPH PUPPIES

For the best picture of your own pooch, he should be sitting still and fixing a loving gaze on you and your camera. Yet the younger the dog, the harder it is to coax out that look. One way to rivet his attention is by rubber-banding a strip of cooked bacon around your lens (protect it with plastic cling wrap first so things don't get too messy—and make sure the bacon's not too crispy, or it'll crumble). A dog whistle works, too, but prepare focus and exposure in advance: Most dogs pay attention to whistles for only about 15 seconds.

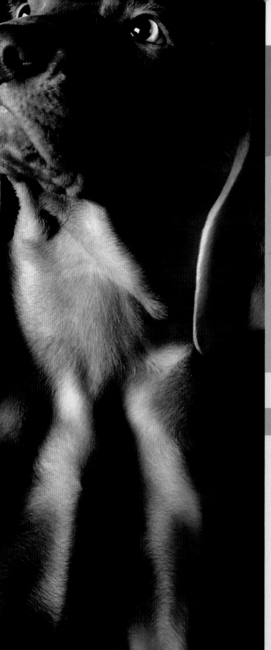

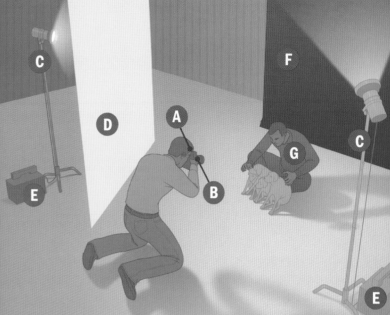

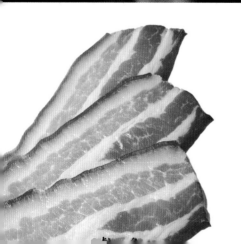

[BIG PROJECT]

282 CAPTURE THE SHINE OF CREATURES' COATS

Snapping adorable puppies is simple. You know what's hard? Making a portrait that conveys the color and sheen of their fur. Especially if you're shooting Weimaraners—made famous by photographer William Wegman, but notoriously nervous and subtle-hued. Pet pro Harry Giglio tackled the challenge with careful setup and lighting. If you'd like to do something similar, follow his example.

He mounted a flash trigger (A) on his camera (B) to wirelessly fire two strobe heads (C) framing the scene. He chose fast-firing, short-duration strobes to freeze the springy pups, mounting the lights on stands so they'd be out of the dogs' way. He placed one strobe behind a spun-glass diffusion panel (D) and shifted that strobe back and forth until he caught the fur's soft texture. He then bounced the other off the ceiling for fill. Power packs (E) drove both strobes, and Giglio selected a background of simple black fabric (F) that wouldn't cast a competing color on the dogs. Finally, a handler (G) helped with doggie wrangling.

283 SHOOT A PORTUGUESE MAN-OF-WAR

Photographer Paul Marcellini captured this Portuguese man-of-war using a simple setup and process that you can borrow when photographing any small aquatic creature, from fish to frogs.

STEP ONE Construct a tank. Buy a 5-gallon (19-L) aquarium and line three of its sides with translucent white plastic, which will transform the tank into a water-filled softbox (leave the front pane clear so that you can shoot through it). Take your rig to your site, then ready the tank by filling it with the water the creature prefers, be it fresh or sea. Cloudy water will wreck your shot, so be sure it's clear. Marcellini filtered seawater through a T-shirt to extract particulates.

STEP TWO Collect your animal. Marcellini carefully netted this jelly-like creature from the sand, avoiding its stinging tentacles. Tuck an extra, freestanding transparent pane in the tank to nudge your subject close to the front pane—for a sharply rendered image, you can't have much water between you and your subject. Let the creature float around in its new environs while you set up your gear.

STEP THREE Mount two accessory flash units—which you'll fire wirelessly—on light stands, and place one behind the tank and the other in front of it.

STEP FOUR Determine exposure. Set your shutter to maximum flash sync speed, and choose a low ISO and small aperture for depth of field. Start your flash units at full power, and find the rear flash's exposure by lowering its power until its light blows out the tank's white background. Then lower the front flash's power until it illuminates the subject without sacrificing color and detail.

STEP FIVE Shoot! Attach a macro lens to your camera so that you can sit some distance away from the tank. Otherwise, your rig could throw shadow on the animal. Keep your camera parallel to the tank's front pane to avoid distortion.

STEP SIX Release. Gently net your animal out of the tank and return it to its watery home.

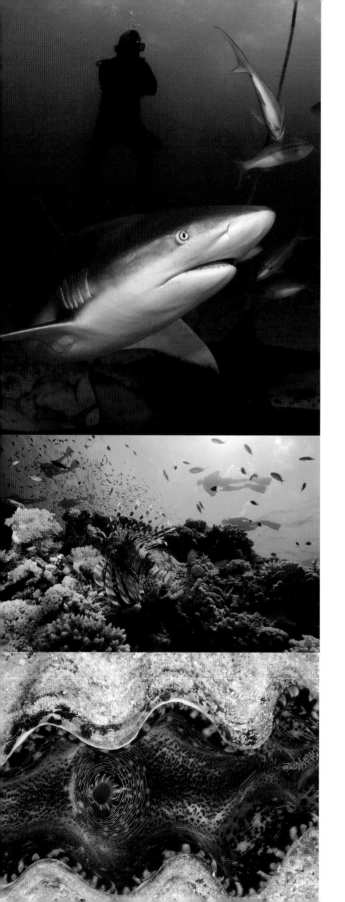

284 SWIM WITH SHARKS

Big carnivorous sharks are among the world's most intimidating photo subjects. If you're courageous enough for a potentially chewy photo session, pick a dive operator that's been in the business a long time, and ask about novice-friendly clear-water sites where you'll enjoy a dive cage's protection.

Not up to a photo-stalking a great white? Sweeter sharks make astonishing models, too. The endearingly polka-dotted (and huge) whale sharks that gather annually off Mexico's Yucatán coast are approachable filter feeders. Innumerable dive trips run you out to their grounds; most permit snorkels but not scuba gear. An ultrawide or fisheye lens helps your camera capture the majestic sweep of these gentle giants. Shoot near the surface so you don't need a flash.

285 PREPARE TO GO DEEP

Deepwater pros shoot in a tough environment and plan accordingly. Saltwater and high pressure eat up equipment, and light and color vanish speedily as you dive downward. But even nonpros can finagle fine scuba shots without costly gear.

PACK THE RIGHT STUFF. Bring a compact, but a DSLR with fast autofocus and a large sensor to admit maximum light is your best bet. You can buy or rent watertight housings: Top-end ones can cost thousands, but even entry-level versions often have protective O-rings, snap latches, external strobes, and interchangeable lens ports.

USE THE RIGHT LENS. Wide-angle lenses capture beautiful sweeps of sea, and macro lenses let you zoom in on tiny sealife. Bring both, and swap optics on the boat.

GET THE LAY OF THE SEA. Hire a guide to show you creatures' hidey-holes. Be patient—wait for shy animals such as eels to emerge, and shoot as many frames as you need to adjust lighting and angle. (See #288 for deepwater shooting tips.)

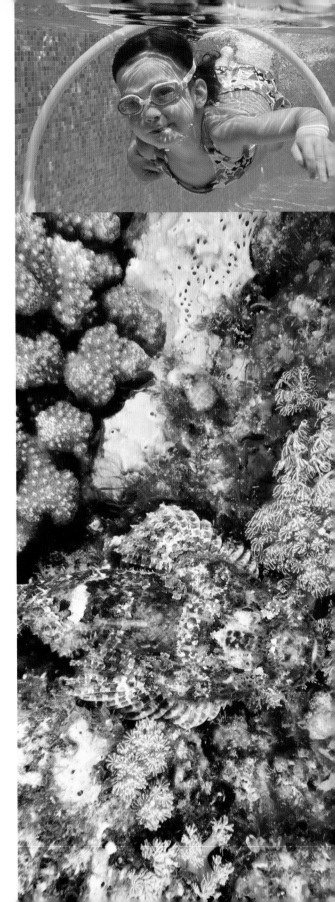

286

PLUNGE INTO THE POOL WITH A COMPACT

Waterproof compact cameras are perfect for casual pool shots, since they can capture both photos and video while totally submerged. To ensure that they'll produce awesome aquatic shots for you, swim close to your subject—light falls off faster underwater than in open air. A wide-angle lens with close-focus capability is a great pool buddy, but turn off your flash. It will create backscatter if waterborne particles intrude between you and your subject. Choose the right white balance, too—some compacts have several, because the WB that works in a pool flakes out under the sea. Composition underwater is challenging but fun: Aim at the bubble explosion that envelops a diver, or shoot a partially submerged, intriguingly distorted subject from just under the surface. Be sure to use your strap, or your camera might fall below its watertight limit—10 to 33 feet (3–10 m) for most models. Finally, rinse the camera with plain water after you towel off.

287

SNAP EASY SNORKELING SHOTS

So you're planning a Caribbean getaway and packing your camera for souvenirs of some heavenly underwater blue. Carry along some essential tips for open-water shots as well.

Your first secret weapon: Google Earth, which can tell you when the sun will rise perpendicular to your site or mask a reef in shadow. Now time your photo. Water reflects and refracts light, but different hues emerge at different times of day. Shooting in the early morning or late afternoon is a time-honored trick, but the "blue hour" around sunset yields astounding azures and fiery skies from below the water's surface. On a windless day, plunge into the shallows at high noon: The sun's rays dive straight down to illuminate Bahamian blues and the white-sand bottom. (To cut surface glare, keep a circular polarizer on your lens's end.) Finally, always bring a buddy; check your snorkel gear dockside; and never touch or stand on coral.

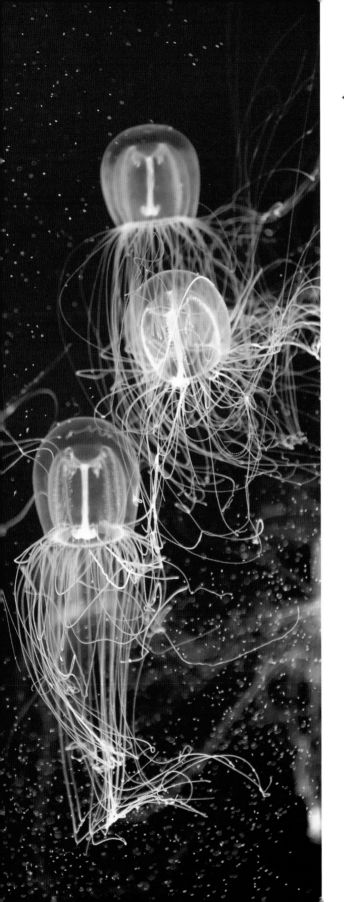

288 LIGHT AND SHOOT DEEPWATER PHOTOS

The moment you slip underwater, you've entered one of the most difficult shooting environments on earth. Yet the world under the waves also offers incredibly photogenic material, so dive right in. Just make sure that you properly light and shoot your aquatic subjects.

LIGHT UP THE SEA Underwater accessory lighting corrects the natural color skew of deep water, where reds look green and blues read as black. Paired external strobes—which should be powerful enough to compensate for the 1 stop of output lost with every 1 foot (30 cm) that light travels through water—and a remote trigger will help you overcome lighting challenges. Always bring extra batteries.

SEEK OUT MIXED LIGHT Shooting underwater is somewhat like studio work: The best shots combine ambient and strobe light. Start off in the shallows, where such mixing is easier, and hold off on depth work until you've found your sea legs. Watch out for excessive light as well, such as that reflected off schooling fish.

EXPOSE PROPERLY Shoot in Raw so that you can add missing color later via software. If your camera can't shoot Raw but does allow you to set white balance, use a warm setting to amp up reds and yellows. You can buy waterproof gray cards to check white balance at various depths.

HOOK YOUR FISH Don't chase sealife. It will simply swim away from you. Instead find a feeding or gathering point, and wait for the fish to approach. When you're shooting speedy animals—sharks, rays, dolphins—you'll probably get only one shot. Make it your best by presetting your strobe and camera settings, and then "track" the animal ahead along its trajectory. A good starting point is 1/250 sec. Shooting with a compact? Keep its shutter partially depressed, and pan with the fish so the camera doesn't need to hunt for focus.

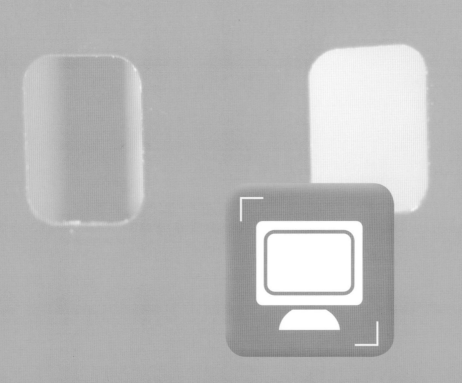

PROCESSING & BEYOND

289 KNOW YOUR IMAGE TOOLS

After you've composed and captured an excellent shot, perfect the final image with photo-editing software. From sweeping changes to barely noticeable adjustments, such programs' tools allow you to experiment with and control color, composition, contrast, exposure, resolution, sharpness, and image size—all the elements that define your final image. Here's a look at key image tools in Adobe Photoshop, the most popular program.

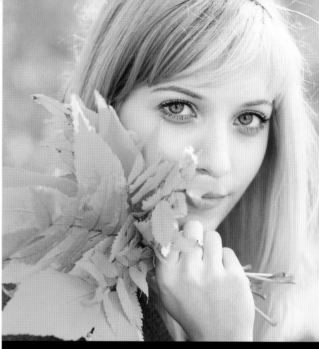

NOISE REDUCTION

New DSLRs have ever-wider ranges of ISO options. This capability makes shooting in low-light situations easy, but it also can make photos look grainy or "noisy." Eliminate or soften noise using the noise reduction tools in Adobe Camera Raw.

SHARPENING

Most digital images benefit from light sharpening—which helps to define lines and edges—though oversharpening can create noise.

IMAGE SIZE

You may want to reduce the size of an image so that it's small enough to email, but try to preserve image quality by shooting for the right size. For computer screens, you need at least 72 pixels per inch, while 300 ppi is ideal for printing.

SELECTIONS

Photoshop's selection tools let you delineate specific areas that you can then adjust without affecting the rest of your image. An especially useful tool is Quick Selection, which gives you a brush to "paint" a selection onto a photo. The Rectangular Marquee tool selects square or rectangular regions. And the Lasso selection tool ropes off sections of your image and allows you to finesse them individually or delete or reproduce them as you choose. Because you're drawing a circle around an area, you needn't fuss with anchor points—it's as easy as drawing a circle on paper.

COLOR

Color management tools allow you to remove, reduce, or add color casts; adjust saturation; add warmth; and adjust tones. A light touch works best. You can also create monochrome, sepia, and split-tone versions of your shots.

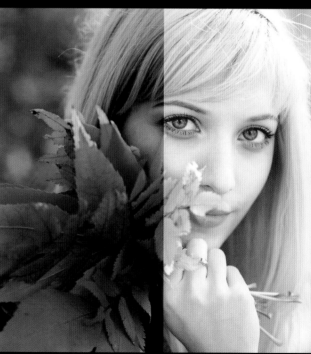

CONTRAST

Adjusting contrast makes a big difference to the impact of a photo. Used properly, it can change the mood of a picture—say, from moody to sunny.

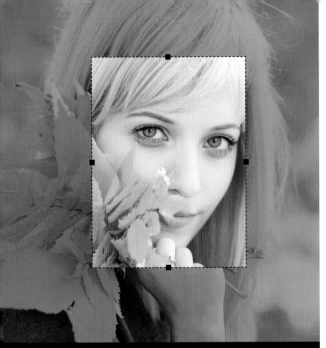

CONTENT-AWARE PATCH, FILL, AND MOVE

These tools seamlessly remove image content you don't want and fill in content that you do want, so you can retouch with great precision. And you can use Move to shift entire objects around your images.

MAGIC WAND

The Magic Wand selects similarly hued areas of images with a single tap. The tool grabs the area for you, so you don't have to trace its outline. Then you can fill that area with another color or fill pattern, or turn it black or white.

EYEDROPPER

Pick up a single color in your image with the Eyedropper—it can select down to a single pixel—and then use that color to paint in other areas of your photo.

SPOT HEALING BRUSH

This retouching tool is a fast way to remove flaws and smudges. It paints with pixels sampled from your photo, and then matches the texture, lighting, transparency, and shading of the sampled pixels to the pixels that you're "healing." For more precise control, choose the main Healing Brush tool.

CROPPING

The Crop tool is invaluable for getting the best possible composition and aspect ratio in your shots. Use it to make a horizontal image vertical or square or to straighten out skew. Keep in mind that you do lose resolution when you crop.

CLONE STAMP

Use this tool to paint part of your image over another section of the same image, or to paint part of one layer over another. It's a great way to duplicate objects and remove image flaws.

GRADIENT

This nifty tool gradually blends colors to smooth out your image. Make sure you select the desired area first, or Gradient will apply its fill to the whole active layer. You can select from preset gradient fills or create your own.

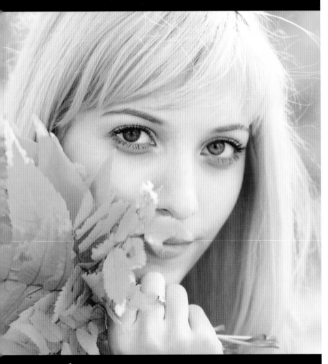

PAINT BUCKET

The Paint Bucket is a fill tool—you simply click a pixel of a color that you like, and the Bucket will fill up adjacent pixels that are similar in hue with the color you've chosen. You can select low or high tolerances so Photoshop knows which pixels to fill.

RETOUCHING

There are tools to tackle everything from cleaning up lens dust marks to eliminating red-eye, fixing lens distortion, and shifting depth of field.

simple ▬▬▬▬▬▬▬▬▬▬▬▬ complex

290 POLISH PHOTOS IN LIGHTROOM

Maybe you want a little more "snap" in a photo—or a more subdued rendition. Maybe you'd like to see more detail in that shadow—or drop it down to dead black. Welcome to post-production: the adjustment of an image after shooting. While you can get started in "post" with the software that came with your camera, the standard of image-editing software, Adobe Photoshop, has huge capabilities for correction, enhancement, and manipulation. Its cousin, Adobe Lightroom, has a simplified yet also powerful tool set that provides you with the ability to manage and edit your photos "nondestructively": It saves unedited originals that you can revert to, along with a record of every edit. Here's what a typical Lightroom workflow looks like.

STEP ONE Plug your memory card into your computer and open up Lightroom. When prompted, tell the application to copy your photos from the card and add them to a Lightroom catalog. Choose a destination on your computer or let Lightroom create a spot—just be sure you have all the photos that you would like to import selected with a checkmark. Click the import button and, if you like, organize them into a specific Collection.

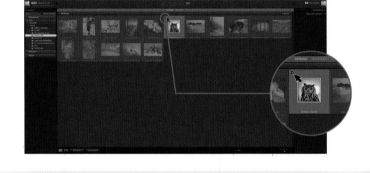

STEP TWO Time to edit. Click on the Develop tab at the top of your screen and head to one of the first things most photographers adjust in post: contrast. In most programs, contrast is handled with a slider. Move it to the right for more contrast; to the left for less. Fancier apps have a levels adjustment, which lets you set the black point (darkest) and white point (lightest) and stretches out the intermediate tonal range.

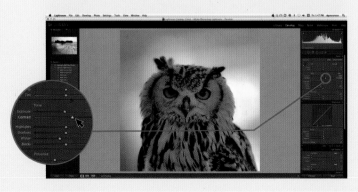

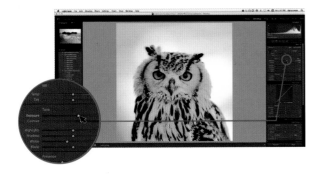

STEP THREE Adjust brightness. This is often called exposure, for good reason—it's the overall darkness or lightness of a photo. Look for a tone that you think should be right in the middle, and adjust the slider until you get it there. Then use the highlight slider to pull down the excess brightness, and the shadow slider to pull up detail in darker areas. You may not be able to restore full detail, however.

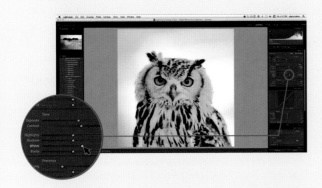

STEP FOUR Tackle color. Move the white balance slider to shift the photo to a more blue or amber look. You can opt for an accurate rendition—the color balance as you remember it—or to manipulate the hues to create a certain mood. While you may want to saturate the colors in vivid scenes (think Mardi Gras), excessive saturation will look very fake. Try lowering the saturation for a more subtle, low-key look.

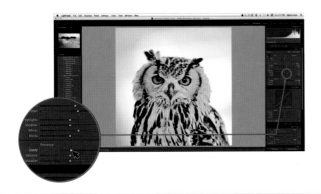

STEP FIVE Whether you shoot JPEGs or Raw, a default level of sharpening—a process by which objects' edges and textures are emphasized for increased definition—has been applied to your photos, so sharpen at your own peril. A little bit of sharpening may be okay if you plan to make a large print. Use the Clarity slider to adjust sharpening.

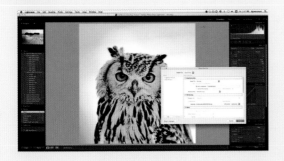

STEP SIX To save your edited image, you'll have to select File > Export. (Again, Lightroom keeps an original, so you aren't overwriting it.) To send over email or post online, save it as a JPEG and at 72 dpi (dots per inch), the standard for computer screens, and a modest size, say 5 by 7 inches (12.7 by 17.8 cm). When you hit Export, make sure you have selected the option to show in Finder, if you'd like to save it on your hard drive or desktop.

291 CUSTOMIZE PHOTOSHOP FOR OPTIMAL WORKFLOW

An efficient software work process is everyone's dream—we all have our pet workarounds and shortcuts. Luckily, there are loads of fresh ways to control and customize your interface. Why customize? Because it can make the program faster and even more efficient to use.

STEP ONE If your screen is a large or high-resolution one, Photoshop's default font might seem tiny. To enlarge it, go to Preferences > Interface. Under UI Text Options, choose UI Font Size: Large. (Restart Photoshop for changes to take effect.)

STEP TWO While you adjust Preferences, you can change the background color behind images if that helps you perceive your shots more clearly. Then click OK to save your changes.

STEP THREE You can also enlarge thumbnails. Right-click on the empty gray part of the Layers panel to see a menu, and choose Large Thumbnails.

STEP FOUR Display only the panels you use regularly. If you use, say, Adjustments, Layers, and History often, keep only those visible. You can also choose a preset in the dropdown menu in the top right corner of your screen. Essentials is a great place to start.

STEP FIVE You also needn't see every menu item Photoshop offers. To pick the ones you want, go to Edit > Menus and click the eye icon to show or hide a given item.

STEP SIX Create or customize your own shortcuts—click the Keyboard Shortcuts tab to edit them. Choose the menu item that you want to access faster, and type the keyboard command you would like to use to activate it.

STEP SEVEN When you have your interface set up as you want it, save it. Go to Window > Workspace > New Workspace. Name it, and check the boxes to save Keyboard Shortcuts and Menus, too.

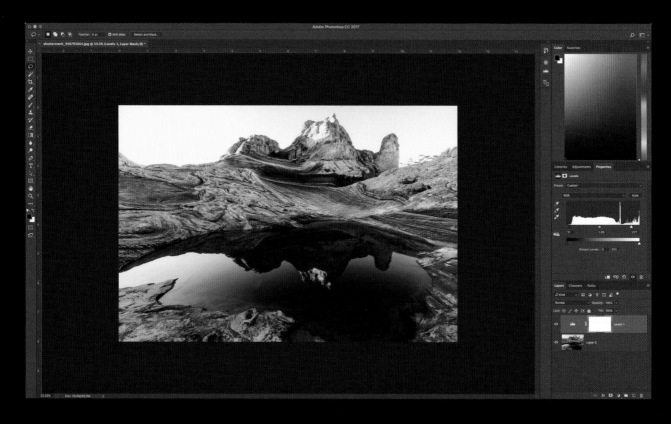

292 OPTIMIZE A COMPUTER FOR EDITING PERFORMANCE

From the drive to the display, a high-performance setup is crucial to successful retouching. If you're shopping around, here's what to look for:

THE RIGHT COMPUTER makes photo-editing software sing. Look for lots of processing power, which means plenty of speed, as expressed in gigahertz (GHz), and a multiprocessor, or multicore, system. Random-access memory (RAM) is another crucial factor, since that's where Photoshop performs most of its calculations. Next time you're working on a large image, check Efficiency in the bottom left corner. If you see a rating of 95 percent or higher, your software is running in RAM, and you're all good. But if it drops to 80 percent or lower, add more RAM to your system.

THE DISPLAY OR MONITOR on which you view your images is also essential. Monitors are primarily made using one of three LCD technologies. Most mainstream displays are twisted nematic (TN); higher-end displays use in-plane switching (IPS). With TN, you see color corruption when you view the screen from any angle besides straight on. IPS displays are wide-view and show more consistent and accurate color across the panel. For improved color accuracy, LED backlight technology is key. Profiling your monitor to get greater color accuracy and accurate black- and white-point balance is also important (use a monitor-profiling package and a calibrating device that attaches to your screen). Some high-end displays have wider color gamuts than consumer-level monitors, which stay calibrated for much longer.

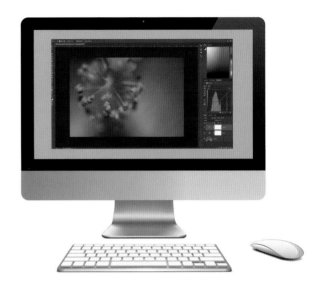

293 PROTECT YOUR PICTURES

If you've ever suffered a computer crash or lost images due to chaotic file organization, you know how vulnerable data can be. That's why you need a *digital asset management* (DAM) system to easily organize, efficiently edit, and safely store your photos. Adobe Lightroom is one of the most popular options, as it allows you to import, convert from Raw, do basic improvements in a nondestructive fashion, organize and archive, and batch print. There's also Phase One Capture One, which is comparable to Lightroom, and Daminion Server, which allows multiple users to access and edit the same images. Look for a tool that allows you to make collections, control versions, store on the cloud (see #353), and add keywords, tags, and ratings for speedy recovery.

294 SAMPLE A SCRUBBY SLIDER

Besides customization, Photoshop's interface has other secrets. Scrubby sliders are among the coolest. Mouse over the word that precedes a number box, such as the word Opacity in the Layers panel, and you'll see a pointing finger with a left- and right-pointing arrow. Click and drag left or right to increase or decrease opacity without using the pulldown menu. Scrubby sliders are in almost every numerical option that appears in the Options bar for a given tool.

295 USE LAYERS FOR SUPERIOR EDITING

Photoshop's layers are the key to making myriad editing changes while leaving your original picture untouched. Understand layers, and you're on your way to understanding the mother of all imaging programs.

Layers are basically images laid one atop another, so you can edit while the original picture remains untouched. Software that includes layers preserves all original image data while you work, so your photo doesn't lose quality as you make each successive edit—this is called a non-destructive workflow. Think of layers as transparencies: You can stack up as many as you like, adding information to each one to build the final image's components.

If you're working with numerous layers, organize them into folders for a streamlined workflow. You can color-code them, too, to quickly identify each layer. This is useful when, for example, you retouch a face—make folders for the eyes, mouth, hair, and so on. If you change your mind about an edit, you can easily delete a problematic layer without starting from scratch.

296 MASTER SELECTIONS

Photoshop's selection tools—such as the Marquee, Lasso, Quick Selection, and Pen—let you make local adjustments to images. There's also the Brush, with which you paint a selection when working in Quick Mask mode. The selection border appears as a line of "marching ants." With the Pen tool, you must convert your path into a selection: Press Ctrl (Command on a Mac) + click on the thumbnail of the path.

Selections are tied to masks (see #298—often, you make a selection so you can turn it into a mask). For example, to change a wall's color, make a selection of the wall via any selection tool. Then use that selection on your mask so that the Hue/Saturation Adjustment Layer affects only the wall. Refine the selection so you can make a precise mask. No old color is left behind, and the new one looks natural.

297 DIVE INTO LAYERS

When you open an image in Photoshop, it automatically becomes a locked layer called the Background Layer. You then can add various layers atop it, including Text Layers, Vector Shape Layers, and Adjustment Layers. When you copy and paste (or drag and drop) a second image into your file, it will automatically appear in a new layer. You can also add empty layers for creating shapes, retouching, and adding background fill to make borders for your picture. When you make any big change, do so on a duplicate layer so you can reduce or intensify its effect by decreasing or increasing its opacity.

Adjustment Layers work differently—there is no image on the layers themselves. They sit atop normal layers, affecting them all so you can tweak exposure, contrast, and colors. To make one, go to Layer > New Adjustment Layer and choose the type you like. If you want it to affect

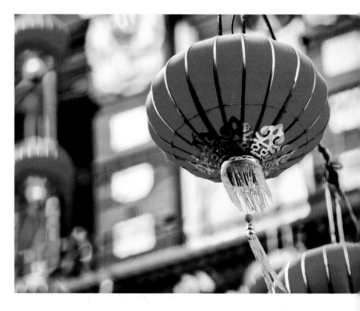

only the layer below it, link the two by holding down Alt (Option on a Mac) and clicking the line between the layers. You'll see an icon with two overlapped circles. When they are linked, the upper layer displays a bent arrow pointing to the layer to which it's linked.

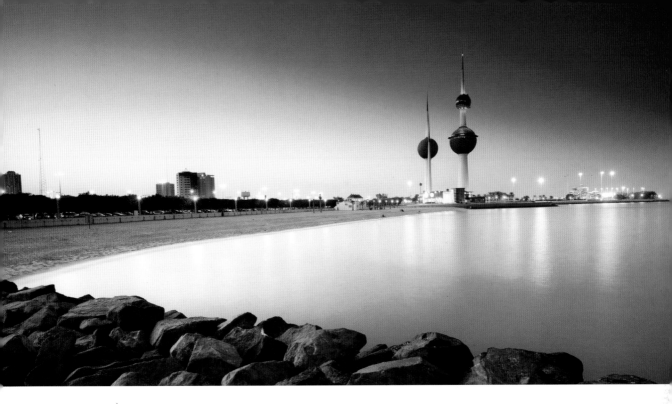

298 MAKE MASKS FOR MORE EDITING CONTROL

Want even more power when editing your photos? Use masks. A mask defines what is visible or hidden on a particular layer, and it can be applied to any type of layer. This allows you to edit targeted portions of your image without affecting the rest of it.

There are two types of masks: layer and vector. Layer masks are saved as alpha channels (which let you load and save selections). Vector masks are pen paths. A layer mask is added by default whenever you add a new Adjustment Layer. If you try to add another mask to that same layer, it will automatically become a vector mask. These masks will be black and white. If

you get confused, think of this handy rhyme: White areas are revealed, and black areas are concealed.

Generally, you use layer masks to specify where you want an adjustment to be applied in your image. Let's say you are working on the skyline image above; you exposed the sky perfectly while shooting, but the land was a bit dark. If you use an Exposure Adjustment Layer to brighten the land, the sky and towers will look overexposed. Instead, fill the mask on your Exposure Layer with a gradient that transitions from black to white at the horizon line so the sky is unaffected while you bring out detail in the land and buildings.

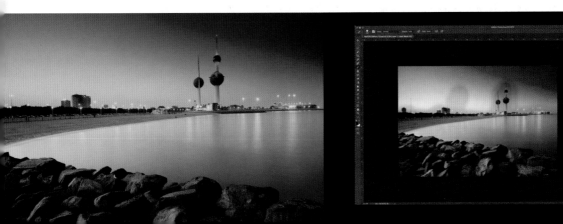

299 DOUBLE UP YOUR LAYERS

If you create an Adjustment Layer in Photoshop to change an image's brightness or contrast and its effect doesn't go far enough, you can double the layer via a quick keyboard shortcut. Select the layer, then press Control (Command on a Mac) + J. The original image here (at left) was overexposed, and an Adjustment Layer failed to sufficiently darken it. So the photographer duplicated the Adjustment layer to achieve an improved image (at right). If the double layers together go too far, dial down the new layer's opacity until you've reached a happy medium.

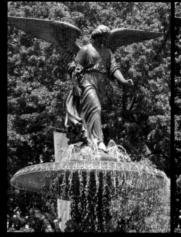
BEFORE

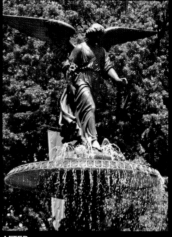
AFTER

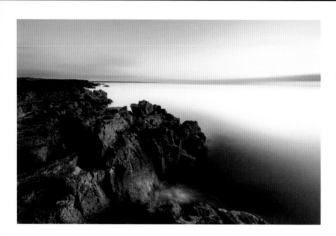

300 FAKE A NEUTRAL-DENSITY FILTER

Landscape photographers rely on split neutral-density filters to help them handle a bright sky and a dark ground. By positioning the dark portion of the filter to match up with the sky, they are able to expose for the ground and come out with a perfectly exposed photograph. If you didn't have an ND filter on hand when you shot, you can mimic its effect with software. The way to do it? Process your photo twice in Adobe Camera Raw—once for the sky and once for the ground—then combine the two in Photoshop.

Start by navigating to your photo in Bridge and open it in ACR. Adjust the colors, contrast, and lens correction. Then expose for the sky, even if this makes the ground look dark. Click Save Image in the bottom left corner. In the dialogue box, rename the file Sky and save it as a TIFF. Then readjust your exposure to brighten the ground. Hit Save Image and name this version Ground. Click Done and return to Bridge.

Select both TIFFs and go to Tools > Photoshop > Load Files into Photoshop Layers. This automatically aligns your images in one file. Make sure the sky layer is on top, and then add a layer mask. Add a gradient to your layer mask along the horizon line, white to black, to hide the ground and show only sky. If you don't get your gradient right the first time, just redraw it until you nail it. The gradient will reset itself each time.

QUICK TIP

301 UNLOCK THE BACKGROUND

If you need to unlock the Background Layer, double-click on the words "Background Layer" and change its name. Then you can adjust its opacity and move it up or down in the stack, just like any other layer.

302
STACK LAYERS TO ENHANCE A MACRO PHOTO

The finest macro lens (see #098) still has a built-in limitation: The greater its magnification, the shallower the depth of field (DOF) in the final image. Even an aperture of f/22 or f/32 sometimes can't keep all of a tiny subject within the DOF, and thus some details are lost. But in recent years software has ridden to the rescue with a startling advance called *focus stacking*. This simple technique involves taking many exposures of the same subject while slightly moving your focus point from frame to frame. Then you stack up these in-focus points to produce a single image that's sharp from front to back. A few systems, such as StackShot, automate the process of sequentially capturing in-focus shots, but many macro photographers prefer to do it manually. Once you've taken the photos, you can assemble them via Helicon Focus or Photoshop. In Bridge, select the images you want to stack and go to Tools > Photoshop > Load Files into Photoshop Layers. Once in Photoshop, go to Edit > Auto-Blend Layers.

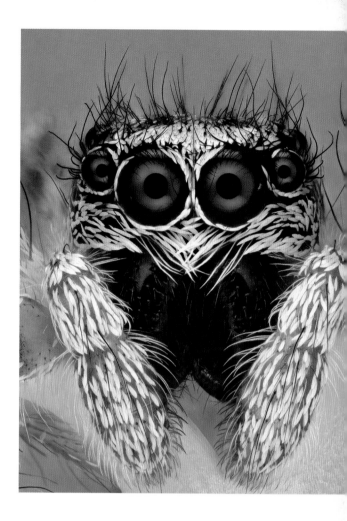

303
EDIT YOUR PHOTOS ON THE GO

MOBILE TIP

When it comes to mobile processing, go beyond your phone's standard camera or photo-sharing apps with advanced tools that let you edit your images without importing to a computer. Photoshop Express is a free, simplified version of the classic that allows for speedy manipulations of color, white balance, and brightness; it also lets you add borders and create collages. Then there's Snapseed, an elegant, Google-backed app that "stacks" edits so you can revisit and adjust them individually. Afterlight is beloved for its stylish, pro-grade filters, while PhotoToaster lets you make selective edits with easy-to-use brushes.

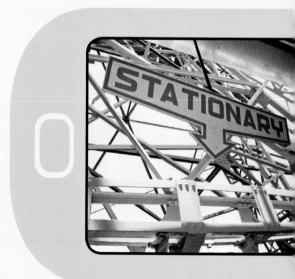

Walking by the lake in a Chicago park near home, I was drawn to the contrast between the cloudy gray sky reflected in the water and the bright green shrubs around it. When I checked the shot on my computer, I noticed the trees in the reflection. To create a subtle horizon, I flipped the image upside down.

—ALEXANDER PETKOV

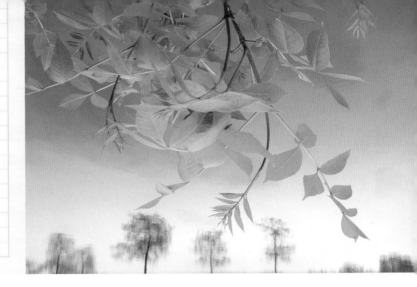

304 ROTATE SHOTS

Easy-to-master rotation tools—found in Photoshop, mobile-phone apps, and other programs—flip photographs horizontally or vertically. You can also use them to rotate images clockwise or counterclockwise, according to your desired degree of tilt.

Yes, rotation lets you correct unpleasantly angled shots, but it's also a powerful creative tool. Use it to turn pedestrian photos into surprising, amusing, or bizarre works of art. You can simply invert an image, such as the one above. And you can even reverse gravity, turning raindrops splashing into a lake into a surreal scene of raindrops arrowing upward.

305 CLEAN UP A BACKGROUND

A distracting background can ruin even the most beautiful shot. When shooting, you can sweep away distant clutter by setting a large aperture to defocus it, or brilliantly light your foreground subject and set an exposure that shadows out background mess. But if you didn't have that foresight, use Photoshop to take the edge off the image.

Struck by the dynamic contrast of richly saturated lights bouncing off a metallic subway bench, the photographer who took the shot below composed it to emphasize the bright reflections. When he noticed afterward that the right side of his picture took in a line of ugly storefronts, he simply cropped off the right half of the image and replaced it with a mirror image of the left. Presto: No more distracting stores, and the final, symmetrical composition has a vibrant vortex that plays up the receding lines of the lights and bench slats.

306 SUPER UNDO IT

To undo a Photoshop error, hit Ctrl (Command on Macs) + Z. To revert further back, go into History and click the last correct step. The default saves 20 steps in History; for more, go to Preferences > Performance and save up to 1,000 states.

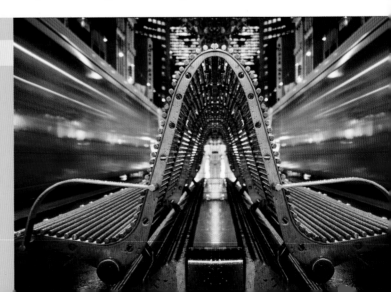

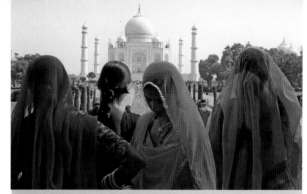

307 CROP TO IMPROVE YOUR SHOTS

Cropping is a simple yet powerful technique. By removing undesirable parts of a shot, you can emphasize or downplay specific elements, bolster or rearrange composition, or zero in on subjects you shot from a distance. Just remember that if you do a radical crop, you'll probably need to sharpen and reduce noise for a crisp and legible image.

Photoshop's Crop tool—hit C or select the icon to get it—is versatile and intuitive, especially when you use it on Raw files so you have the optimal amount of data to manipulate. Its menus offer you preset aspect ratios (such as a basic square) as well as Unconstrained, for freehand cropping. Once you select a crop and hit Enter, deleted areas will gray out; if they distract you, go to the Gear icon menu to darken them.

To reposition an image within a crop, click and hold on the picture as you move it. Grab the "handles" at the crop's corners and sides to reposition the crop frame atop your image. You can also straighten out misaligned photos via the Straighten button—draw a horizontal or vertical line, hit Enter, and Photoshop reorients your image accordingly. An important refinement in Photoshop's recent versions is the Delete Cropped Pixels checkbox. Check it to permanently delete extraneous areas; uncheck it if you want to retain them (hitting the Crop tool again gives you the entire original photo).

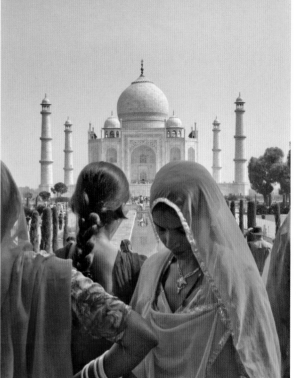

AFTER

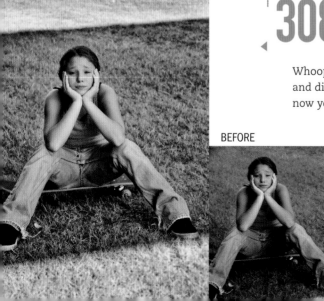

BEFORE

308 UNCROP A PHOTO

Whoops. You've followed the rule book, cropping out extra space and distracting details around the edges of your photograph. But now your composition feels crowded and airless. A dose of negative space can give your shot breathing room, balancing composition and emphasizing its subject.

Working in Photoshop, pull up your original, uncropped file. Extend the picture canvas and then use Content Aware Fill to add extra space around your subject. Then tweak the subject itself a bit, boosting contrast using Curves or Hue > Saturation Adjustment Layer to shift colors and add dimensionality.

309 PUT A TWIST IN YOUR SHOT

Take a nothing-special photo and warp it into a vortex with software that allows you to distort an image around a center point. For arresting results, pick an image with a dynamic perspective: Tunnels, bright flowers, landscapes, and architecture are all great subjects to distort and transform into psychedelic art.

To start, choose an image with strong, graphic lines and contrasting colors. These qualities will lend structure to the image, keeping it crisp and sharp despite the applied distortion. Next, go to Filter > Distort > Twirl. Don't swirl your photo beyond recognition—torque it just enough to get the visual impact you want without obscuring your scene or subject into a featureless blur. (Note: The Twirl tool works only in 8-bit mode—if you choose a converted Raw file in 16-bit mode, reduce it to 8-bit before trying this technique.)

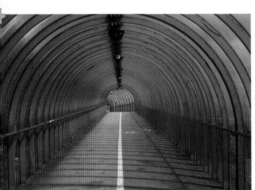

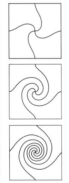

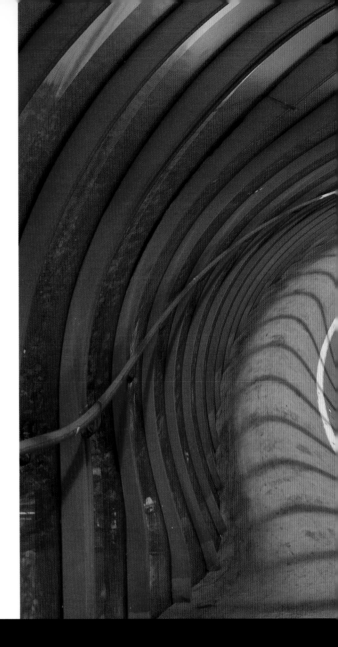

310 SCRATCH UP SOME POLAROID ART

Take retro-cool Polaroids a step further by lightly scratching them with a blunt-pointed object, such as the nonbristled end of a paintbrush. When you put pressure on a Polaroid's surface, you're moving the chemical emulsion inside, altering the image's appearance. Make it look like a cartoon by amping up outlines, as in the Polaroids shown here, or add shapes, draw patterns, or scratch away elements

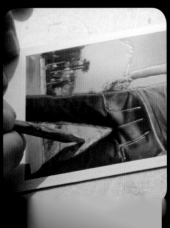

■ Draw, scrape, or scratch the Polaroid a few minutes after it begins to develop.

■ Experiment! Be open to blocking out large areas of your image with pattern and delving into abstraction.

■ You can also peel apart the Polaroid's layers (the black backing and the white top) for direct access to the emulsion.

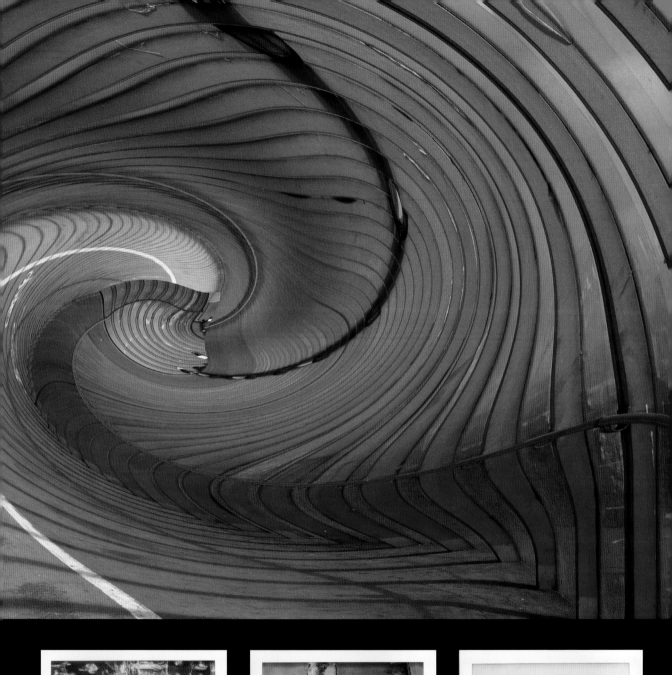
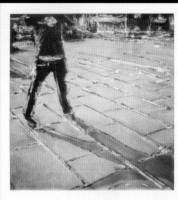
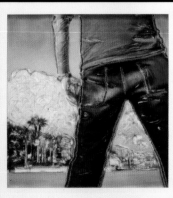
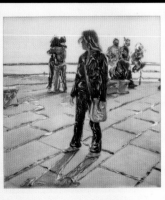

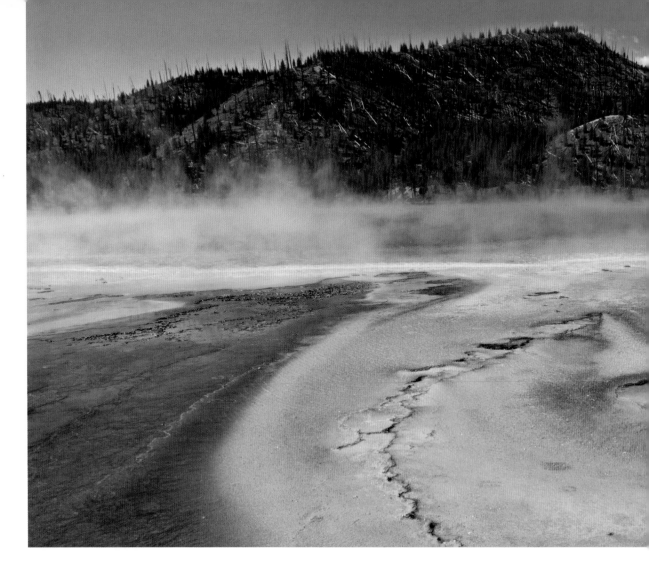

311 COOK WITH RAW FILES

As their name says, Raw files are powerful raw material. Unlike a JPEG, which is "cooked" (meaning that sensor data is heavily processed in-camera), a Raw file contains a ton of unadulterated data that you must manipulate before editing the image. But Raw files are worth the work—they give you total control over all the parameters of image processing. Here are the essentials for working with Raw files.

STEP ONE Before you begin conversion or adjustments in the Basic panel, scroll down to Lens Corrections. Check the Enable Profile Corrections box. If your lens has a profile made by Adobe or you've added one of your own, use it. Otherwise use Manual corrections.

(It's wise to do this before doing any basic adjustments because Lens Corrections—especially its vignette removal function—can really alter your image's appearance.)

STEP TWO Return to the Basic panel. Adjust the Exposure slider, which (unlike the other sliders) is measured in increments of stops. In earlier versions, Exposure set the white point. Now it works on midtones and won't clip highlights. As you adjust any slider, the tones you affect are highlighted in the histogram. Now dial in proper contrast via the Contrast slider.

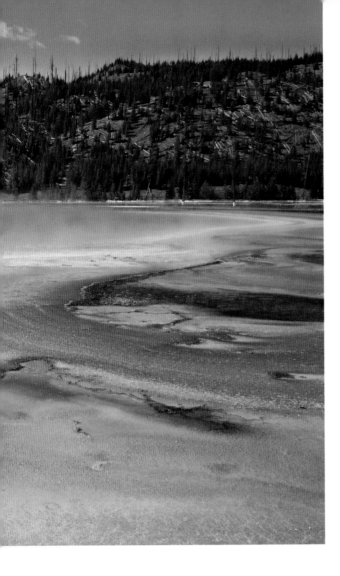

312 LEARN WHEN TO GO RAW

Sometimes JPEGs are your best option: when your memory card is almost full or you don't plan to print photos. But JPEGs have limits. They're compressed as they're taken, so settings are written in stone. Set the wrong white balance, for example, and fixing tone later will be a bear. Here are other times when Raw is best:

☐ **YOU WANT TO DIG DETAIL OUT OF SHADOW** A Raw image captures about 2 more stops of dynamic range than a JPEG, so shadow detail that might be pure black in a JPEG retains detail in Raw.

☐ **YOU WANT TO SHOOT FIRST AND BALANCE LATER** You don't have to set the camera's white balance when shooting Raw. You can adjust it to your taste when you convert the Raw file. Click on a preset (such as Daylight or Tungsten), and custom-tune it to your heart's content.

☐ **YOU NEED TO OPEN A FILE MULTIPLE TIMES** Raw converters create images without altering the original Raw files, so you can open a Raw file repeatedly to try new things. It's like a film negative: Endless interpretations of one original are possible.

☐ **YOU DON'T WANT TO FUSS WITH PHOTOSHOP** Raw converters control exposure, contrast, color balance, and saturation. Some sharpen and reduce noise. And that might be all the image control you want.

313 CHOOSE A RAW-SPECIFIC PROGRAM

Most cameras let you shoot Raw + JPEG at the same time—a great idea when you're shooting photos that you want to immediately share online. But the option speedily devours memory-card and drive space, because Raw files are big boys. Most Raw devotees instead deploy programs dedicated solely to Raw, such as Phase One's Capture One or Adobe Lightroom, to quickly process Raw files into JPEGs.

STEP THREE Shift the Shadows slider right to bring back detail in any overly shadowed areas, or the Highlights slider left to restore detail in overly bright ones. Adjust Whites and Blacks to control clipping.

STEP FOUR In the Presence section, move the Clarity slider to add contrast and definition to midtones (taking it up to 100 will net you an HDR-like look). Up Clarity to add punch, and Vibrance to intensify colors.

STEP FIVE If your changes produced noise, go to the Details tab and add as much noise reduction as needed. Use the Adjustment Brush for localized noise removal. Finally, in the Lens Corrections tab, check the box to remove chromatic aberrations.

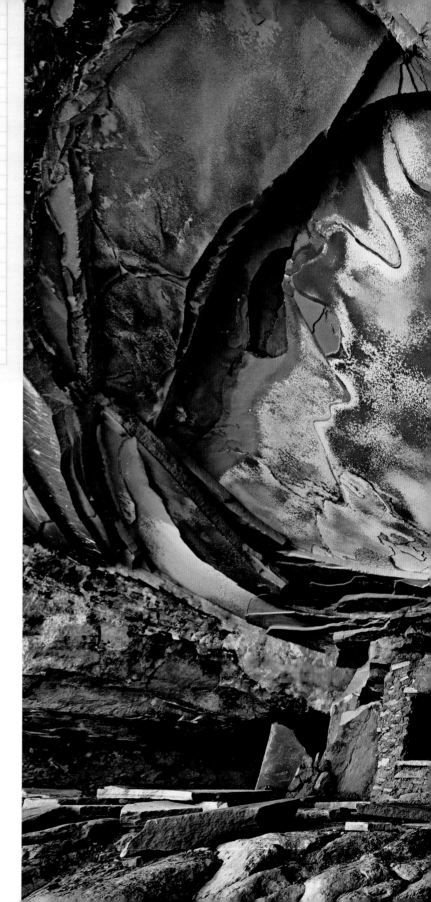

I was shooting this ruined Anasazi cliff dwelling in Utah when I realized the full range of tones wouldn't fit into a single exposure. I decided to sacrifice shadow detail rather than lose the highlights, since those had the most interesting details of the masonry. So I kept my histogram bunched to the right without clipping it off. The image appeared very bright, but it gave me the most detail possible. Then I tweaked the highlights and shadows in Photoshop.
—GUY TAL

314

DODGE AND BURN DIGITALLY

To adjust shadows and highlights in digital processing, you can use Photoshop's equivalents of tried-and-true darkroom staples. The Dodge tool lets you brighten shadowy areas, and the Burn tool darkens brighter spots. For this shot, photographer Guy Tal picked the Dodge tool to shed some light on upper portions of the image, then used Burn to darken lower areas. Photoshop's Dodge and Burn can permanently alter pixels when applied to a background image layer, so Tal made the changes on a copy of his background layer, using a Soft Light blending mode for subtle effects.

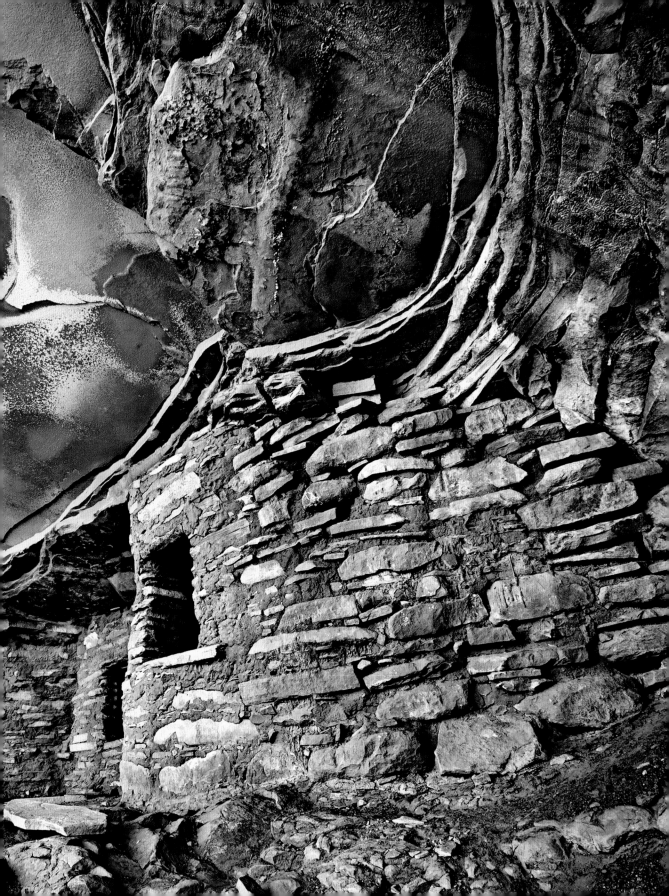

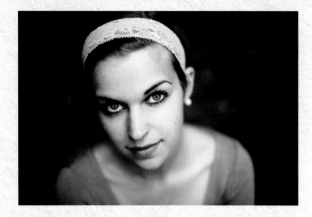

315 CONVERT AN IMAGE TO B&W

The secret to a beautiful monochrome: Start off with a great color image and let its wealth of tonal information help you make choices about which hues should go bright and which dark. Then follow these tips.

☐ **ADJUST TONAL RANGE** Make sure your color image contains true black and true white before you delete its colors. To do so, create a Levels Adjustment Layer in Photoshop. Drag the white triangle inward until it abuts the beginning of the histogram. Do the same with the black triangle. If necessary, drag the center triangle left or right to brighten or darken midtones.

☐ **USE THE B&W TOOL** In Photoshop, click the Black & White button in the Adjustments Panel, and then hit the Auto button. Grab the hand tool and place it on your image. Drag right on a tone to lighten it, left to darken it.

☐ **TRY FILTERS AND PRESETS** In Photoshop, use the Black & White tool's pulldown menu to experiment with different looks. If you go for the High Contrast Blue Filter, you'll get a gritty, dirty effect. Try a red filter for soft skin tones, but if this effect is too much, move the Reds slider left to mellow it out.

☐ **ADD GRAIN** Adobe Camera Raw (ACR) has a more sophisticated method for adding filmlike grain than Photoshop does. So save your image as a flattened TIFF and close the file. Double-click the Mini Bridge panel at the bottom of your screen and navigate to your TIFF. Right-click its thumbnail and select Open with > Camera Raw. Choose the Effects tab, and zoom to 50 percent. Once you increase the grain by moving the Amount slider to the right, the automatic Size and Roughness will kick in. The defaults add subtle texture, but you can increase all three sliders to make your photo really grainy.

☐ **SPLIT TONE** ACR's Split Toning tool adds a bit of tint to highlights and shadows to distinguish them. A classic split-tone shows warm highlights and cool shadows. To create one, click on the Split Toning tab and select a warm, yellow-orange hue for the Highlights and a cool blue for Shadows. Then slowly increase the Saturation for each.

316 MAKE YOURS MONOCHROME WITH EFEX

The digital darkroom provides many ways to turn color into monochrome. Although no single method works for every image, Google's free Nik's Silver Efex software, a Photoshop plug-in, often does the trick. Among its preset styles are High Structure, High Contrast Red Filter, and Dark Sepia, all of which are particularly good for landscapes. You can customize these presets with brightness, contrast, and structure slider controls, or use color filters to alter an image's tones as you would when shooting on B&W film through lens filters. Go with a green filter to lighten foliage or a red filter to darken a blue sky. Efex also lets you apply effects that mimic the look of B&W film. If you come up with a look you love, save those settings as a new preset.

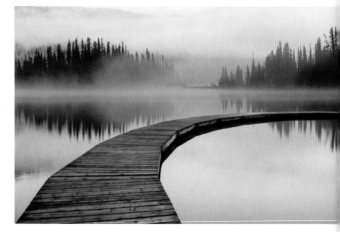

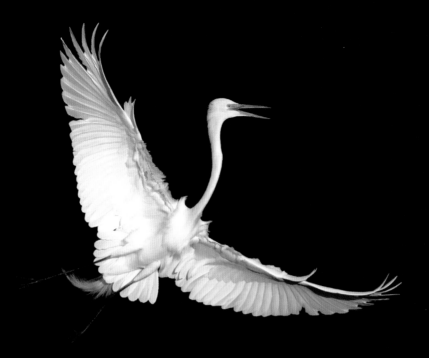

317 FADE (A BACKGROUND) TO BLACK

Darkening your background draws your subject forward so it shines out as the central focus of your composition. You can easily create this effect through Brightness/Contrast in Adobe Photoshop, as the photographer of this brilliant egret did. You'll get the best results if you preserve your subject's highlights and allow the background to fall away while you're out shooting. Then clinch the effect with software.

STEP ONE Begin by hitting W on your keyboard and selecting the subject using the Quick Selection tool. Then start painting on the subject until it's nearly all selected. This first go-round can be rough.

STEP TWO Zoom in to the subject's edges and hone your selection. In Quick Selection, hold down the Alt (Option on a Mac) key to get the Subtract from Selection tool. Now paint in areas where you want to remove the selection. To make the brush smaller, tap the left bracket key ([) on your keyboard. To make it bigger, tap the right bracket (]). Just do the best you can. For the shot here, the toughest parts to fine-tune were the bird's feet and wispy feathers.

STEP THREE You now have a usable selection, so go to Select > Inverse, switching the selection from enclosing the subject to enclosing the background. Then create a Brightness/Contrast Adjustment Layer by clicking on Brightness/Contrast in your Adjustments Panel. This makes a mask in the shape of your selection so your adjustments will apply only to the background. Then bring Brightness down and Contrast up until the background goes black.

STEP FOUR You'll immediately see where your selection looks good and where it doesn't. Any color from the original background will appear glaringly fake against the black background. To fix it, right-click on the Background Layer and choose Duplicate Layer. Then hit O for the Sponge tool. In the Options bar, choose Mode: Desaturate, and Flow: 100 percent. Zoom in and, with a large brush, paint away the distracting color.

STEP FIVE Getting rid of errant color helps, but it doesn't erase hard edges around soft details such as feathers. Click on your mask again and hit B for the Brush tool. In the Options bar, set Opacity to 50 percent. Set the foreground color to black (hit D, then X on your keyboard to do so), then paint on small areas to bring them back in. If you go too far, hit X to switch to painting with white, and repaint to cover mistakes.

318 CRUISE WITH CURVES

The Curves tool is among the most powerful in Photoshop, and it's the most versatile, too. Use it to add contrast just where you want it, to brighten or darken an image, and even to correct color. Curves simply graphs the tones of your image. As in a histogram, the darkest tones are represented on the left, and the brightest on the right. When you're viewing an RGB image, you'll see that the curve line begins at bottom left and travels along a straight diagonal to top right. You add points on that line and move it up or down to change your image.

The good news: The Curves tool is much harder to explain than it is to use. So, to make it a little easier to understand, here are a few of the most common curves you can implement, plus details on what they do. Try them on your shots to test-drive this creative tool.

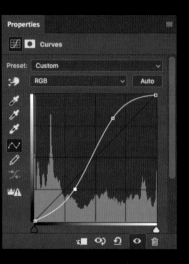

ADD CONTRAST Behind the curve, you'll see a histogram. If it doesn't touch the edges, add contrast by moving the small black and white triangles inward to the histogram's edge. This makes the angle of the curve line steeper. Note: Use this method only when your histogram doesn't touch the edges. If you do it on an image with a good histogram, you'll end up clipping highlights and shadows.

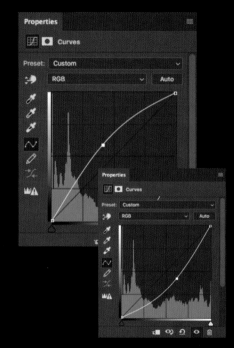

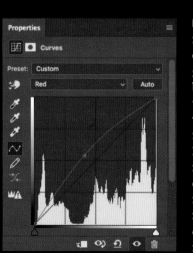

FIX COLOR Curves lets you manipulate your image's colors. Add or subtract red, green, or blue from a photo by using the pulldown menu to select the color that you would like to change, then manipulate that color's curve. For a warmer version of an image, pull down the blue curve to make the image more yellow. To make the image more magenta, pull down the green. To make it more cyan, pull down the red.

BRIGHTEN If your image is too dark, call up Curves to brighten it. Here's an exaggerated example: Grab the midpoint of your curve and lift it up. The whole image brightens. The great thing about using Curves for this? Your black and white points don't change, so you won't clip highlights or shadows.

DARKEN To darken an image, just do the opposite of what you did to brighten it. Grab the curve by the center point and bring it downward.

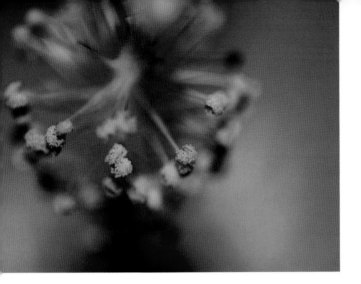

319 UP A SILHOUETTE'S CONTRAST

Silhouettes and shadows make great graphic elements, but there is such a thing as too much darkness—sometimes a photo's features need a little rescuing from the dark side. To cast a light on the gritty textures and stark figure hiding in a nearly monochromatic shot such as the street scene you see here, navigate to the HSL/Grayscale tab in Adobe Camera Raw and check the box to convert to Grayscale; the slider options below will change automatically. Pull the appropriate slider to the right to brighten your image, then adjust the Shadows slider to reveal more detail and the Clarity function to up the midtone contrast.

320 GET PERFECT CONTRAST

When you edit with Curves, first get the contrast right. Control dark tones by adjusting the graph's left side, and bright ones by adjusting the right side. Pull down the curve on the left, and dark tones darken further. Lift it on the right, and light tones brighten. Often, the curve ends up looking S-shaped.

STEP ONE Create a Curves Adjustment Layer by clicking the Curves button in the Adjustments panel. Now add contrast with the histogram as a guide. Pull the black arrow right until it aligns with the start of the bumps on the histogram's left side. This ensures that the photo's darkest tones are truly black. Drag the white arrow left until it aligns with the start of the bumps on the right so the lightest tones are close to true white.

STEP TWO Since the pollen is the focal point, use it to determine how you'll refine contrast. Zoom in, grab the pointed finger in the Curves dialogue box's top left corner, click on a bright point, and drag up. The image brightens based on the chosen tone, and the point on the curve where the adjusted tone lies is now marked.

STEP THREE Click and drag down on a shadowy area until these tones are as dark as you want them.

STEP FOUR Zoom out, then click on the points you added to the curve. Pull them up or down to refine your image. If the highlights and shadows are pleasing but the midtones could be brighter, work with the curve's center. Click directly on the curve to add a point, and drag it up until the midtones are as bright as you wish.

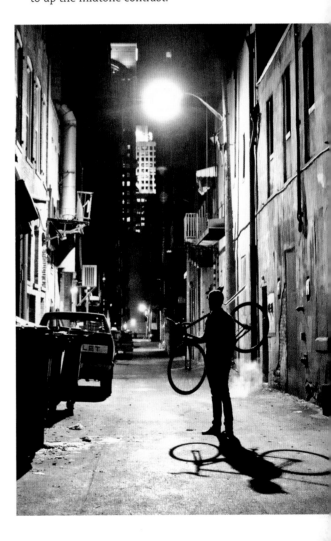

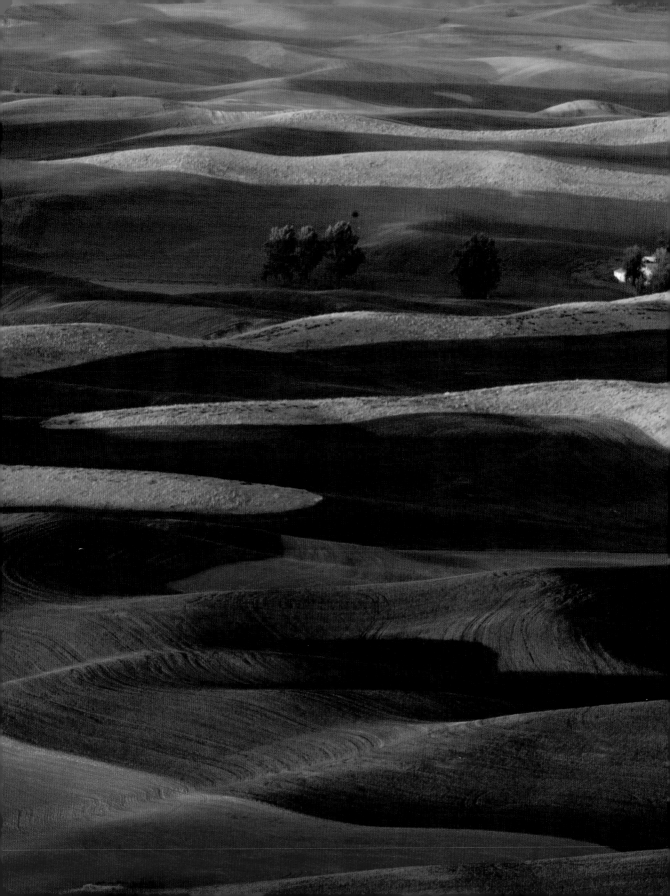

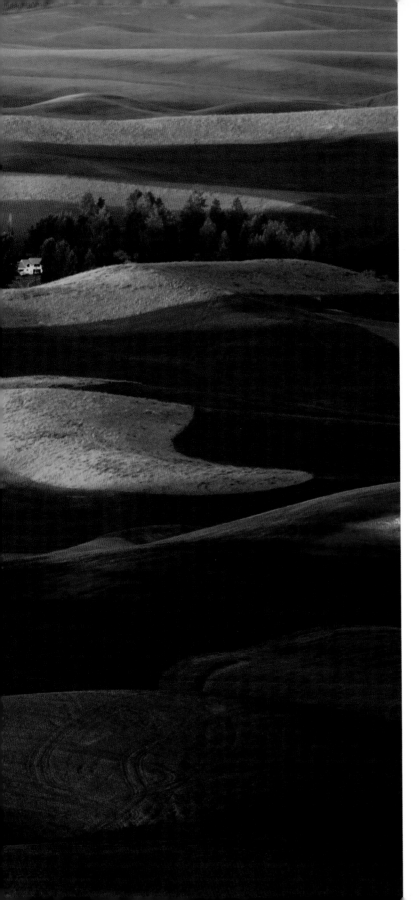

321 FIX IT WITH LEVELS

Photoshop's Levels is a powerful histogram-based corrector that zaps ugly color casts and adds convincingly natural contrast. Here's how to use it:

STEP ONE First find the image's black and white points—its darkest and lightest spots—with a Threshold Adjustment Layer (hit the Threshold button on the Adjustments panel).

STEP TWO The image turns B&W. In the histogram at right, pull the tiny gray arrow right until just a bit of white remains in the photo. That's the white point. Click and hold the Eyedropper tool in the toolbar, and choose the Color Sampler tool from the pop-up menu. Zoom in on the white spot. Click it with the Color Sampler. A target numbered 1 appears on it. To find the black point, drag the white arrow in the Threshold Adjustment Layer left until a bit of black remains. Zoom in and click with Color Sampler. Target 2 appears.

STEP THREE Delete the Threshold Adjustment Layer and make a Levels Adjustment Layer. Pick the white dropper. Hit Caps Lock to turn the cursor into a target, and align it with target 1. Click—the whites (and the whole image) brighten. Click the black dropper and then target 2. Levels resets the tones for better contrast and cleans up the blacks to neutralize color.

322 FIX IT WITH CURVES

Want to fix contrast or hue with Curves? Use a Threshold Adjustment Layer to mark the black and white points, then simply grab the black and white droppers in Curves' dialogue box to edit.

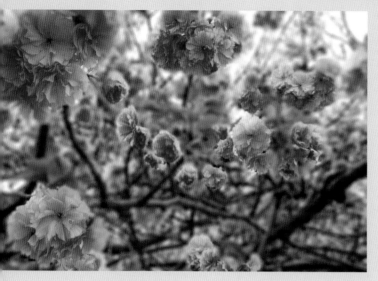

323 SOFTEN WITH BLUR

Photoshop's spanking-new Blur Gallery sports a trio of sophisticated image-smudging tools that turn your shots into impressionistic works of art. Field Blur blurs an entire photo. Tilt-Shift applies a targeted blurring effect like that of a tilt/shift lens. And Iris Blur mimics a Lensbaby, sweeping sharpness over a selected area while blurring the rest. You can finesse the size, shape, and edges of sharp areas, as well as the degree of the sharpness. Test-drive Iris Blur on a classic floral image, such as these cherry blossoms.

simple ▬▬▬▬▬▬▬▬▬▬ complex
▲

STEP ONE Duplicate your background layer (it's always wise to preserve an untouched version of an original shot on its own layer). Then go to Filter > Blur and choose Iris Blur from the submenu.

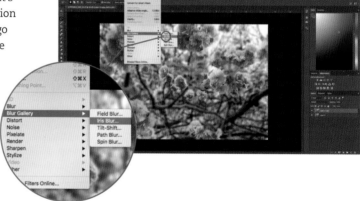

STEP TWO You'll see a circle of sharpness sitting on the image. Grab it by its center and pull it where you want the image to be sharpest. To adjust the blur level, shift the slider in the toolbar or grab and move the circular slider in the center of the Floating Blur tool. As you adjust, a display shows you level of blur.

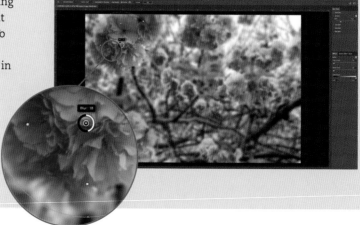

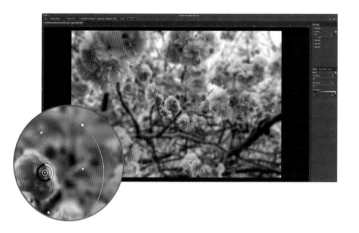

STEP THREE To adjust a sharp zone's size and shape, click and drag anywhere on the tool's outer circle to enlarge or shrink it. You'll see two small dots on the circle—drag one to make an ellipsis of sharp focus or rotate its orientation. Pull out on the little square on the circle to make an equilateral sharp region. Inside the circle are four more dots. These mark the transition between sharpness and blur. Pull them inward for a gradual transition, outward for a sharper edge.

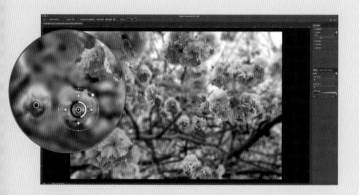

STEP FOUR Now add another sharp area. Click on a spot you want to be in focus, adjust its size and shape, and do the same across the image as many times as needed. To remove focus from an area, click on a point and hit Delete. All these circles and points might confuse you; hit Ctrl (Command on a Mac) + H to see the image without them.

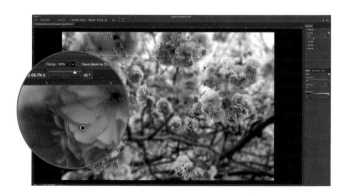

STEP FIVE Your image could look odd if many areas have the same degree of sharpness. Click on a point to select an in-focus area, then use the Focus slider in the Options bar to dial down sharpness. Do the same in other areas until your image looks smooth and balanced, then click OK. Want to save the mask for further modification? Check the Save Mask to Channels box at the top of the screen.

324 REPLACE ODD COLOR WITH ONE COLOR

You can't be fussy with grab shots. Imagine, for example, that you've captured a photo in the pouring rain, through a car windshield, on a point-and-shoot camera. While the resulting murkiness adds to the shot's atmosphere, the color looks strange. This flaw is easily remedied by using Photoshop's Black & White tool in the form of an Adjustment Layer. Then add back some color with a selenium-like tone, using a Color Fill Adjustment Layer set to Soft Light Blend mode. Dial back the layer's opacity to 25 percent to keep it from turning into purple haze.

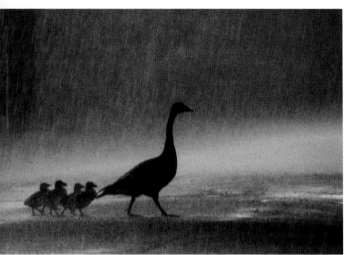

325 USE GRAYSCALE TO FIX COLOR

If the hues in your color image appear muddy, take it into monochrome. Start with a flat conversion of your Raw file to make sure you have as much detail as possible. Then, using the Photoshop plug-in Google's Nik Silver Efex, turn your image B&W with the preset called Full Dynamic Harsh. Next, modify the preset by using different control points for the sky and land areas, which will keep the latter darker and less contrasty. Finally, try adding a very light selenium tone for a hint of color across the image.

326 RESTORE SOME ORIGINAL COLOR

As an alternative to converting a color image entirely to B&W, consider desaturating its overall color until it displays a subtle wash of tone. Using a full-color photo, create a Black & White Adjustment Layer, and move the sliders until you like the conversion. Then reduce the opacity of the Black & White Adjustment Layer to restore just a trace of the image's original color.

327 TONE WITH MASKS

All the color-tweaking methods described here work even better when you combine them and use masks. Click on a layer or an Adjustment Layer to select it, then click the mask icon at the bottom of the Layers panel to add a layer mask. With the mask selected, paint on your image—use a soft-edged black brush to selectively hide any previously applied tone effect, or use a white brush to restore it. Vary your brush's opacity as needed.

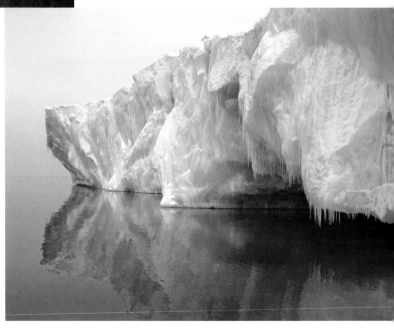

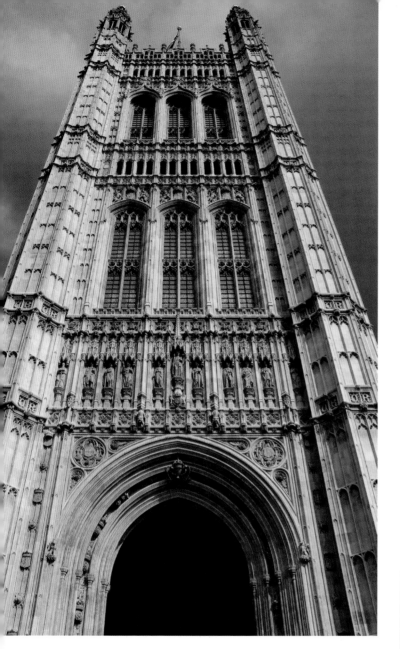

ADD SELECTIVE GRAYSCALE WITH HUE/SATURATION

Black-and-white images are beautiful, but some are even lovelier with a bit of tone. In the past, film photographers added color via their choice of printing paper (such as silver gelatin prints) or printing process (such as platinum or cyanotype for warm- or cool-toned prints), or they selectively added color by hand. These days, you can tone your B&W digital images in virtually unlimited ways. In Photoshop, adding an overall wash of color is simple: Make a Hue/Saturation Adjustment Layer and set its blend mode to Color. Check the Colorize box, and use the Hue slider to choose the color you'll add. To adjust its intensity, move the Saturation slider. (Disregard the Lightness slider.) Potentially the most intense of Photoshop's toning methods, this technique affects an image uniformly.

330 ADD COLOR BY HAND

Working manually, you can augment any area of your image with any hue you choose. First make a new, blank layer, and set its blend mode to Color. Grab a soft-edged brush and double-click on the foreground color in the toolbar to choose the tone you want. Paint it in wherever you want it. If the color is too intense, reduce the opacity of the brush (not the layer) to control the hue's effect. If you find you've built up too much color, use the Eraser tool at any opacity to reduce or remove it.

329 SPLIT TONES WITH CURVES

Use this technique when you want to apply two different tones—one for highlights and one for shadows. Make a Curves Adjustment Layer and set its blend mode to Color. Then use the pulldown menu to choose the Blue Channel rather than RGB. Make a subtle S-curve, lifting the shadows and pulling down the highlights. This will bring a blue tone into the photo's shadows and put blue's opposite, yellow, into its highlights.

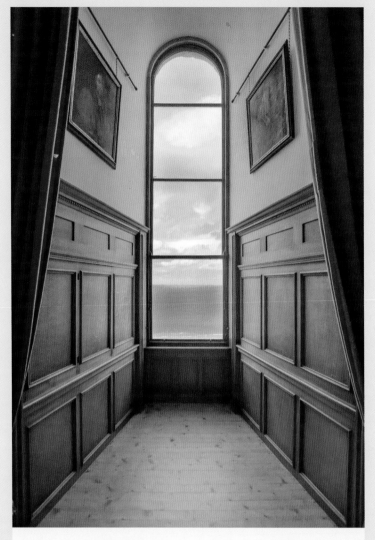

CONTROL TONE WITH LIGHTROOM

Adobe Lightroom, with its easy-to-navigate interface, allows selective adjustments via its Adjustment Brush tool, which you can use to brush white balance onto your image. Thus you can easily correct mixed lighting, or apply zones of varied white balance for creative effects. This Magritte-like shot by Andrew Wood nicely illustrates the power of both selective adjustments and Lightroom's Camera Raw processing engine. Take on a similar project to work multiple zones of an image and create a final Raw conversion that really glows. The best part? No layers are required.

simple ▬▬▬ ▬▬ ▬▬ ▬ ▬▬ ▬▬ complex
▲

STEP ONE Before you go local with adjustments, go global via a basic conversion. Adjust white balance and exposure, and decide whether to use a built-in lens conversion. Wood took three shots of this hallway, and the one with the best highlight detail was, unfortunately, also the darkest. If you have a similar dilemma, restore as much shadow as possible, then use the Color and Luminance noise-reduction tools so the image is usable.

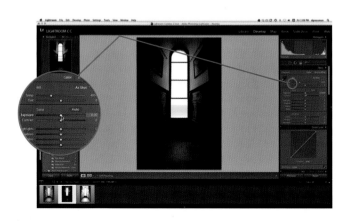

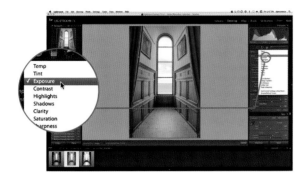

STEP TWO Click on the Adjustment Brush icon and, via the Effect pulldown menu, choose the adjustment to apply. Here, more detail was needed in the window's view. In such a case, choose Exposure and then set up your brush (check Auto Mask so Lightroom will help you paint within your edges). Mouse over your image and use the right and left bracket keys to expand or shrink the brush to match the area you'll paint.

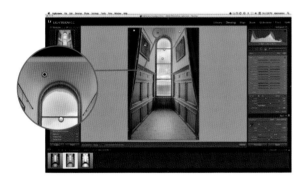

STEP THREE Now paint in your effect. Moving the sliders before you paint is tricky, so go with the default and, after you're finished painting, adjust the Exposure slider to further decrease exposure in areas where detail is needed.

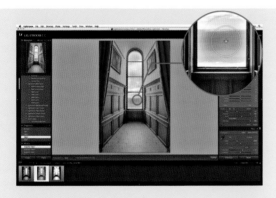

STEP FOUR Further edits might be required—here the curtains and paintings were overbright and color shifts on the ceiling required selective white balance adjustment. To add a new adjustment point, click the New button. As before, choose an effect from the pulldown menu, paint it in, and adjust the slider. To re-edit an area, click on its gray dot. Note: Clicking on your adjustment point gives a preview of its location.

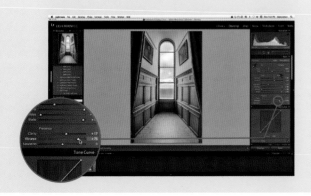

STEP FIVE Once you've done all your local tweaks, the final product might need a global goose. If the image looks flat, edge up the Clarity and Vibrance sliders so it will pop.

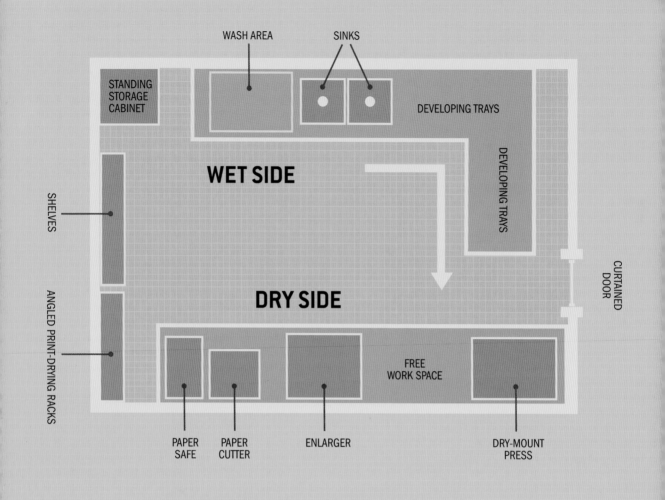

WASH AREA

SINKS

STANDING STORAGE CABINET

DEVELOPING TRAYS

WET SIDE

SHELVES

DEVELOPING TRAYS

DRY SIDE

CURTAINED DOOR

ANGLED PRINT-DRYING RACKS

FREE WORK SPACE

PAPER SAFE

PAPER CUTTER

ENLARGER

DRY-MOUNT PRESS

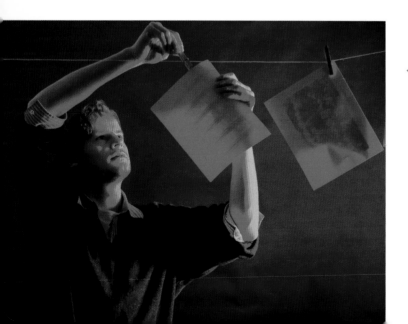

332

LIGHT-PROOF YOUR DARKROOM

Before you process your first print, make sure your new darkroom is truly lightproof. Close the door, draw the shades, and sit there for ten minutes. If any light is leaking in, your eyes will detect it by then.

333 SET UP A HOME DARKROOM

If you're a passionate film shooter, you'll soon long to do your own processing. Why leave all the home alchemy to digital photographers—or consign your film to commercial processors? If you have a small room to devote exclusively to processing gear, constructing your own darkroom is a great option. (Don't work in your kitchen or bathroom. Darkroom chemicals are smelly and messy.)

For B&W processing—color work is best left to pros because it requires costly equipment—you need a small spare room or even an empty closet. Any space will do if it has an electrical outlet and a sink (ideally a long, shallow one) with running water. Lightproof it by taping or Velcroing opaque shades to window and door frames.

All darkrooms have a wet and a dry side. On the wet side is the sink, with four developing trays nearby. Your prints move through these trays from left to right, from developer to stop bath to fixer to hypo-clearing solution in the last tray (see #336).

On the dry side, your enlarger—buy one with a good lens and a timer—should sit on a sturdy counter. This is also the area where you'll handle negatives and print composition. You should invest in a sturdy easel that can hold photo paper flat under the enlarger as you make exposures, plus a stainless-steel tank and reels set for processing film rolls. Ideally, your darkroom should also have a safe for photo paper and shelves for chemical bottles and other storage. Other essentials include:

☐ A print-drying rack or clothesline with pins

☐ An amber or red safelight

☐ A digital darkroom thermometer to test chemicals' temperature

☐ Latex gloves and an apron to protect clothing

☐ A small, soft paintbrush to whisk dust off negatives

☐ Dodging and burning tools (wire, cardboard, scissors, and tape)

Setting up all this equipment should keep you busy for a while. But be warned: You'll covet other retro darkroom toys after you've fallen in love with making your own prints.

334 BUY THE RIGHT ENLARGER LENS

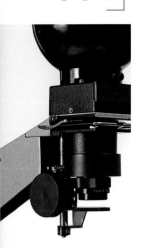

An enlarger is a projector that allows you to make prints from a film negative. The enlarger lens's focal length is determined by your film's format. Here's a guide to standard focal lengths:

☐ 50mm length: 35mm film

☐ 75–90mm length: Medium-format (120) roll film

☐ 150mm length: Large-format film

335 CLEAN A NEGATIVE

It's not necessary to clean negatives unless they're smudged, but if you do have to remove some gunk or smears, use a specialized film cleaner. The best ones evaporate rapidly so as not to leave residue. Use a microfiber cloth for cleaning—specialized anti-static cloths are available from camera gear vendors.

336 MAKE YOUR FIRST DARKROOM PRINT

You've set up your basic home darkroom (see #333), and now an envelope of freshly developed B&W negatives is begging to be printed. What to do? Close the door, flick on the safelight, and get to work.

STEP ONE Line up the chemicals and mix them per manufacturer directions. Pour developer, stop bath, fixer, and hypo-clearing solution into four separate trays, left to right, on the counter by the sink. Developer activates photo paper's chemical emulsion, shading in parts exposed to light. Stop bath halts the developer's work, and fixer takes off unexposed emulsion so the photo won't darken in regular light. Hypo-clear washes off the fixer and other chemicals.

STEP TWO Choose a negative and load it into the enlarger's negative carrier (carrier sizes vary, depending on film size) emulsion side down. When you turn on the enlarger's light and shine it through the negative onto the enlarger base, the image should appear right side up. Bring the image into focus and turn the light off.

STEP THREE Make a test strip to decide how long to expose your photo. Cut a 1-inch- (2.5-cm-) wide strip of photo paper, set the enlarger lens's f-stop to a moderate aperture such as f/8, and set its timer for 30 seconds. Now block out the light with a cardboard square in small increments: one for 5 seconds, one for 10, one for 15, and one for 30. Develop the strip and decide which time works best for your image.

STEP FOUR Place a full sheet of photo paper, emulsion side up, on the enlarger base. Turn on the light for the selected amount of time.

STEP FIVE Place the paper in the developer and rock the tray back and forth a little. (Follow each chemical's manufacturer instructions on how long to keep your paper in each tray.)

STEP SIX Move the paper to the sink with rubber-tipped tongs. Rinse it, and drop it in the stop bath. Rock the tray again.

STEP SEVEN Rinse the paper again and put it in the fixer. Rock the tray. Then do a final hypo-clear rinse.

STEP EIGHT Hang the image on your drying rack. Congratulations: You've now created your very first B&W print!

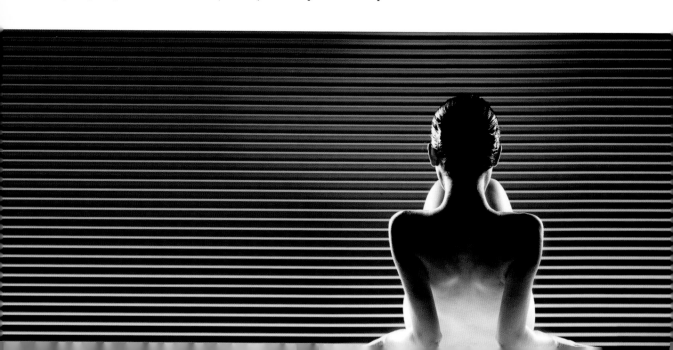

337 STORE FILM SECURELY

Unexposed film rolls are somewhat like uncooked eggs—keep them cool to keep them fresh. Room-temperature storage can eventually cause film emulsion to degrade, and generally color film has a shorter shelf life than B&W. Stash the rolls in zippered bags in the fridge if you plan to use them within a few months. For longer storage, put them in the freezer (warning: Never freeze Fuji or Polaroid instant film). When you're ready to shoot, just set out the rolls until they return to room temperature and condensation dries up. If they're past the expiration date, consider keeping them anyway; there may be times when you'll want the look of aged film (see #249). Cold storage is also a great way to stockpile beloved films that manufacturers might soon stop making, or that crate of discontinued film you couldn't resist buying on eBay.

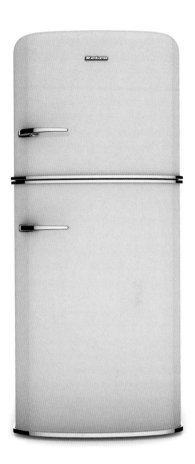

338 DODGE AND BURN

If part of a print is too light, you need to "burn" that section, or expose it for a longer time to darken it. Conversely, if part is too dark, you "dodge" it, or expose it for less time to lighten it. This basic definition is easy to grasp, but dodging and burning are acquired skills requiring lots of trial and error. The tool you employ is an opaque cardboard form (or your own hand, if you like), which you move around as the print is exposed. To burn, let a dark area sit for a longer time under the enlarger's light while you block light from the rest of the image. To dodge, block light from reaching the overly dark area, or expose it for only a brief time. Move your cardboard or hand slowly during the exposure so that the light gradient looks natural and you don't make silhouettes on the final print. (For details on digitally dodging and burning, see #314.)

339 PROTECT YOUR PHOTO PAPER

In home darkrooms, the best place to store unused photographic paper is in the black bag you bought it in. Don't carry the paper outside the darkroom unless it's in the bag. Remember that even safelights can, over time, expose paper, so don't leave unprotected sheets lying around the darkroom. To store paper for long periods, put unopened packages in the fridge. As with film, wait until it returns to room temperature before you handle it, then use it promptly.

340 GO PRO FOR TOP-NOTCH PRINTS

Printing at home is convenient and fast. But professional labs are best if your printer can't wrangle a certain size or you can't get an image to look right in your own software. Photo labs range from easy-to-use online services to high-end shops where you work directly with master printers. To ensure you'll get the prints of your dreams, follow these pointers.

FIND THE RIGHT LAB Don't like fussing over proofs and color settings? Choose a do-it-all service offering preset print sizes (and fun extras such as photo mugs). Save serious jobs for a local shop where you sit down with a seasoned pro to work files under optimized lights on a color-correct monitor.

CALIBRATE AND PROFILE YOUR OWN DISPLAY Your home edits translate best into pro prints when you standardize your monitor's color and contrast with a calibration device. (Top-drawer labs offer downloadable profiles for their printer/paper combos, too.) If you don't have a device—or an eagle eye for color—let the lab do the color corrections. They know their printers and papers best.

FIND OUT WHAT THE LAB CAN HANDLE Ask questions: Does the lab limit file sizes? Can it just handle JPEGs? Can it accept Adobe or ProPhoto RGB images, or must you submit in the narrower sRGB color space? (sRGB means "standard red, green, and blue" and is the standard color space for printing and online sharing.)

PICK YOUR MEDIUM Most labs offer digital c-prints, made via laser projection onto the photo paper you specify (choosing from matte, metallic, and so forth). High-end shops make longer-lasting inkjet prints as well, besides allowing you to choose from a dizzying variety of papers and sizes.

THINK IN B&W Some labs convert color files to B&W for you. Others ask you to send grayscales. C-print shops sometimes offer B&W prints on optimal resin-coated paper; inkjet labs also offer fiber-based papers for that traditional darkroom look. Ask before you upload.

CONSIDER ASPECT RATIO If your shot doesn't fit the lab's printer dimensions, a technician can crop for you. Or you can do it yourself at home before you send the file.

ORDER TEST STRIPS Before you print, select some representative images and send them to the lab for a trial run. Ask the technicians to print your tests on a few different paper stocks so you can pick the one that pleases you most.

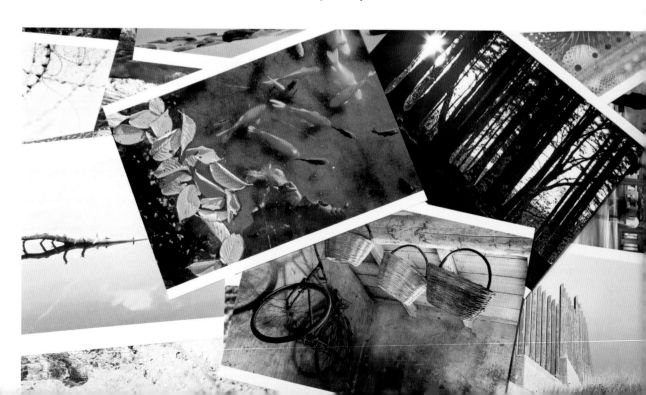

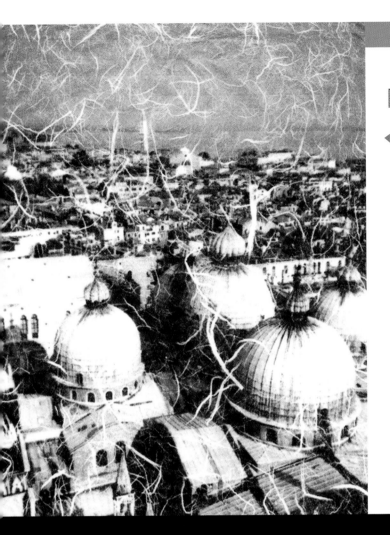

341 FAKE AN ANTIQUE PHOTO

Handmade natural-fiber paper—specialty stock using bark, linen, cotton, or other plants—can make shots you took yesterday look as if they've aged for a century. Unlike regular photo paper—made to produce crisp, snappy prints—soft, fibrous paper produces weathered-looking images.

Buy a few kinds of paper at a stationery store so you can experiment. Gluestick a sheet of ordinary printer paper to a fiber sheet's back so it won't jam the printer. Select your image and load the paper "sandwich" in the printer, ensuring that the fiber sheet is the one that will receive the ink. Hit Print, gently peel apart the sandwich, and inspect the results. Too soft? Return to the file, amp contrast or color saturation, and print again. Sections dropping out? Try a smoother-fibered paper. Now find an old-fashioned frame, and you've got a genuine digital antique.

342 CREATE CONTACT SHEETS

Miss squinting through a loupe at image thumbnails? Want to plan crops with grease pencil rather than software? Use Adobe Bridge to print contact sheets—it lets you make PDFs without leaving the program.

First select your images or folders. Then, in the Bridge menu, go to Tools > Photoshop > Contact Sheet II. Fill in the contact-sheet dimensions and color specifications you want in the Document area; specify your preferred image layout and arrangement in the Thumbnails area. Then choose Use Filename as Caption to label the thumbnails with their source-image file names. Now click OK, name your PDF, and print out your contact sheet whenever you are ready.

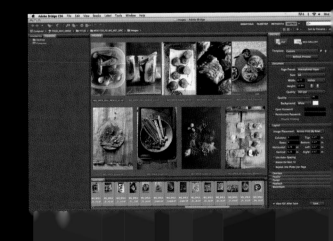

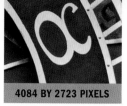

5184 BY 3456 PIXELS
21.6 by 14.4 inches (54 by 36 cm)

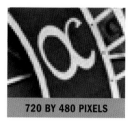

4084 BY 2723 PIXELS
17 by 11.3 inches (43 by 28 cm)

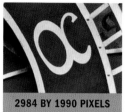

2984 BY 1990 PIXELS
12.4 by 8.3 inches (31 by 21 cm)

720 BY 480 PIXELS
3 by 2 inches (7 by 5 cm)

343 DETERMINE MAXIMUM SIZE

Pixel count, though not a hard-and-fast indicator of resolution, provides a handy rule of thumb for an image's enlargeability. The point of having lots of pixels in an image is that you can stuff them together tightly to make a continuous-tone image. The minimum necessary for "photo-quality" enlargements is 240 pixels per inch (ppi). So if you're using a 3000-by-2000-pixel camera, simply divide those numbers by 240 and you'll get maximum enlargement size: about 12½ by 8½ inches (32 by 22 cm).

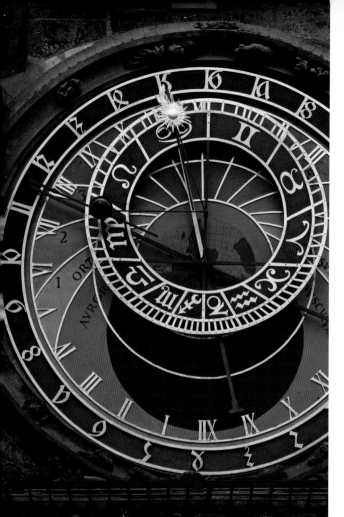

344 UNDERSTAND RESOLUTION

These days, there's a lot of confusion over resolution and pixel count. Because digital images are made up of dots, and because dots are recorded by pixels, people assume that the more pixels, the higher the resolution and the sharper the picture. But factors besides pixel count affect resolution—which itself is an umbrella term for the amount of data that an image holds. The size of a camera's processor makes a difference, and, in fact, sometimes bigger individual pixels make for better resolution. So pixel count is just an indicator of potential resolution, and resolution is more than a measure of pixels—it's the level of detail that a camera can capture. A camera with a good resolution score offers you more options for cropping and zooming.

345 SAVE FILES AS TIFFs

A debate rages among software aficionados: Is it better to save a layered file in Photoshop as a PSD (Photoshop data file) or a TIFF (tagged image file format)? PSD, usually, because you'll probably want to reopen that file in Photoshop, which can reveal and make the most of those layers. Double-clicking a PSD file tells Photoshop to open it; double-clicking a TIFF could call up a program that doesn't use layers. Plus, PSD files can pack in more metadata than TIFFs.

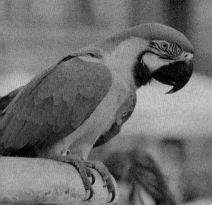
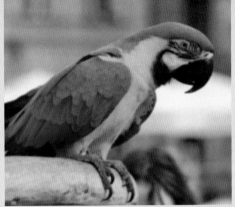
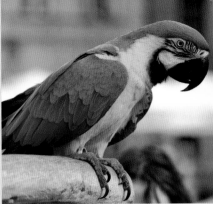

▲ BEFORE Graininess reduces the vibrant detail and colors in the bird's feathers and in the background.

▲ TOO MUCH The noise is gone, but so is the detail. Reduce noise on a duplicate layer and add a mask on the bird.

▲ JUST RIGHT When noise is reduced only in the background, the subject retains detail and pops to life.

346 FIX NOISE WITHOUT LOSING DETAIL

Too much grain can make for an ugly picture. But go too far in taking the noise out and your subjects will look plastic. The good news: Noise reduction can improve your pictures. The bad news: It's a rare occasion when a single noise-reduction setting works for your whole image.

To start, find the noise-reduction tool in your image-editing software. Adjust the sharpness of the photo with your sharpening tools, but not so much that it ceases to look natural. If it's the defocused areas in your image that need smoothing most, dial down the tool that sharpens details all the way.

Do your noise reduction on a duplicate layer, then add a mask (see #298). Simply paint out the areas where noise reduction does more harm than good, leaving detail where you need it.

347 PICK THE RIGHT PRINTER

Each printer model has a maximum printing width. If you want to make mostly small prints, a printer that tops out at just 4 inches (10 cm)—perfect for making 4 by 6 prints—may suit your needs. Other printers (mostly for commercial use) can be up to 44 inches (112 cm) wide. A big size may be tempting, but if you print large only occasionally, it makes sense to buy a smaller printer and send those few big ones to a lab.

348 CHOOSE A PRINTER INK

Some printers use dye-based ink, some use pigment-based, and some use a mix of both. In general, dye is less archival: On some papers, prints tend to fade faster (especially on matte ones) or smudge, and there may be color shift. Some dye-based inks have recently undergone an upgrade in longevity and resistance to moisture, so if you like the look of dyed inks, ask around or experiment with various options.

349 DISPLAY YOUR BEST SHOTS

Reward yourself for all your hard photographic labor with a thoughtful display of your favorite images. Creative ways to show your work are limited only by your imagination.

FRAME IT UP Choose a solid, attractive frame to mark a photo as an artwork and protect it from damage. Select high-quality mats and frames that will last a lifetime. Hang photos alone or in complementary pairs, or line a hallway with a series of shots that tell viewers a story as they walk through your home.

SWING THEM FROM A STRING Hang clothesline or wire between two nails and attach your photos with binder clips or clothespins. Multiple strands of photos draped across a wall lend a casual, artistic air to a room.

GO INVISIBLE In a modern space, mount photos without frames, spray-mounting them to foam board and then using Velcro or small hooks to attach them to walls.

MAKE A PHOTO BOOK You can design and craft a photo book via numerous services, picking size, paper, and cover style, and then designing the book in the services' own software (templates range from cute to gritty). Selections, prices, and ease of use vary widely, so research several before you order.

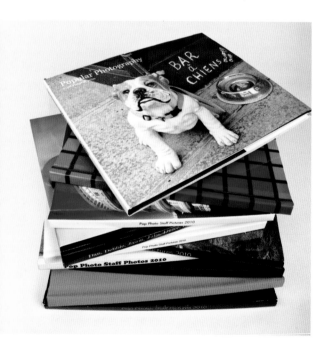

350 COMPREHEND COPYRIGHT

Under U.S. law, the creator of an image owns its copyright. But if you're shooting for another person or company, read the fine print on your contract before you sign—you might not be able to retain rights.

Another area of concern is the Internet: When you upload photos, it's hard to control where they'll end up. Protect them by uploading only small versions to image-sharing sites—thus they'll be useless to printing pirates. Add a watermark, too, via editing software, so your name and copyright symbol are displayed on each image.

351 PROTECT WITH METADATA

It's wise to add your name and copyright info to images' metadata. Open Bridge, then choose File > Get Photos from Camera. Click Advanced Dialogue, and then, under Apply Metadata, type in your copyright text. For detailed metadata on all images you import going forward, make a template in Bridge by going to Tools > Create Metadata Template. And if you've already imported and want to add metadata after the fact, do it via the Metadata tab in Bridge. Highlight all your photos and enter your name and copyright. The details will be applied to all photos' data at once.

352 CHOOSE THE RIGHT COLOR PROFILE

The color profile in which you edit and print photos isn't always the same one you'll use to share them. It makes sense to shoot JPEGs in Adobe RGB—a color model that defines an image's hues by their relative amounts of red, green, and blue—and to open Raw files in ProPhoto RGB. But when you upload shots to a website or print them at a drugstore lab, first convert them to sRGB (standard red, green, and blue). In Photoshop, go to Edit > Convert to Profile. The Source Space is the current profile. From the pulldown menu under Destination Space, choose the profile to which you want to convert your photo.

353 | STORE IMAGES IN THE CLOUD

It sounds like a bunch of hovering photons, but the cloud is simply composed of server banks—and it's an increasingly popular place to securely stow photos. The best way to access it is to sign up for one of the many online storage systems.

Apple's iCloud backs up photos—when you take a picture, it's wirelessly transferred to Apple's online storage system and syncs to all your enabled devices. Other services let you pull photos from your own devices into cloud storage and access them anywhere.

Carbonite's service stows everything—images, audio, video, and text—automatically. Google, Amazon, Microsoft, and Dropbox are just a few of the other online storage giants out there who are eager to keep your assets safe; most programs are free up to a certain storage size. If security is a concern, you can always stick to external hard or flash drives. Just mind the old 3:2:1 rule: Keep at least three copies of your data, making sure that two are stored on different types of devices and one is housed off site.

354 | BE A PICKY EDITOR

To put together a first-rate image library, you must be selective. Here are five tips that will help you see your work with fresh eyes so you can edit and streamline your photo collection, giving photographic gems the attention they deserve while relegating lesser images to the trash (or recycling) bin.

INVERT TONES For B&W photos, break free from preconceived ideas of composition by viewing the image with its tones inverted, as in a negative. The Photoshop command is Image > Adjustments > Invert.

SWITCH COLORS This works the same way. If the inverted colors are garish, convert the image to B&W and then use tonal inversion.

GO TOPSY-TURVY View your images upside-down. This upends your notions of how the subject looks, freeing your eyes to consider the composition anew.

SEE YOURSELF AS OTHERS SEE YOU Visualize a photo published on a magazine cover, perhaps even superimposing type or a logo with an image editor. This overrides your emotional attachment to the image, so you can evaluate your photograph as if it had been taken by someone else.

BE RUTHLESS It can hurt, but have no mercy in discarding images. The more you throw away, the more you'll shift your focus to the standouts in your collection of digital artworks.

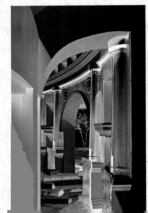 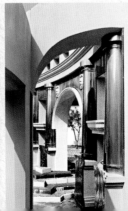 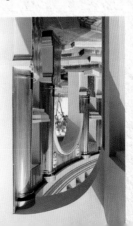

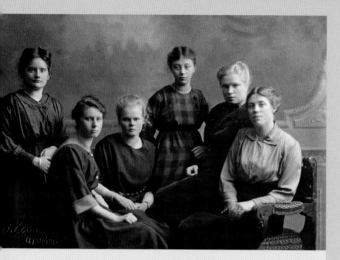

simple ▰▰▰▰▱▱▱▱▱▱▱▰▰▰▰ complex

355 BRING AN OLD PHOTO BACK TO LIFE

Restoring antique or historic photos is a labor of love: It takes time and patience to fix faded, torn images. It also takes software: Photoshop's Content-Aware Fill, Content-Aware Patch tool, and Content-Aware Spot Healing Brush are fabulous restoration tools. Content Aware is an advanced replacement technology that analyzes an image and seamlessly substitutes new texture and tone for unwanted image information. Its tools can rid even the most challenging photos of rips, cracks, dust, mold, and other indignities of age.

STEP ONE Before scanning or photographing your original, gently blow or brush off loose dirt and dust. Remove the frame only if the photo comes out easily. If the photo has been taped together, don't peel away the tape—that could further damage the image. If the photo is in pieces, scan its sections into a single file. Then place each piece on a separate layer: Type W to get the Quick Selection tool, and select one part of the image. Type Ctrl (Command on a Mac) + J to jump the selected part to a new layer. Do the same to the other segments, naming each layer as you go. Then turn off your background layer.

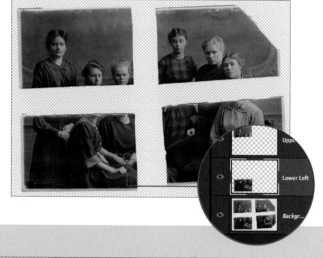

STEP TWO Move and rotate the pieces into place as if you were assembling a puzzle. Select a segment's layer, then tap the V key to activate the Move tool. Tap the arrow keys to move the sections into position, or, to rotate them most accurately, choose Edit > Free Transform and move the pivot point (centered by default) to the corner to act as a fulcrum. Then grab the opposite corner's Transform handle and rotate the piece into place. Hold down Shift as you tap the arrows to move the pieces faster.

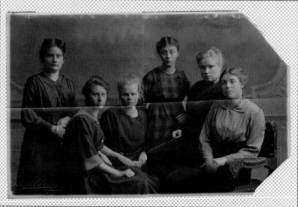

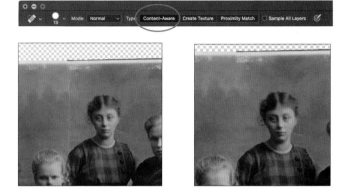

STEP THREE This step is best done on a dedicated layer. Click on the top layer, hold down Alt (Option on a Mac), and choose Layer > Merge Visible. Select the Spot Healing Brush (J); Content-Aware should be on. Make the brush slightly larger than the first crack that you'll repair. Now, starting at the outside edge, paint over the thinnest cracks first. To repair straight tears, click once at the start of a crack, release the mouse, hold down Shift, and click at its end. To repair large rips where white paper shows, first use the Clone Stamp (S), and then use the Spot Healing Brush to refine your cloning.

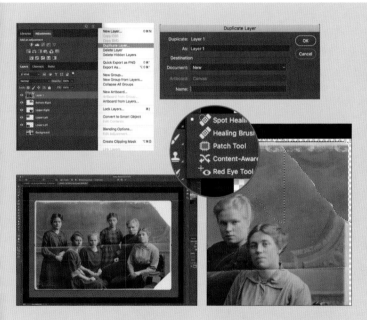

STEP FOUR Use the Patch tool, set to Content-Aware, to replace missing bits. First make your top layer into a new file: Go to Layers > Duplicate Layer and change the Destination to Document: New. Use the Crop tool to crop and straighten it. Click on the Patch tool and select the upper right corner. Click and drag your selection to the left until it fills the empty corner, then release your mouse. Conceal any telltale seams with the Spot Healing Brush.

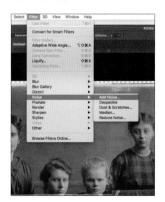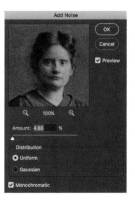

STEP FIVE Cloning and healing can create softness. To conceal it, select Filter > Convert for Smart Filters, then add a hint of noise. Go to Filter > Noise > Add Noise. Select Uniform, check the box for Monochromatic, and use an amount from 4 percent to 6 percent.

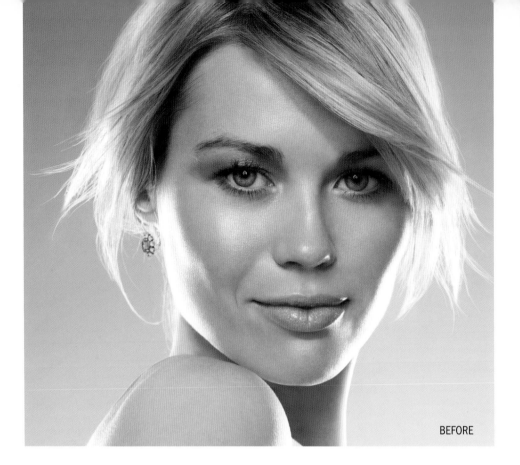
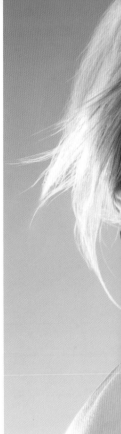

BEFORE

356 EDIT EYES

Enhancing your subject's eyes really brings a portrait to vivid life. Begin with a bit of simple retouching. Clone away bushy eyebrows and other distractions, get rid of red veins in the eyes, soften any rough skin texture, and lighten any shadows. When you have a cleaned-up portrait, you're ready to go to town with Photoshop. (Use a stylus and tablet for best results.)

STEP ONE Set the Lasso tool with a generous pixel feather and make a loose selection of the color of the shadow around the eye. With the selection active, create a Hue/Saturation Adjustment Layer, then move the sliders until you like the color.

STEP TWO You can add contrast to just the pupil and iris, or choose the whole eye area from lower lashes to eyebrow. Use Lasso to make a generously feathered selection. Then create a Curves Adjustment Layer. Make an S-curve, or leave the curve untouched and simply set the blending mode to Soft Light, reducing

layer opacity until you like what you see. For this image, Soft Light with 38 percent opacity worked well.

STEP THREE To brighten the eye's iris and white, select them with a feathered Lasso (choose about 10 or 15 pixels). Use a Curves Adjustment Layer to hold the darks where they are but lighten the midtones a bit, staying fairly close to natural.

STEP FOUR Return to the layer where you did your initial retouching, and use Lasso to make a selection around the eyes, including the eyebrows. Type Ctrl (Command on a Mac) + J to copy the selection to a new layer. Go to Filter > Other > High Pass, and, on a high-resolution file, set Radius to around 8.

STEP FIVE Change the layer's Blend Mode to Soft Light. Add a mask to the layer and fill it with black, then use a white, soft-edged brush to paint back in the eyes and the brows.

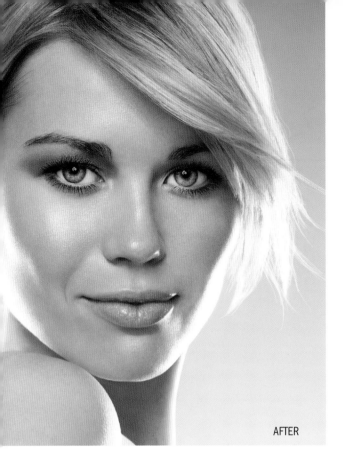

AFTER

357 UNDO A SQUINT

Open up half-closed eyes with the Liquify filter in Photoshop or Elements. Select Liquify and zoom in on one eye. Next, choose an appropriate brush size in the Tool Options palette. Make the brush no larger than the width of the eye's iris. (If the smallest brush size is too big, zoom in closer.) Select the Forward Warp tool, place the brush in the iris (above the pupil), and gently nudge upward to create a smoothly arched eyelid. Repeat on the lower eyelid.

358 REMOVE RED-EYE

Getting rid of the red-eye that results from on-camera flash is easy in Photoshop. First, zoom in on your subject's eyes. Select the Red Eye tool found in the Spot Healing Brush tool's fly-out menu. In the Options bar, you can choose the amount you want to darken the pupils—40 to 50 percent usually works well. Then hover over each red pupil and click. The Red Eye tool will sample the pixels in this area and replace anything red with a natural pupil color.

359 EXTEND EYELASHES

Eyelashes, especially fair ones, sometimes fade out in portraits, but you can restore them to life with a judicious application of software mascara. Open Photoshop, and then tweak the Brush control's setting to create an eyelashlike brush. Select the brush and, in the Options bar, click the Airbrush icon to activate Flow. Click the button to open the Brush panel and hit Transfer. Set the Opacity Jitter control to Pen Pressure, then click on Shape Dynamics. Set the Size Jitter control to Fade, the Size Jitter to 80 percent, and the Control to 80. (If an 80 percent Jitter appears too rough, simply reduce the size until the brush matches the lashes you're editing.) Make a new, blank layer and sample a color from one of your subject's existing eyelashes. Now draw in improved lashes.

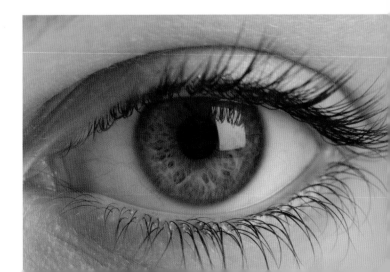

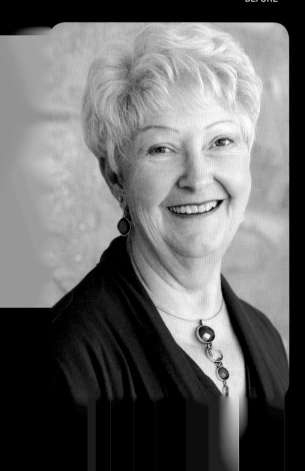

BEFORE

360 RETOUCH SUBTLY FOR PERFECT PORTRAITS

This is a lovely portrait of a lovely woman, and it doesn't require retouching. But if you're aiming for a somewhat idealized or younger version of your subject—or yourself—try out these steps. They'll let you subtly brighten eyes, whiten teeth, and minimize wrinkles and skin flaws.

   Remember: With great power comes great responsibility, so don't go too far! The trick to beauty retouching is making subjects look like slightly better versions of themselves.

STEP ONE Eyes are often the most important feature of a portrait, so make them stand out. Duplicate the background layer and name the new layer Eye Whites. Now grab the Dodge tool, set it to midtones, and leave Exposure set to 50 percent. Zoom in close, and dodge the white parts of the eyes until they're looking a bit brighter.

STEP TWO Duplicate your Eye Whites layer and name the new layer Teeth. Double-click on the color swatches in the toolbar to get Color Picker. Use the dropper to select one of the teeth's whiter tones as the foreground color. Create a new blank layer and change its Blend Mode to Screen.

STEP THREE Switch to the Brush tool, and paint your subject's teeth with a small brush until they're white and bright. If they seem too bright, lower this layer's opacity until they look realistic. When you like their appearance, go to Layer > Merge Down to blend your whitened teeth layer with the Teeth layer that you created in Step Two.

STEP FOUR Now create a new blank layer and call it Blemishes. Grab the Spot Healing Brush, check the box for Sample All Layers, and choose Content-Aware. Then, zoomed in at 100 percent, paint out any blemishes on your subject's complexion.

STEP FIVE Make another new blank layer, and name it Wrinkles. Switch to the regular Healing Brush and set it to Sample Current and Below. Sample a spot with smooth skin on your subject's face, and then paint over a wrinkle to erase it. You need a light hand here, so if your work looks too smooth, go to Edit > Fade and turn down the effect until it looks flattering but natural. One hint: Since wrinkles grow longer as we age, especially around the eyes, just shorten them to make someone look younger. Don't take them out altogether.

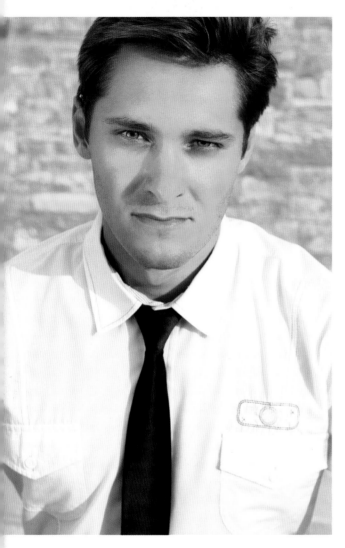

361 SAVE FACE WITH SOFTWARE

Give your portrait subjects a youthful glow with a bit of all-over skin smoothing in Photoshop. First duplicate your background layer by going to Layer > Duplicate Layer. Name the new layer Blur. Go to Filter > Blur > Gaussian Blur. Set the radius to 50 and click OK. Now add a black layer mask to the Blur layer. Holding down Alt (Option on a Mac), click the Layer Mask button. Next hit B for the Brush tool. In the Options bar, pick a medium-sized, soft-edged brush, and slide the brush's opacity to 30 percent. Be sure that white is set as your foreground color, and paint the skin until it is smooth and glowing. Overdid it? Just reduce the layer's opacity.

362 PREVIEW YOUR RETOUCHING

In Photoshop, you often zoom in to adjust a portrait. From such a close view, it's hard to gauge how edits affect the whole image. Here's a trick that neatly solves the problem: Go to Window > Arrange > New Window For, and choose the file you're working on. Line up the images on your screen (or, better yet, on two monitors). Zoom in on one, out on the other. All edits you make to the zoomed-in image show on the zoomed-out one, so you see the results of your edits as you work.

363 FIX FACIAL FLAWS WITH YOUR PHONE

Smartphones can, with the right apps, flatter portrait subjects and transform even a flawed complexion into a glowing, natural-looking one. Numerous free or cheap apps for iPhone and other devices automatically reduce the visibility of freckles, moles, zits, and wrinkles and zap red-eye, and they do it all without slapping on a thick pancake of color. After shooting, you can modify the smoothing and brightness levels until you—and your subject—are pleased with the results.

MOBILE TIP

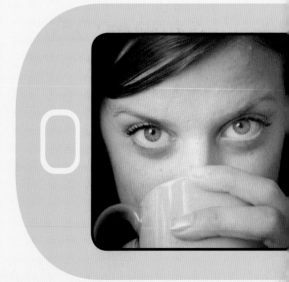

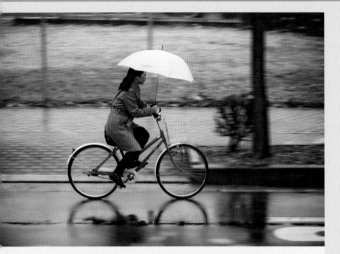

simple ▬▬▬▬▬▬▬ complex

364 EMPHASIZE MOTION BY FAKING BLUR

Sometimes you find yourself in a situation where, as much as you want a panning effect, you're unable to manage it—for example, when you're shooting a moving subject out of a train window, as with the image here. Fortunately, motion blur, like many effects, can be created with software. This tutorial takes advantage of tools found in CS6 and later, such as Content-Aware Fill and Smart Objects. But you can do this in older versions of Photoshop and Elements—you need only Layers and the Motion Blur filter.

STEP ONE First, as always, duplicate your background layer before you start (this crucial step ensures that you'll have your original to go back to if you mess up). To fake the blur, you'll need to select the subject, move her to her own separate layer, then blur the background. If you blur the background without first cloning out the cyclist, you'll see a blurry cyclist behind a sharp one. So before you add the motion effect, she's got to go.

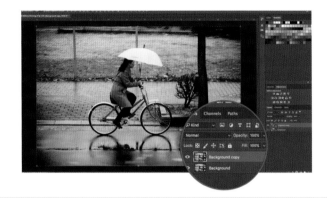

STEP TWO Select the figure and her bicycle. Type W for the Quick Selection tool and paint to make the selection. Hold down Alt (Option on a Mac) to paint and remove a selection from where it shouldn't be. Then zoom in and, with a small brush, paint to correct any over- or underselecting that this tool has done.

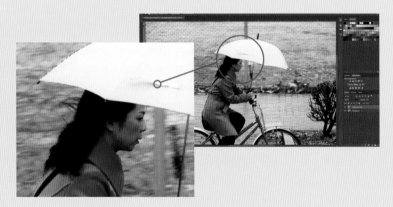

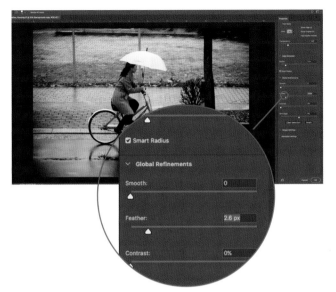

STEP THREE In the Options bar, click Refine Edge to perfect your selection. Keep the feathering low, and add a little smoothness to even out jagged edges. Check the box to use Smart Radius for edge detection. To mask along a straight edge, click at the beginning of the line, hold down the Shift key, and click at the end of the line.

If your selection is still imperfect, exit Refine Edge and then hit Q on your keyboard for Quick Mask mode to adjust it manually. For instance, here the basket was so close to the background color that it was undetectable by the auto-selection tools. The solution was to paint the entire basket with the Brush tool. When you're done, hit Q to exit Quick Mask and see your selection again.

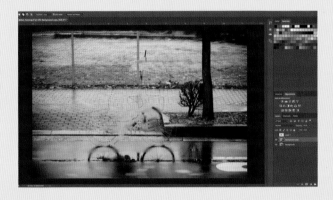

STEP FOUR Type Ctrl (Command on a Mac) + J to jump the selected subject to its own layer. Your marching ants will disappear. Reactivate your selection by holding down Ctrl while clicking on the Layer 1 thumbnail. Now click on the Background Copy layer. Expand the selection by going to Select > Modify > Expand, and expand by at least 15 pixels. Then go to Edit > Fill and choose Use: Content-Aware. Hide Layer 1 to see the results. If they're acceptable, continue, as you'll later apply a blur anyway.

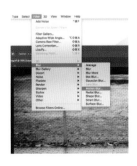
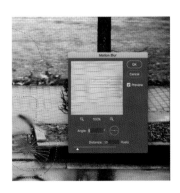

STEP FIVE With the Background Copy selected, go to Layer > Smart Objects > Convert to Smart Object. Then go to Filter > Blur > Motion Blur. Set Angle to zero, and play with the distance until it looks realistic. Click OK, then turn on Layer 1. If you need to adjust the blur, double-click on the Motion Blur Smart Filter to redo it.

Photoshop versions CS3 and older don't have Smart Filters, so if you're using an older version, simply apply the filter to your layer.

365 DECIPHER DISTORTED IMAGES

Most lenses create slightly distorted images, and their linear distortion is usually worst at the frame's edge. Very wide-angle lenses are notorious offenders, but inexpensive telezooms can yield distortion, too. Some lenses also add vignetting. In specific subjects—such as those with plenty of straight horizontals and verticals—perspective distortion introduced by a tilted camera is a problem. So, if your images seem to squish or expand in the middle, or the buildings in your skyline shots seem to topple toward one another, either your lens or your angle of view may be at fault. Here's how to straighten out these two common types of distortion using Photoshop.

LENS DISTORTION is the culprit to blame when you see lines bowing inward or outward around a photograph's center. To fix the warp, use the Lens Correction filter to apply the opposite radial distortion weighted between the center and edges. Images that include long, straight lines often need the most lens-distortion correction.

SHOOT A TARGET to create lens-correction profiles for particular combinations of your cameras and lenses, and then save and use these profiles to automatically apply corrections to any later images that you shoot with the same combination of gear. If you don't wish to craft your own profiles, you can use the ones that came with the program or download ones created by other shooters and apply them to your shots.

PERSPECTIVE DISTORTION is easily spotted—lines that are parallel in reality converge in your image, either vertically or horizontally. You'll find this problem frequently in architectural shots. To fix the issue, go to Edit > Transform > Perspective and then pull the lines into proper orientation.

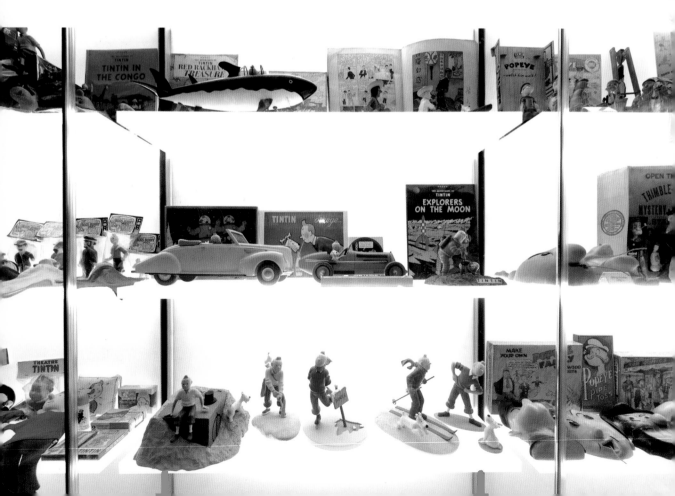

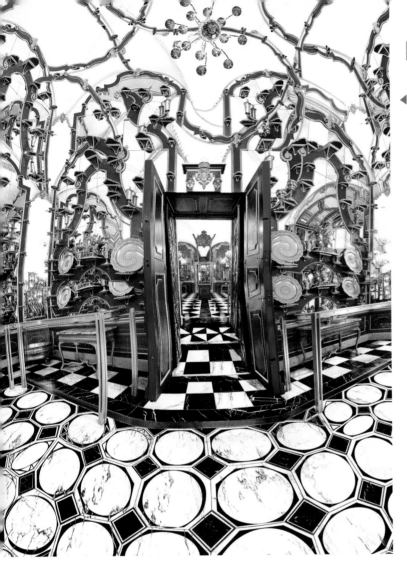

366 | WARP A WILD PANORAMA

At its highest levels, image editing is a fine art. Photographer Raïssa Venables cannily combines panorama techniques (see #369), compositing (see #374), and Photoshop layering and masking to craft distorted, baroque interiors for her series "All That Glitters." If you're eager for a challenge, sample a few of her techniques.

STEP ONE Shoot in the highest resolution available to you, pivoting a tripod-mounted camera 360 degrees from a single position to capture an entire interior. (Venables likes rooms that are, she says, "excessively opulent," but a simple room is a better first project.) Bracket for all you're worth—for focus so that all elements stay sharp, and for exposure so you'll have lots of highlight and shadow detail for editing.

STEP TWO Make work prints of the photos and manually assemble them with tape and scissors, as Venables does, into a rough sketch. Venables warped this image outward to emphasize the dizzying spin of her mega-panorama, but you might prefer an easier arrangement. After this planning stage, make new, high-res scans—Venables employed 17 separate images in this shot—and open Photoshop to begin the high-art phase of your work.

STEP THREE Open the first image and expand the canvas around it to the dimensions you plan for the final print. Venables printed this one at 79 by 62 inches (2 by 1.5 m), so the image is as imposing as the room itself. Then draw together all the images in a panorama, hiding seams via layer masking, the Transform tool, and the Warp tool.

STEP FOUR Now let your imagination run free. Craft multiple layers and masks to "paint," collage, and distort your image. Venables twined the green and gold trim all over the distorted ceiling, relocated parts of the room, and mirrored, rotated, and erased at will, proving that image-editing software is as powerful as any paintbrush.

367 | WIELD THE WARP TOOL

A tidily aligned photo is all very well, but sometimes you want a touch of the bizarre. Photoshop's Warp is the tool for the job. Make a selection of part of an image via your preferred method, and go to Edit > Transform > Warp. Simply grab the selection's handles to skew it in any direction.

The separate Puppet Warp tool lays a mesh over an image and fastens it with small "pins" that you use to control or resist distortion. Both subtle tweaks and surreal twists can be made with this nicely granular tool. It's similar to the Liquify tool, and it's equally skilled at generating intriguing distortions. (Note: Puppet Warp won't work on the background layer.)

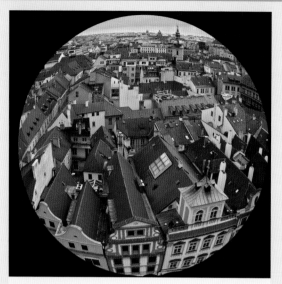

simple ▰▰▰▰▰▱▱▱▱▱▱▱▰▰▰▰ complex
▲

368 GIVE A PHOTO THE FISHEYE LOOK

People often use Adobe Photoshop just to fix pictures: correcting white balance, adding contrast, or removing elements that don't belong. But sometimes it's fun to use Photoshop to get a bit wacky, taking an image to an entirely different place.

To get started, try out this quick and easy trick to make an ordinary photo look like it was shot with a circular fisheye lens, complete with its telltale shape and black background. You'll need the Warp tool, first introduced in Photoshop version CS2. The technique works best on images that have lots of horizontal and vertical lines so the distortion really stands out.

STEP ONE Begin by cropping your photo into a square, ensuring the distortion you'll add later will look more realistic. Get the Crop tool by typing C. In the Options bar, click on the drop-down menu and choose 1x1 (Square) to automatically constrain the proportions. Make sure Delete Cropped Pixels is checked so that the distortion will be applied only to the square you have selected, and not to the pixels outside the frame. Drag the edges of your square to crop your image with a circular final product in mind, and hit Enter.

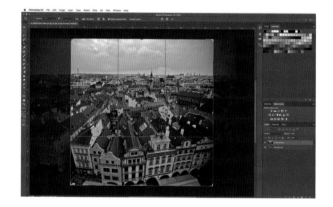

STEP TWO Since the Warp transformation can't be applied to the background layer, work on a duplicate. Go to Layer > Duplicate Layer. Name it Fisheye, and click OK.

If you're looking for a shortcut, a quick way to duplicate your background layer is to drag it down to the New Layer button in the Layers panel.

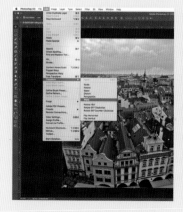
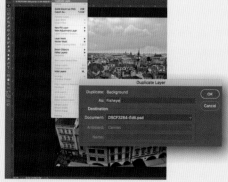

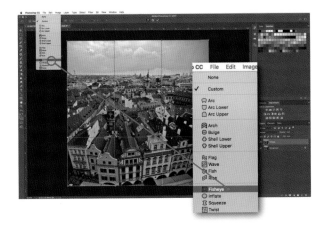

STEP THREE Now it's time to add some distortion to your photo. Go to Edit > Transform > Warp. Then, in the dropdown menu in the Options bar, choose Warp: Fisheye. The default usually provides enough distortion, but if you want more, increase the Bend percentage. (With a real fisheye lens, the closer you are to your subject, the more distorted it becomes.) When you like the way it looks, hit Enter on your keyboard to keep your transformation.

Want another way to increase the Bend? Try grabbing the small square in the center of the grid's top line, then pull it upward.

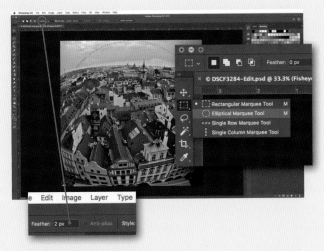

STEP FOUR With the distortion all set, add the black circle. Get the Elliptical Marquee tool and set a very slight bit of feathering: Two pixels should do it. Then put your cursor in the top left-hand corner of your photo, just inside the border. Hold down the Shift key and drag the cursor diagonally to make a circle that fits inside the image. If your selection isn't in exactly the right place, use your arrow keys to nudge it so that it encompasses all the important elements of your picture.

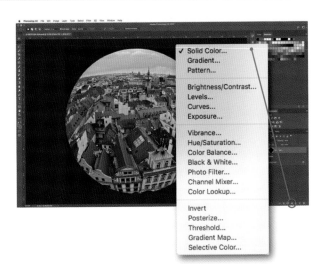

STEP FIVE Now reverse your selection by typing Ctrl (Command on a Mac) + Shift + I on your keyboard. Doing this will ensure your selection encloses everything outside the circle you just drew. From the Adjustment Layer menu at the bottom of your Layers panel, choose Solid Color. Select black in the color picker, and then hit OK to see how your faux fisheye photo looks.

369 WIDEN YOUR WORLD WITH PANORAMAS

Ever looked at a landscape, then peered through your viewfinder to discover that even your widest lens couldn't capture the entire scene? That's when a panorama comes in handy: You take a series of photos and piece them together later, capturing the widest possible scene with the greatest amount of detail.

You can stitch the panorama together yourself by dragging and aligning all the images in a single canvas sized to the approximate pixel dimensions of the final version: roughly the dimension of a single frame times the number of component frames you're including in your stitched-together composition. Then use layer masks to blend the overlapping areas into a seamless whole. If you'd rather not do it on your own, let your software take over. For instance, Photoshop's Photomerge tool does an excellent job.

370 GO GLOBAL

Want to turn a panoramic photo into the whole wide world? Use this trick to transform a 360-degree panorama into a globe. Start with Photomerge and stitch your images together to make one long horizontal image. Then crop your image so that it has no border and rotate it upside down. Go to Filter > Distort > Polar Coordinates. This somewhat obscure filter is your ticket to globalization. But depending on how fast your computer is and how large an image you're rounding out, it may take time to process. Make sure Rectangular to Polar is selected, then click OK.

Now you have something that looks like a globe, albeit one that was stepped on by a giant. That's easy to fix. Choose Edit > Free Transform. That gives you handles on all sides of your image so you can change its shape. Grab the handle on the left and drag it right until the oval becomes a circle. Some white will remain, so crop it out to finish your global image.

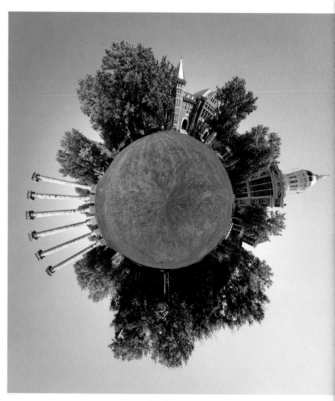

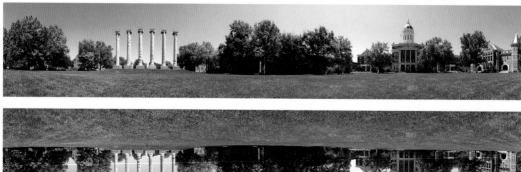

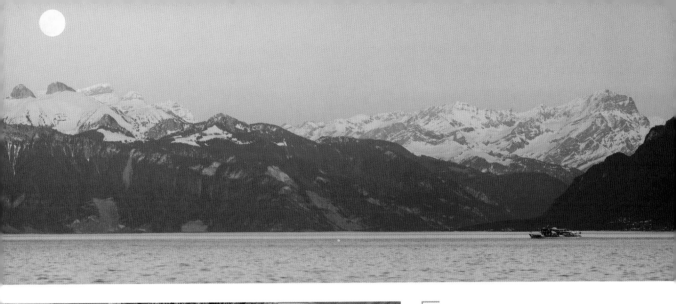

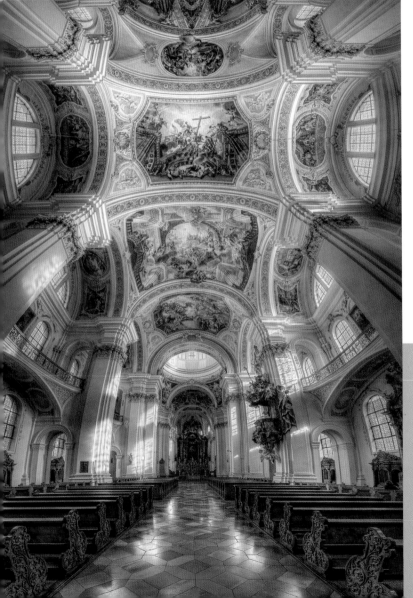

371 MAKE A VERTORAMA

You've heard of panoramas, but how about a vertorama? Yes, it's a real term: It's a panorama-like image made up of vertical slices of a scene stitched together in software. Klaus Herrmann, a German computer scientist, did just that for this interior of the St. Martin Basilica in Weingarten. It's five verticals joined together. Why vertoramas? They let you shoot an expansive interior or landscape to include far more detail than you would get in one wide-angle capture, and you end up with something like a traditional pictorial aspect ratio (i.e., 3:2), not the long sliver typical of stitched horizontals.

372 DITCH DISTORTION

Adaptive Wide Angle, a filter in Photoshop, can correct the distortion inherent in panoramas, straightening buildings and horizons and reducing wide-angle distortion. It's compatible with Smart Objects—use it as a Smart Filter, which you can edit at any time.

QUICK TIP

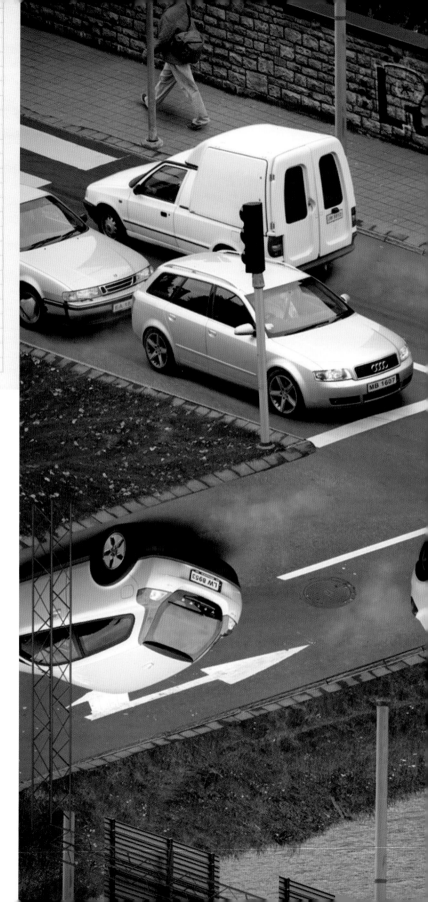

BACKSTORY

I began learning image editing as I learned digital photography. I sketch an idea, then use photography and software to make it happen. To combine photos, you have to capture your elements in the same lighting and from the same angles, with the same shadows. To get multiple perspectives on a scene, I shoot from different elevations. Combining is less difficult when the photos are planned carefully in advance. I love the ability to imagine a scene and make it look real—and digital photography and editing let you do that.

—ERIK JOHANSSON

373

CREATE AN OPTICAL ILLUSION

Hundreds of shots—and inspiration from mind-bending artists such as M. C. Escher—enable Erik Johansson to craft trompe l'oeil masterworks. They're composites (see #374)—very precisely planned ones.

To combine the vertical and horizontal lines of traffic in this image, he shot from multiple hills along a road, standing far enough away to capture perfectly straight lines. He assembled the photos into a rough composite in Photoshop and added background and fill from a stock library of elements such as skies and trees. The last stage—compositing—required days as he adjusted color temperatures across layers and fine-tuned contrast.

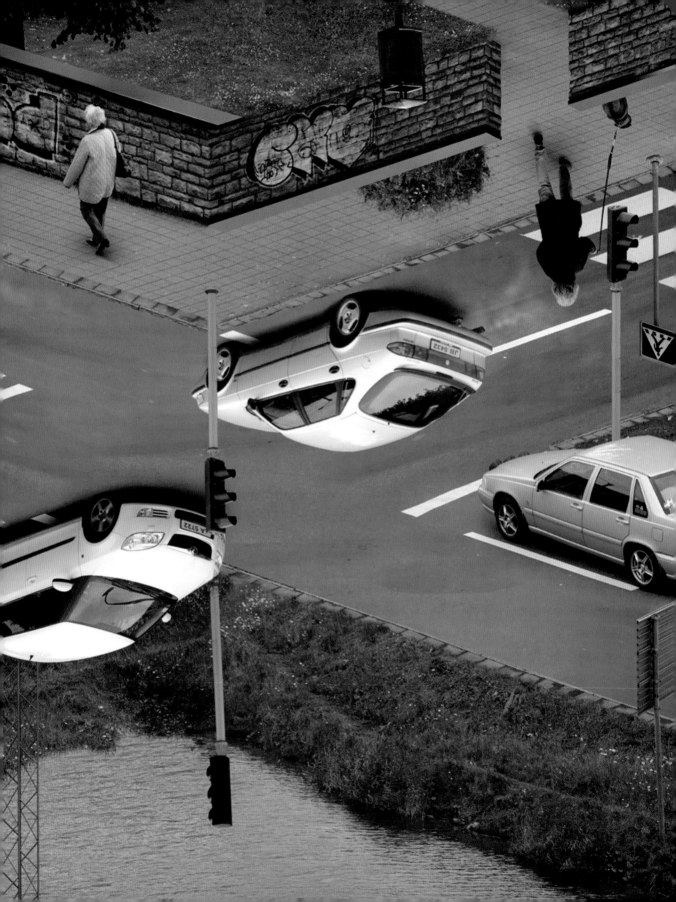

374 CRAFT A COMPOSITE

This image from Romain Laurent's "Tilt" series is so seamless and simple, it's hard to believe it's composed of many elements. But it's actually a composite of numerous separate images. To create a vertigo-inducing shot of your own, try out his method:

STEP ONE First take an empty background shot (here, the cobblestone street) for your image's base layer.

STEP TWO The second layer is your trick shot of your model. Bring along a friend to support her as she leans to the side, and capture multiple images from the same perspective, making sure they all line up.

STEP THREE Postshoot, convert your Raw files (see #312) and ensure their colors match as closely as possible. Then open Photoshop to begin compositing.

STEP FOUR Choose the best overall shot of your model, then use Photoshop's high-precision Pen tool to excise your helper and separate the model as smoothly as possible from her original background. Now layer her figure atop the base-layer background of the empty street, placing her where she was in the initial shot.

STEP FIVE Check for telltale flaws. If you can spot the assistant's shadow, remove it using a combination of the Pen tool and masks. Look, too, for areas missing from the street because your assistant's body covered them, and patch in fill from other shots.

STEP SIX Do all details look their best, or are there better versions in alternate shots? Laurent cut out and layered in superior images of the model's right shoulder, tote bag, dress bow, and left hand.

STEP SEVEN Minimize cloning and healing by using your clean base layer, and employ masks to show or hide areas as needed. Your final file, which will include many masked Curves Adjustments Layers, should skew perspective just enough to intrigue the viewer.

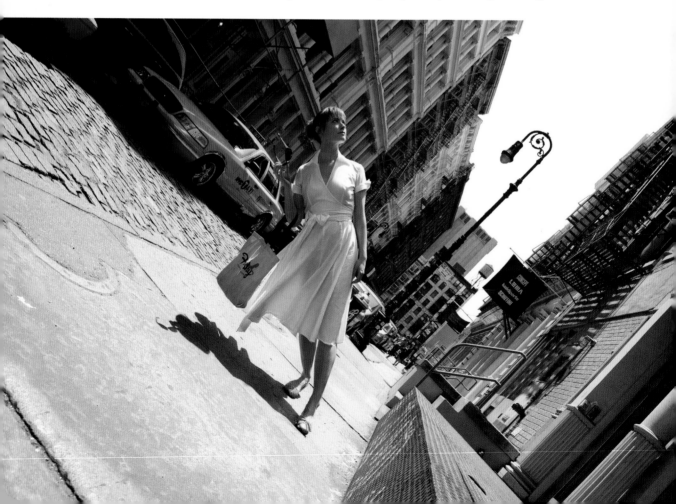

375 ANIMATE A GIF ON A SMARTPHONE

Several free apps let you conjure animated GIFs (graphics interchange format files) out of smartphone shots in mere seconds. Use them to amuse Facebook friends—or shock Granny. Giphy Cam, a popular choice, works on Androids and iPhones, as does the built-in GIF maker on Tumblr's app. Their functions permit you to shoot brief sequences to convert to GIFs or work with existing photos, adding special effects and previewing GIFs before you upload them.

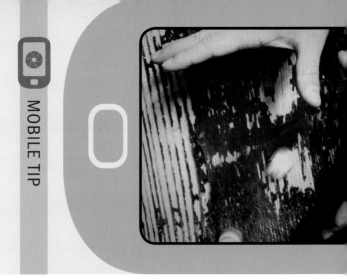

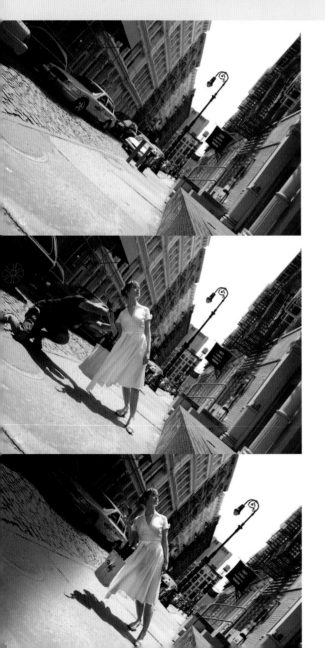

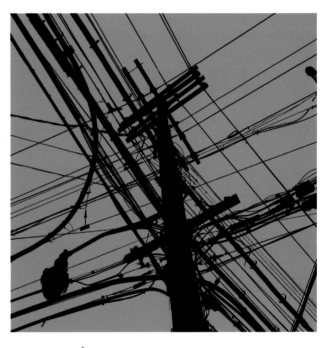

376 SWITCH OUT COLORS FOR GRAPHIC POP

Philip Habib shot these utility towers and lines against a gray sky. Looking at the image files later, he was disappointed by their weak contrast, so he swapped out the colors. If you find yourself in a similar fix, try borrowing his trick. Mask off the background using Photoshop's Color Range tool, then fine-tune lines with a hard-edged brush. Now replace the background with the shade you desire—Habib was inspired by painter Piet Mondrian's bold palette—to enhance contrast.

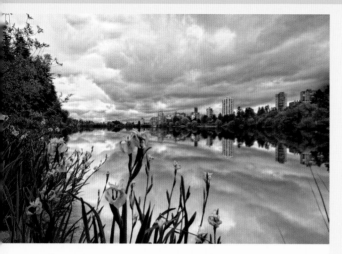

simple ▮▮▮▮▮▮▮▮▮▮▮▮▮▮▮▮▮ complex

377 FAKE A REFLECTION

Not every scene photographs the way you see it in your mind's eye. Say you find a beautiful lake and position yourself for a composition with a strong foreground, midground, and background. The scene is lovely, but it's windy and the water is choppy, not tranquil. You take the shot, and the final result lacks both serenity and symmetry. There's no need to live with it—you can fake a mirrorlike reflection in Adobe Photoshop even if Mother Nature didn't have the grace to provide one.

STEP ONE Since the sky will be doubled in your final picture, clean it up first. This photo shows a bright spot on the top left portion of the sky—use the Healing Brush to remove that kind of visual distraction. Then ensure you like the image's exposure and color tones. When your photo is at a good starting place, grab the rectangular Marquee tool by hitting M on your keyboard. Use it to select the whole top section of your image— the section that you want "reflected" on the water's surface.

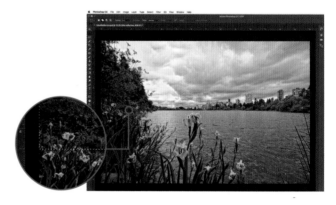

STEP TWO Type Ctrl (Command on a Mac) + J to copy the selected area and jump it to a new layer of its own. Then go to Edit > Transform > Flip Vertical to turn it upside down. Type V to get the Move tool, and, holding down the Shift key so it doesn't wiggle left or right, drag the top half down until it meets the horizon line. If it doesn't quite fit, type Ctrl (Command) + T to transform it, and stretch it until it meets the bottom.

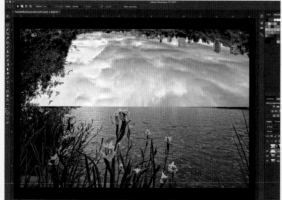

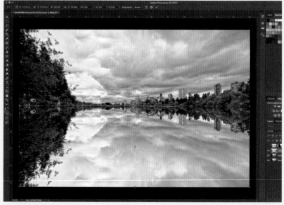

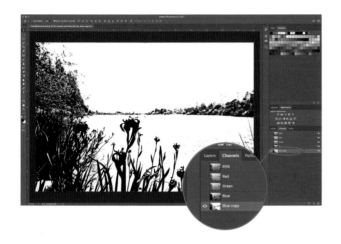

STEP THREE Now make the selection. Turn off the layer with the fake reflection, select the layer below it, and use your preferred method to select anything that isn't water. Various methods work best for specific photos—here the Blue channel is a good starting place for a mask. Duplicate it, then use Levels to add enough contrast to blow out the water. Click OK, then hit Ctrl (Command) + A to select the whole layer and Ctrl (Command) + C to copy. Click on the thumbnail of the Blue copy. Turn off your extra channel so you don't see it, but save it in case you want to go back.

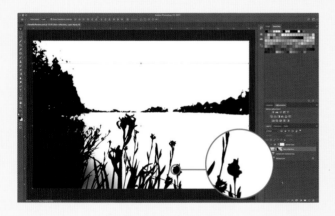

STEP FOUR Head back to your layers, then add a mask to the layer that contains your reflection. Press Alt (Option) + click on it to show the mask, then hit Ctrl (Command) + V to paste the contrast version of your Blue channel into it. Deselect it, then use the Brush (B) to finish whiting out the water and blacking out the foreground grasses. The foreground here is detailed, so take time to perfect it with the Pen and Quick Selection tools.

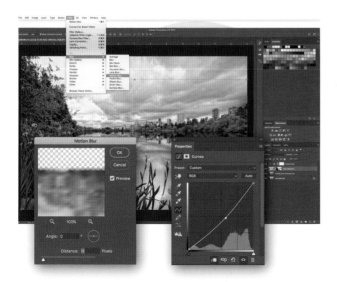

STEP FIVE Now for the fun part: making the water look realistic. Click on the layer thumbnail for the upside-down sky. Then go to Filter > Blur > Motion Blur. Choose a nearly horizontal angle (4 degrees or so) and a distance you like. Click OK. Now run that filter again, this time choosing a more vertical angle (such as 60 degrees). Finally, darken the water. Make a Curves Adjustment Layer, and lock it to the water layer by holding down Alt (Option) and clicking on the line between the two layers. Bring down midtones until your water looks real. Presto: You've got the flawless reflection you envisioned when you first composed your shot.

378 QUICKLY SHARPEN A LANDSCAPE

Most pictures, especially landscapes, turn out just a bit blurrier than they should be. Whether the blurriness is the fault of your lens, Raw processing, resizing, or other digital-workflow tasks, you'll want to subtly sharpen your images before you print or share them.

Photoshop and Elements both offer several fast options for sharpening. Adjust Sharpness in Elements, and its cousin Smart Sharpen in Photoshop, are popular options. But there's another method—High Pass sharpening. Quick and simple, it won't amp noise, create oversharpened or "crunchy" edges, or sharpen areas where you want to preserve blur. Instead, it provides just the right amount of contrast and snap.

STEP ONE Wait to sharpen until you've resized and finished the rest of your editing work. Then, in Elements, copy your background layer by right-clicking it with the mouse and choosing Duplicate Layer. Now hit Ctrl (Command on a Mac) + Shift + U to completely desaturate your duplicated background layer. By zapping color, you'll avoid oversharpening or increased color noise.

STEP TWO Now it's time to add the High Pass filter. Go to Filter > Other > High Pass. Move Radius slowly upward until you can just barely see your image's edges in the gray preview. (Note: The smaller your original image, the smaller Radius you will need.) Anything beyond five or so pixels won't truly sharpen, so don't push it too far—that would give the photograph a fake-HDR appearance. When you're done, click OK.

STEP THREE To check out the effect of your High Pass filter, change your background copy layer's Blend mode. Use the pulldown menu found at the top left of your Layers Panel to switch your mode from Normal to Overlay.

STEP FOUR Now you should have a presentably crisp image. If it looks too sharp, simply lower the layer's opacity. But if it still isn't sharp enough, experiment with another Blend mode. Linear Light will probably take the photo over the edge into crunchiness, so give Hard Light a try to see if that mode will take the effect up just a bit.

STEP FIVE When you're finished with your sharpening work, flatten your final image by going to Layer > Flatten Image. Then simply Save As. Remember to use a new file name.

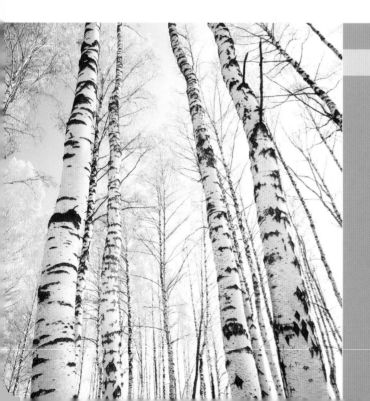

QUICK TIP

379 CUT OFF FRINGE

Ever shoot a landscape only to notice that backlit branches or mountains show purple edges where they meet the sky? Or that one side of a backlit object is cyan and the other red? The purple stuff is called fringing, and the split color is known as chromatic aberration. Both are so common in digital pictures that they're often accepted. But fixing them makes photos look cleaner and more professional. In Photoshop's Lens Correction filter, Adobe Camera Raw, or Lightroom, simply check the Chromatic Aberration correction box to clean up your landscapes.

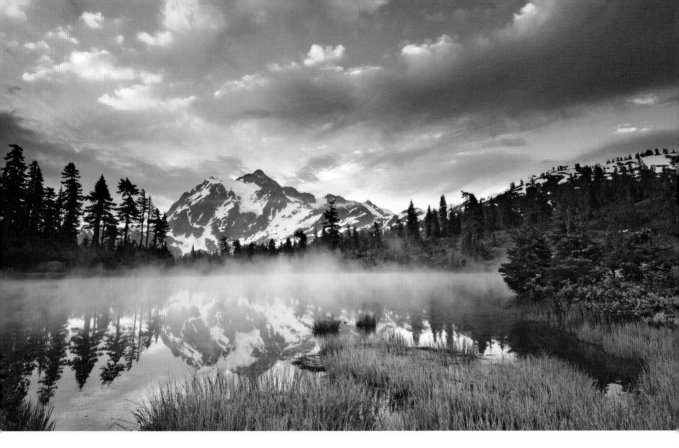

380

LEVEL YOUR HORIZON

A slanted horizon can mess up an otherwise wonderful landscape. Even when you're shooting with the support of a tripod, however, it's hard to tell by eye if you've properly captured the horizon.

If your horizon turns out wonky, use the straightening capability that's in Photoshop's Ruler tool. Find it by clicking and holding the Eyedropper icon in the toolbar. Use the ruler to draw a line along the horizon, and then click the Straighten Layer button in the Options bar at the top of the screen. The world should return to an even keel.

381

PUMP UP THE CLOUDS

To add drama to a cloudy sky in Photoshop, duplicate your Background layer, then use the pulldown menu to choose the Multiply Blend mode. The effect will most likely be too strong, so dial down the layer's opacity until you get a more realistic sky. Add a mask to the layer, grab the Brush tool, and paint with black on your mask to hide all the areas that you don't want your Multiply Blend to affect.

382

ADD SPOT CONTRAST

Sometimes you'll shoot a landscape with excellent contrast in certain sections but a flat look in others. Zap dull spots one at a time using a Curves Adjustment layer and a mask. First, select the Curves button in the Adjustments panel. Click on the pointer finger in the Curves dialog (on the left in the Properties panel), place it on an area you wish to lighten, and drag upward. Do the same on an area with a tone you want to darken, but drag downward. Fill the mask with black to hide all adjustments. Set the Brush to white, with 30 percent opacity, to slowly paint them back in.

GLOSSARY

AMBIENT LIGHT The available light in a scene, whether from natural or artificial sources, that is not explicitly supplied by the photographer for the purpose of taking pictures.

APERTURE The adjustable opening inside the lens, the aperture determines how much light passes through to strike the image sensor. The size of the aperture is measured in f-stops, and higher numbers signify a smaller opening.

APERTURE-PRIORITY MODE A camera mode in which the photographer chooses a specific aperture setting, and the camera automatically selects a complementary shutter speed to achieve a proper exposure.

APS-C An image sensor format used in many DSLRs that's smaller than a full-frame format sensor (and thus captures a smaller angle of view).

ARTICULATED LCD A flip-out image screen that can rotate and swivel away from the camera body, giving the photographer flexibility in the angle of view.

AUDIO FLASH TRIGGER This device allows you to sync your camera with a microphone so that the shutter is triggered by sound rather than the pressing of the shutter button. Useful for capturing very fast action because it eliminates the photographer's reaction time from the process.

AUTOEXPOSURE A mode in which your camera automatically calculates and adjusts exposure settings in order to match an image with the subject as closely as possible.

AUTOFOCUS A mode in which the camera automatically focuses on the subject in a designated point of the LCD or viewfinder.

BACKGROUND The elements in an image that appear farthest from the viewer.

BARREL DISTORTION Distortion in which straight lines curve outward in the image. These barrel-shaped lines are most noticeable along the edges of a photograph.

BOUNCE Light that is redirected toward a subject by a reflector or other reflective surface. Usually soft light, it helps spread light and fill shadows.

BRACKETING The technique of taking a number of pictures of the same subject at different levels of exposure, usually at half- or one-stop differences.

CENTER-WEIGHTED METERING A metering system that concentrates the light reading mostly in the central portion of the frame and feathers out to the edges.

COMPOSITE A picture made of multiple, separate images that have been pieced together with software.

CONTINUOUS (HOT LIGHTS) Traditional tungsten or halogen lights that stay on continuously while you're shooting.

CONTINUOUS MODE Also known as burst mode, this is the digital camera's ability to take several shots in less than a second with just one press of the shutter button. The speed and total number of frames differs between camera types and models, and is sometimes adjustable.

CONTRAST The range and distribution of tones between the darkest and brightest points in a photograph.

DEFOCUS Defocusing a subject seen through the camera's lens makes it appear softened and less defined.

DEPTH OF FIELD The distance between the nearest and farthest objects that appear in acceptably sharp focus in a photograph.

DIFFUSER Any material that softens and scatters light that passes through it.

EXPOSURE The total amount of light allowed to fall on the photographic medium (determined by aperture, shutter speed, and ISO) during the process of taking a photograph. Also refers to a single shutter cycle (that is, a frame).

EXPOSURE COMPENSATION A feature that lets you increase or decrease your camera's exposure settings in small increments to achieve proper exposure. Usually controlled by a button marked with plus and minus symbols.

FILL LIGHT A technique usually used to soften the contrast in a scene by shining a light that's softer than the main light into a scene's shadows to erase them.

FILTER A camera accessory that can be attached (either screwed on or clipped) to the end of a lens to alter or enhance its effect.

FLASH The brief illumination of a subject during the moment of exposure.

FOCAL LENGTH With a lens focused at infinity, this is the distance from the point in the lens where the path of light rays crosses to the film or sensor. Longer focal lengths magnify images, while shorter focal lengths reduce magnification and show a wide angle of view.

FOCUS When an element in an image is distinctly defined and its outlines are clearly rendered, it is said to be "in focus."

FOCUS RING A ring on the lens barrel that a photographer rotates to adjust focus manually.

FOCUS TRACKING A camera feature that can calculate the speed of a moving subject in order to properly focus and position the camera's lens to capture it.

FOREGROUND The elements of an image that lie closest to the picture plane, appearing nearest to the viewer in a photograph.

F-STOP A number that indicates the size of a camera's aperture. The larger the number, the smaller the lens opening, which works in conjunction with shutter speeds to accomplish correct exposure.

FULL-FRAME A camera sensor format that has the largest sensor (measuring 36 by 24mm) commonly found in DSLRs.

HARD LIGHT Light that has a narrow focus and falls off quickly into shadow on striking a subject.

HIGH-DYNAMIC-RANGE (HDR) IMAGING A technique in which several versions of the same picture taken at different exposure values are overlaid to get an image with the widest range of tones possible.

HISTOGRAM An electronic graph on a digital camera showing the distribution of tones in an image, from completely dark (on the left) to completely light (on the right). Displayed on the camera, it's a useful tool for determining whether an image contains the correct range of tones for a proper exposure.

HOTSHOE A connector on top of the camera, where accessory flashes and other devices can be mounted to sync with the camera.

HYPERFOCAL DISTANCE The closest distance at which a lens can focus while keeping objects at infinity in acceptably sharp focus. It varies with f-stop. Landscape photographers exploit hyperfocal distance to create the feeling of deep space in photos.

IMAGE SENSOR The medium in the camera that captures light and converts it into an electric signal.

IMAGE STABILIZATION A camera or lens function that can be switched on to reduce blurring created by the movement or jostling of a camera during an exposure.

ISO The setting that regulates a camera's digital sensitivity to light. The higher the ISO, the greater the sensitivity, and the greater the low light and/or high-speed capability.

JPEG The most common type of image file, useful because it compresses images into convenient sizes and can be read on any platform. JPEGs can be resized easily in image editors; large ones are suitable for most image edits and for large prints and viewing on big screens. Small files are ideal for emailing and web use. High levels of compression will cause more data loss and image degradation.

LCD (LIQUID CRYSTAL DISPLAY) A thin, flat display screen on a digital camera that provides a live feed of what the camera is seeing, allows you to play back images after shooting, and offers access to menus and information such as exposure settings, autofocus points, and histograms.

LENS FLARE Unwanted degradation of an image caused by light scattering inside a lens, resulting in odd spots, streaks, and veiling fog.

LIVE VIEW A function that sends the image through the lens to the LCD rather than the optical viewfinder. Using this function affords a larger view of the frame, easier depth-of-field preview, magnification for manual focusing, and other benefits. But it can be hard to use in bright light and when shooting handheld.

MACRO Close-up photography of very small subjects. The image on the sensor is close to the size of the subject or even larger.

MIDGROUND The elements of a photo that appear to lie in the middle of the space relative to the viewer.

MOTION BLUR The streaking in an image that results when either the subject or the camera moves during exposure.

NOISE Undesirable graininess and flecks of random color in a portion of an image that should consist of a single smooth color. Noise in an image generally increases with higher ISOs.

OVEREXPOSURE When too much light strikes the sensor, the image is overexposed, meaning its colors and tones appear very bright or white, and highlighted areas are washed out.

PANNING The horizontal movement of a camera along with a moving subject. The technique is used to suggest fast motion, and brings out the subject from other blurred elements in the frame.

PANORAMA An image that depicts an extremely wide angle of view, typically wider than the human eye can see and than most lenses can capture. Often created through compositing.

PENTAPRISM A multisided device built into a DSLR that corrects the orientation of the image and directs it to the viewfinder.

PIXEL The smallest single component of a digital image. Also refers to the light-gathering cells on a camera's sensor.

POST-PROCESSING The work done with software on an image after a camera has captured it. It ranges from converting the image into a different type of digital file to editing and altering the picture.

PRIME LENS Any lens that has a fixed focal length, as opposed to a zoom lens, which has a variable focal length. Often referred to as a "fast" lens.

RAW FILE Also known as a digital negative, losslessly compressed RAW files are created in your camera. To output them, you must modify them with a converter, such as the one provided with your camera. RAW files allow you to alter camera settings, such as white balance, after the fact, and provide the most possible original data in an image.

REFLEX MIRROR A mirror that reflects light coming through the lens upward to the pentaprism for viewing through the optical viewfinder. It then pivots up when the shutter is pressed, creating a path between the lens and the image sensor.

RULE OF THIRDS A compositional guideline stating that visual tension and interest are best achieved by placing crucial elements of a photograph one-third of the way from any of the frame's edges.

SATURATION The intensity of color in an image. A saturated image's colors may appear more intense than the colors did in the actual scene, an effect that can be achieved with software.

SELF-TIMER A camera mode that gives a predetermined delay between the pressing of the shutter release and the shutter's firing. Can be used on a tripod-mounted camera for self-portraits or to eliminate the effects of camera shake when you press the shutter.

SHUTTER A mechanical curtain that opens and closes to control the amount of time during which light can reach the camera's image sensor.

SHUTTER-PRIORITY MODE A camera mode in which the photographer chooses the shutter speed, while the camera automatically adjusts aperture to achieve a proper exposure.

SHUTTER SPEED The amount of time during which the shutter stays open to light, generally measured in fractions of seconds. (1/8000 sec is a very fast shutter speed, and 1/2 sec is very slow.)

SINGLE-AREA AUTOFOCUS A shooting mode in which the camera focuses on a specific element or point within the frame.

SOFT LIGHT Whether diffused or coming from multiple or broad sources, this light falls on a subject without casting deep shadows or creating much contrast.

SPOT METERING A camera function that measures the light in only a small area, generally in the center of the frame. Use this feature when you want to precisely meter a particular point or element, and don't want other areas of the scene to affect the exposure.

TIFF A type of digital image file that is great for editing with software because it retains image quality and doesn't compress files.

TUNGSTEN LIGHT An incandescent type of continuous lamp that gives warm-toned light.

UNDEREXPOSURE When too little light strikes the sensor, the overall tone of an image is dark, shadows are dense, and colors are muted.

VIEWFINDER The opening the photographer looks through to compose and (if using manual focus) to focus the picture. A viewfinder can be electronic or optical.

WHITE BALANCE This camera setting defines what the color white looks like in specific lighting conditions and corrects all other colors accordingly.

ZOOM LENS Any lens that is constructed to allow a continuously variable focal length, as opposed to a prime lens, which has a fixed focal length.

ZOOM RING A ring on the barrel of a lens that, when rotated, changes the focal length of the lens.

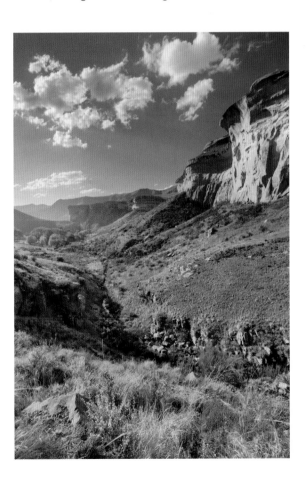

INDEX

IMAGE CREDITS

All illustrations courtesy of Francisco Perez. All images courtesy of Shutterstock Images unless otherwise noted.

Half title, page 1: Nicky Bay (lower right) **Contents, page 4:** (left to right): Atanu Paul, Allyeska Photography **Contents, page 5** (right): Subhajit Dutta **Contents, page 6** (left to right): Regis Lefebure, Jim Wark **Contents, page 7** (right): Daniel Soderstrom **Contents, page 8** (left): Stephan Edwards **Contents, page 9** (far right): Ian Plant **Introduction, page 11:** Charles Lindsey

CAMERA BASICS

004: Pablo Hache (bottom), Andrea Lastri (top right) **005** (top to bottom): Ian Plant, Eric Chen, Dorothy Lee **014:** Ulderico Granger **015:** Laura Bello **018:** Stocksy **019:** Scorchy Designs **021:** Laura Barisonzi **025:** Stocksy **026:** Francesca Alvarez **029:** Stocksy **030:** Stocksy **032:** Stocksy **033** (left to right): Maciej Bednarz, Stocksy **035:** Stocksy **036:** Stuart Fisher **039:** Chris Tennant **040:** Stocksy **042:** Ian Plant **043:** Stocksy **048:** Christopher Stewart

COMPOSING & SHOOTING

049: Stocksy **050:** Stocksy **051:** Sabina Miklowitz **053:** Glenn Losack **054:** Tom Haymes **055:** Guillaume Gilbert **057:** Mike Cable **058:** Martin Wallgren **059** (top to bottom): Daniel Whitten, Adam Oliver **060:** Brett Cohen **062:** Pascal Bögli (left) **064:** Stijn Swinnen **065:** Erin Kunkel (from *Williams Sonoma Salad of the Day*) **066:** Ali Zeigler **067:** Alex Farnum (from *Williams Sonoma This Is a Cookbook*) **068:** Kate Sears (from *Williams Sonoma Two in the Kitchen*) **071:** Dave Bunnell **073:** Javier Acosta **074:** Jim Wark **077:** Jason Hawkes **078:** Ben Ryan **080:** Justin Gurbisz **081:** Alex Wise **085:** Subhajit Dutta **091:** Trent Bell **092:** Ian Plant **093:** Satoru Murata **094:** Michael Baxter **095:** Philip Ryan **100:** Andy Teo **102:** Dan Bracaglia **103:** Ricardo Pradilla **105:** Aaron Ansarov **106:** Ben Hattenbatch **107:** Fotolia **121:** Meghan Hildebrand **124:** Kenneth Barker **115:** Marisa Kwek **125:** Sandy Honig **127:** Jeff Wignall **129** (small): Nick Benson **131:** Allyeska Photography **133:** Andreas Jorns **134:** Stocksy **136:** Rick Wetterau **138:** Cary Norton **141:** Byron Yu **142:** Laura Barisonzi **143:** Michael Soo **145:** Lucie Debelkova **146:** Tom Ryaboi **148** (left to right): Douglas Norris, David B. Simon, Ray Tong **150:** Ralph Grunewald **154:** Giorgio Prevedi **157:** James St. Laurent **162:** Cameron Booth **163:** Pan-Chung Chan **166:** Edwin Martinez **167:** Nabil Chettouh **172:** Carl Johan Heickendorf **173:** Maurizio Costanzo **174:** Oyo **175:** Paul Hillier **176:** Brandon Robbins **178:** Brooke Anderson Photography **179:** Charlotte Geary **180–181:** Ashley Pizzuti–Pizzuti Studios **184:** Mat Hayward **188:** Mat Hayward **189:** Jeffrey Ling **190** (all): Delbarr Moradi **191:** Herman Au **192:** Greg Tucker **193:** Tafari Stevenson Howard **196:** Gary Reimer **200:** Martin Bailey **201:** Paul Burwell **203:** Daniel Soderstrom **204** (top to bottom): Lisa Pessin, Gerardo Soria

GEAR & SETUP

207 (left to right): Alberto Feltrin, Shawn Miller, Leonardo Miguel Cantos Soto, David O. Andersen **208** (left to right): Rick Barlow, Yew Beng **211:** Michael Soo **212:** Danny Ngan **215:** Connor Walberg **218:** Carol Weinberg **226:** Matthew Hanlon **227:** Jason Petersen **228:** Scott Markewitz **230:** Donald Miralle **233:** Regis Lefebure **234:** Andrew Wong **235:** Ryan Taylor **236:** Dan Taylor **237:** Stefano De Luca (bottom left), Simon Jackson (bottom right), Graham Gamble (top right) **238:** David FitzSimmons **240:** Matt Haines **241:** Skip Caplan **244** (left to right): Barbosa Dos Santos, Laurens Willis, Darren Constantino, Thomas Fitt, Stephanie Carter **243:** Rhea Anna **246:** Stephen Bartels **247:** Bud Green **249:** Chuck Miller **253:** Lisa Elmaleh **254:** Kari Orvik **255:** Stocksy **256:** Nathan Combes (top), Cameron Russell, Stephane Giner, Mathieu Noel (left to right) **258:** Allison Felt **261:** Matt Parker **263:** David Becker **265:** Lisa Moore **266** (top to bottom): Gareth Brooks, David Yu, John Petter Hagen **268:** Ryan Finkbiner **270** (top to bottom): Alexis Burkevics, Larry Andreasen **271:** Stocksy **273:** Stocksy **277:** Debbie Grossman **278:** Meghan Hildebrand **279:** Teru Onishi **282:** Harry Giglio **283:** Paul Marcellini **285:** MaryAnne Nelson (bottom)

PROCESSING & BEYOND

291: Peter Kolonia **292:** Timothy Vanderwalker **297:** David Yu **298:** Saleh AlRashaid **299:** Philip Ryan **302:** David Maitland **303:** Debbie Grossman **304:** Alexander Petkov **305:** Jesse Swallow **307:** Subhajit Dutta **308:** Regina Barton **310:** Stefano Bassetti and Filomena Castagna **311:** Debbie Grossman **314:** Guy Tal **315:** Luisa Mohle **316:** Darwin Wiggett **317:** Cheryl Molennor **320:** Timothy Vanderwalker **319:** Ian Momyer **321:** Kevin Pieper **323:** Debbie Grossman **324:** Jamie Lee **331:** Andrew Wood **341:** Helen Stead **342:** Maren Cuso (from *Williams Sonoma Spice*) **349:** Peter Kolonia (stack of books), Dan Richards (dog book) **354:** Timothy Edberg **355:** Katrin Eismann **356:** Charles Howels **360:** Carol Delumpa **363:** Filip Adamczyk **364:** Lluis Gerard **365:** Xin Wang **366:** Raïssa Venables **368:** Anna Pleteneva **370:** Ben Fredrick **371:** Peter Kolonia **373:** Erik Johansson **374:** Romain Laurent **375:** Jess Zak **376:** Philip Habib **377:** Lee Sie **381:** Dan Miles

Last page: Priska Battig
Front endpaper: Daniel Bryant
Back endpaper: Geno Della Mattia
Back cover Lisa Pessin (first row, middle), Tim Barto (second row, left), Matthew Hanlon (second row, middle), Dan Bracaglia (third row, left), Kenneth Barker (third row, right), Lucie Debelkova (fourth row, far left), Luisa Mohle (fourth row, middle)

POPULAR PHOTOGRAPHY

P.O. Box 6364
Harlan, IA 51593
www.popphoto.com

ABOUT *POPULAR PHOTOGRAPHY*

With more than 2 million readers, *Popular Photography* is the world's largest and most noted photography and image-making publication. The magazine brings 80 years of authority to the craft, and in its advice-packed issues, website, and digital editions, its team of experts focus on hands-on how-to hints and inspiration for everyone from beginners to top-notch professionals.

Editor-in-Chief Miriam Leuchter
Art Director Jason Beckstead
Features Editor Debbie Grossman
Senior Technology Editor Philip Ryan
Assistant Technology Editor Adam Ryder
Assistant Editor Sara Cravatts
Group Photo Editor Thomas Payne
Photo Editor Fiona Gardner
Contributing Editors Richard Bernabe, Tim Fitzharris, Peter Kolonia, Harold Martin, Ian Plant, Dan Richards, Julia Silber, Jeff Wignall
Popphoto.com Editor Stan Horaczek
Assistant Online Editor Jeanette D. Moses
Editorial Production Manager Glen Orzepowski

Popular Photography is a division of **BONNIER**

ACKNOWLEDGMENTS

WELDON OWEN

Weldon Owen would like to thank Dan Richards for writing the Camera Basics section, Marisa Kwek for art direction, Moseley Road for initial design development, and Jessica Bandy, Ian Cannon, Katie Cavanee, Emelie Griffin, Linzee Lichtman, Marianna Monaco, Peggy Nauts, Jenna Rosenthal, Katie Schlossberg, Michael D. Shannon, and Mary Zhang for their editorial and design assistance.

weldon**owen**

Weldon Owen is a division of Bonnier Publishing USA.

1045 Sansome Street
San Francisco, CA 94111
www.weldonowen.com

WELDON OWEN, INC.

President, Publisher Roger Shaw
VP, Sales Amy Kaneko

Senior Editor Lucie Parker
Project Editor Laura Harger
Consulting Editor Maria Behan
Editorial Assistant Molly O'Neil Stewart

Creative Director Kelly Booth
Art Director Lorraine Rath
Senior Designer Meghan Hildebrand
Project Designer Diane Dempsey Murray
Designer Michel Gadwa
Image Coordinator Conor Buckley

Associate Production Director
Michelle Duggan
Imaging Manager Don Hill

A WELDON OWEN PRODUCTION

Library of Congress Control Number is on file with the Publisher.

ISBN: 978-1-68188-270-3

10 9 8 7 6 5 4 3 2
2017 2018 2019 2020 2021

Printed in China.

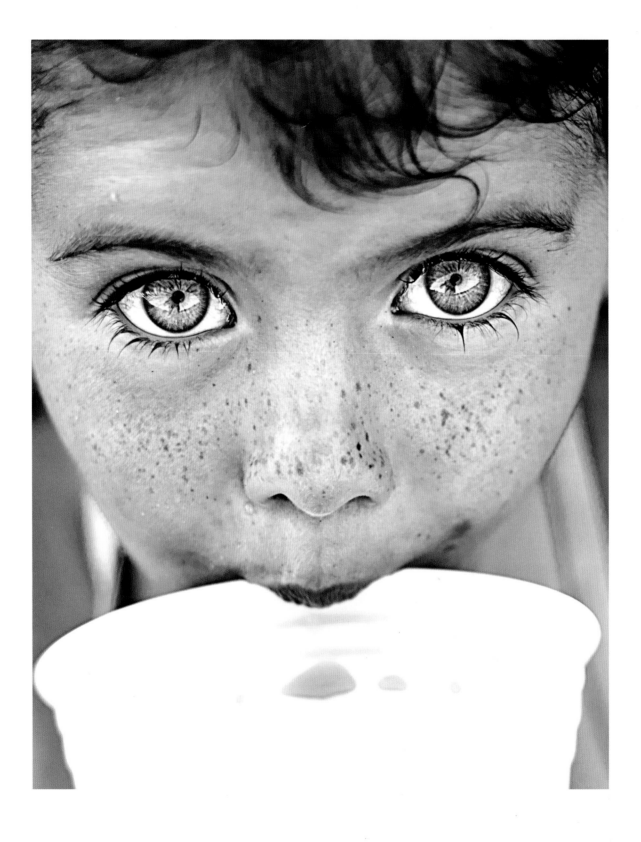